GW01607457

John Piper
in Kent & Sussex

Curated by Nathaniel Hepburn

MASCALLS GALLERY, PADDOCK WOOD
TUNBRIDGE WELLS MUSEUM & ART GALLERY
SCOTNEY CASTLE, LAMBERHURST

09.03.11 - 21.05.11

TOWNER, EASTBOURNE

02.07.11 - 25.09.11

Published by Mascalls Gallery

ISBN 978-0-9567676-0-8

British Library Cataloguing in Publication Data.

A catalogue record for this book is available from the British Library.

Contents

Foreword

Richard Ingrams

Photographs of John Piper suggest a gaunt, solemn and rather forbidding looking figure – an impression that is utterly false. He was a warm hearted, generous man with a great sense of humour and, unusually for an artist, someone who was appreciative of many diverse attitudes and styles both in fellow artists and his fellow human beings.

I was lucky enough to get to know him as a result of his friendship with my weekending neighbour in Berkshire Osbert Lancaster. Later when I collaborated with landscape photographer Fay Godwin on a book about Romney Marsh, a favourite place of his, I came to know him and his wife Myfanwy very well, visiting them frequently at their home near Henley.

It was typical of John that when publisher Hugo Brunner proposed that I should write a book about him (Piper's Places, 1983) he welcomed me without reservation. I was a satirical journalist with no special knowledge of art, but he saw no objection to that, as many famous artists would have done. For me, it was a wonderful opportunity to spend hours talking to him – hours often spent gossiping about his fellow artists or his aristocratic patrons. What impressed me about John was that in spite of an exceptionally busy routine he was invariably calm and composed. I don't think I ever saw him angry or even flustered.

Now, nearly twenty years after his death, this new exhibition is proof that there has been no decline in his popularity with the public. It is one in the eye for those condescending critics who in his lifetime dismissed him as a provincial artist who had unwisely turned his back on the Modern Movement. Not that the criticism really bothered him. He went on 'doing his thing' and in the years since his death he has been triumphantly vindicated.

Introduction

Nathaniel Hepburn

John Piper was a versatile artist: this exhibition includes painting, printing, photography and collage; stage design, costume design and travel guides; as well as tapesty, stained glass and church vestments. Using geography as the parameters for the exhibition, rather than chronology or subject, allows the strands of Piper's works to be seen together. Some of Piper's most important works were produced in Kent and Sussex: his experiments as a young artist in the 1930s took place on this coast, the Brighton Aquatints were a revolution away from abstraction, his Romney Marsh churches solidifed his mature style and his Chichester Cathedral tapestry is one of the greatest pieces of modern religious art.

Within weeks of starting my research I realised there were too many works for Mascalls Gallery alone. I am grateful to Emma Slocombe, Chlöe Tapping and Joe Lloyd at Scotney Castle, and Jo Wiltcher and Ian Beavis at Tunbridge Wells Museum for their enthusiasm as the exhibition grew. Thank you to the staff and interns at Mascalls Gallery - Caroline Derrick, Helena Copsey, Sophie Coles and Laura Campbell - as well as all our volunteers.

I am delighted that Matthew Rowe requested that Towner, as the largest new gallery exhibition space in the region, present the exhibition in a single venue in Sussex over the summer period, extending the reach of the exhibition across both Kent and Sussex. Thank you to Matthew Rowe, Sanna Moore, Sara Cooper and all the staff at Towner.

The many private lenders to this exhibition cover the UK and they all opened their doors to me, and let me take away their prized Pipers - it is greatly appreciated. Thank you to the public galleries who have lent works; particularly Simon Martin and Julie Brown at Pallant House Gallery, the staff at the V&A and Tate - especially Emily Down in the Tate Archives.

The authors of the catalogue essays have shone new light on Piper's work and their ideas have greatly influenced this exhibition. The Piper family have been supportive from my first contact as have four people who have been the recipients of a constant flow of emails and phone calls - David Fraser Jenkins, Frances Spalding, Hugh Fowler Wright and Stephen Laird - thank you for being so generous with your knowledge, time and encouragement.

The Road South: John Piper in Kent and Sussex

Alexandra Harris

Stane Street, the great Roman road which led south out of London, passed through what is now Epsom in Surrey on its firm straight progress down to Chichester. As a boy, John Piper read about this road, and imagined it: 'When I was ten, and read Hilaire Belloc's *Stane Street*, about the road from Epsom to Chichester, I was already trying to draw trees to go with it'.[1] That early bit of drawing seems peculiarly appropriate because, over the course of his long life, John Piper did indeed forge a route from Epsom to Chichester – from the town where he grew up and became a solicitor, to the city in whose cathedral he installed one of his most audacious commissioned works.

But Piper's routes were rarely like those of Roman roads. He preferred to get from A to B via as many other places as possible, and Chichester was only one among hundreds of destinations across Sussex and Kent towards which Piper made his winding way. This exhibition is the first to bring together his work in this area. Piper is one of the twentieth century's great interpreters of England, both in words and in pictures, and to look at his work from these counties is to feel a deeper sense of their unique moods and textures. It is also to get a fuller sense of what topographical art can do.

The south-east corner of England was never the centre of Piper's world: from 1935, when he moved to a remote unheated farmhouse with his partner Myfanwy Evans, that centre was Fawley Bottom, in the Chiltern Hills, on the border of Oxfordshire and Buckinghamshire. And Fawley remained 'home' for the rest of his life. But he would always be drawn back to the South. He knew Sussex from his earliest camping trips and recorded it in his 'journey books' with passionate precision. During the five years he spent with his father's firm of solicitors, he would sometimes go off with a friend on a Friday evening and return to the office on Monday morning having seen more of the county than most people manage in years. When at last, in his late twenties, he was able to devote himself to being an artist, he set out for the Sussex coast and found his inspiration by the sea.

Because Piper worked in Kent and Sussex at intervals all his life, this exhibition gives the contours of his career: the main stylistic developments, and his work in an amazing number of different media: oils, watercolours, collage, mixed media, tapestry, stained glass, set design, photography and much else besides. So this show is, in a way, 'representative' of Piper's work. But Piper himself was usually more interested in specifics than in the general or representative view, and the exhibition offers ample opportunity for appreciating his responses to the distinctive feel of particular places. His sketch of hopfields (cat 66), with its brilliant fusion of geometric lines and organic blotchiness, was called not just *Hopfields*, but *Hopfields at Ospringe*. That difference mattered.

Piper left the Royal College of Art in 1929 and faced the task of establishing himself as an artist. He found he could make a living as a literary journalist, but the need to keep writing for money put added pressure on the time left for painting. He was 26, and already he felt belated, too old to be just starting. He had married a fellow student at the Royal College, Eileen Holding, but the relationship was increasingly difficult. As he moved between his cottage in Surrey and a series of rented flats and studios in London, Piper tried to find his own imaginative space.[2] He found it not in London, but on painting trips to the sea.

The earliest paintings shown here are those of a young artist working out his relationship to his contemporaries. In the haunted and haunting *Custom House* (cat 3), the influence of Christopher Wood is so pronounced that this might even, in retrospect, be called a memorial painting, a tribute to a man who died that year, at the age of twenty nine and would enjoy the shapes of the seaside no longer. The windows are empty (de Chirico has left his mark), low light catches the arches, and the monument is black against the sea. The picture has a sombre twilight feel, and yet there is something that smiles in the naïve style of the custom house itself. Perhaps it is the pleasure that Piper seems to have taken in those exaggerated quoins: he would enjoy a good quoined wall for the rest of his life. And then there is the boat resting in the wittily stuck-on sand, suggesting all the possibilities of collage.

The triumphant ingredient of his collages over the next two years would be the humble paper doily (cat 9-13). It might have been twee, but it was nothing of the sort. Piper's harbour views through windows evoke not prim tea-tables but all the warming, old-fashioned, tobacco-stained atmosphere of seaside pubs and fishermen's cottages. He used the doily as a stencil for brightly coloured, densely patterned paintings in 1932, and then the following year the master of modernism found himself attracted to the doily too. Picasso included one in his collage for the cover of *Minotaure* and Piper would almost certainly have seen it. When Piper subsequently included doily curtains to frame his cobbled quays he was alluding to Picasso but also taking the idea in his own directions. He was starting to explore the close relationship between paintings and interiors, and he was signalling his interest in Georgian and Victorian design, reaching back to the hey-day of the doily (crocheted, not the later paper imitations) when pattern was welcomed into the home. The appreciation of exuberant design that first showed itself in those doilies would later make Piper a champion of the curlicued frosting on pub windows and an influential advocate, more broadly, of overlooked traditions in English decoration.[3]

Like a room with oversized furniture, Piper's harbour views give a sense of intimacy and generosity. Things seen through the window appear very close, but not threateningly so. The world is touchable and asking to be explored. The same paddle steamer seems always to be chuffing past, and in *Seaford Head* (cat 19) there is a nice companionship between the ancient fossils on the beach and the contemporary newspapers whose lines of text form stratified cliffs and a sloping road, and even a felicitous passing albatross.

These beach collages first came to public notice when Piper was elected to the 'Seven and Five Society'. His work was clearly connected with that of other members like Winifred Nicholson and Frances Hodgkins, both bringing new vibrancy to still-life painting, and exploring its relationship to landscape. But it was the 'Seven and Five' which also encouraged Piper towards abstraction. In 1934, under the leadership of Ben Nicholson, the group voted that everything in its next exhibition should be abstract.

Piper could see the possibilities of abstract painting, and was deeply admiring of pioneers like Jean Hélion and Piet Mondrian. He produced clean, taut, beautifully balanced collages and constructions. But his abstracts were connected with places, and they were always courting figuration. A curving shape becomes for a moment the side of a bottle, perhaps, half-hidden in the sand; a few inky arches hint at buildings along the promenade; a stripe suggests a lighthouse or a buoy (cat 21). Hence the teasing title of the 1938 abstract exhibited here (cat 30): *Sea Buildings*. We look for the buildings, of course, but this is only the groundwork for that other complementary part of the process, which is to recognise the abstract design in the world around us. Piper educates the eye in the language of shapes and rhythms, the relationship between an attention-catching architectural detail and the whole surrounding scene.

Piper himself felt that his abstract paintings were an education, and he would always acknowledge their role in developing his sense of composition and formal clarity. But his responsiveness to particular places was too strong to be satisfied by abstracts. He was hungry for detail. 'Pure abstraction is undernourished,' he wrote in an essay called 'Abstraction on the Beach': 'it should at least be allowed to feed on a bare beach with tins and broken bottles'.[4] A more appealing feast was waiting for him on the South Coast, from Newhaven to Dungeness. Piper packed his bag with ink and watercolours, subtle shades of coloured paper to be cut and torn and pasted together, and gouache for the bright splash of a flag or a red life-ring on the harbour wall. He went down to the seaside and sat with a board on his knees, inking in jetties, masts and telegraph poles, or cutting from paper a steep run of steps. He liked the combination of pleasure and practicality in seaside buildings. As he wrote in his essay on 'The Nautical Style': 'They are functional but they are something else as well. They have strength, gaiety of design and colour (even if it is only the gaiety of black and white) and they are usually in startling contrast with their surroundings'.[5]

Piper's collages of 1936-8 are among the most joyous works of his career. Their tonal delicacy and structural complexity is mixed with all the appeal of childish exaggeration. *Newhaven* (cat 25) might be an image circling round a child's magic lantern. In Piper's imagination, the most dauntingly remote of places could take on this playfulness without losing their power. Who else could go to Dungeness and be reminded of a nursery?

> Coastguard cottages, huts, stores, railways, flagpoles, where flags are constantly run up to salute passing vessels (which come close inshore here, rounding the point in deep water) make a museum of maritime structures and appliances. The whole area looks like an oversized nursery floor, very untidy at first sight, but having an underlying pattern.[6]

If Dungeness looked like a nursery floor with toys left in odd places, the coast in turn inspired Piper's lithograph *Nursery Frieze* (cat 28), made in two sheets which could be joined together, and designed to run round the walls of a child's room. 'Run' is the word because the frieze is full of motion: the waves coming in, boats going past, the wind filling out a striped windsock, a train puffing its way out of a coastal station and into a tunnel. We go with the train into darkness and emerge happily in a night-time scene full of fun and light: the moon is out, there are lights on at the house, and in the garden there is a bonfire and fireworks leaping into the sky. Time passes from day to night, and from the summer-seeming beach to the autumnal fires, and then to the pinky glow of a winter sky against which the bare trees are silhouettes.

Nursery Frieze shares in the spirit of other 1930s wall decorations like Rex Whistler's picturesque fantasias, Edward Bawden's witty murals, and (closest to Piper) Eric Ravilious's wall paintings for the Midland Hotel at Morecambe. Ravilious had also chosen coastal scenes by day and night, and had also made dramatic use of fireworks. Both men were devotees of a good firework display and Piper would in time become an expert in firework choreography. Like fireworks, the designs of Ravilious and Piper were sophisticated entertainments, while also appealing to a simple sense of wonder.

With the declaration of war, of course, the fireworks had to stop. The South Coast was now vulnerable territory, and mounted its defences against invasion. Fighter planes flew over Kent and Sussex in formation, training for what was to come. Virginia Woolf, who lived at Rodmell near Lewes, set her novel *Between the Acts* on a June day in 1939, and the atmosphere is tense with intimations of violence that seem painfully at odds with the quiet fertile countryside. Piper visited Hamsey, just north of Lewes up the river Ouse, and painted St Peter's church, with its Norman chancel and largely unrestored medieval interior (cat 31). Piper's joy in churches that had not been thoroughly 'scraped' and polished up by the Victorians was linked with his admiration for the work of John Sell Cotman, who had painted churches in an 'exquisite state of decay'. At that time in the early nineteenth century, wrote Piper, 'clear glass windows let in the sunlight that streamed over the faded umbers, ochres and greys of the walls, furniture and walls'.[7] Cotman's churches were in Norfolk, but the same mood and the same colouring characterises Piper's study of Hamsey. The church had no heat or light, but the painting is a study in tranquil warmth. The walls and arches are ancient and bear the marks of centuries, but Piper's translucent watercolour and lightly inked lines give the feeling that this place is a fragile haven. In its quietness and in its subtle elegiac note, the painting is akin to the watercolours commissioned from Piper and many other artists for the wartime Recording Britain project, which sought to preserve the memory of endangered places.

Other of Piper's wartime 'recording' exercises took a different attitude to vulnerability and showed buildings fighting back. When Edward Sackville-West asked Piper to make a series of paintings of Knole, the enormous seat of the Sackvilles near Sevenoaks, Piper responded with images of drama. His *View of Knole* (cat 41) shows the sprawling buildings (in reality a whole village) hunkering down, offering an inviolable face to the thunderous sky. *The Gatehouse, Knole* (cat 38) is similarly unbreachable. Piper layers his impasto to evoke the stoutness of these walls, which are worn and scarred and wise with age. This was the great house of Virginia Woolf's *Orlando*, the book in which Woolf restored Vita Sackville-West to the beloved family home she had not been able to inherit. In Woolf's fantasia, both Orlando and her house thrive for five centuries and show no sign of stopping when they reach the present day. Piper's paintings have a similar surviving spirit and, as ever, he turns buildings into extrovert characters. 'This vast old war-horse of a house was built with a splendid sense of drama, and acts up', he wrote of Seaton Delaval.[8] And though all his houses are individuals, Knole has that same protean, defiant turn.

When Piper went back to the coast after the war, it was not the gay flag-flying place he had known in the 1930s. Barbed wire was stretched along beaches; harbours bore the debris of a long military campaign. At Dungeness in 1947 (cat 45-6), Piper applied thick oils and scratched through to the board beneath, evoking a tough, forbidding place. But though at first sight these paintings look like visions of elemental chaos, they settle into shape as soon as the eye finds the horizon. The water is divided from the air and the land from the sea; the sea itself seems to calm. These are survival paintings again, with which one struggles and gets through. Introducing an exhibition of his work in 1948, Piper expressed the deep awareness of threat and change which must colour the work of a modern artist:

> Today, I hope to be a painter who reacts in favour of early loves without being reactionary, and who paints churches both medieval and Victorian, mountains, beaches, downs and valleys, without for a moment forgetting that on most downs there is an aerodrome, from most mountains you can see factories in the valleys, that many churches are nearly empty on Sundays, and that on any English beach there may be an unexploded mine.[9]

Piper's return to Dungeness was connected with a commission from Nikolaus Pevsner to write and illustrate a King Penguin book on Romney Marsh. If only every area of England had a Piper Penguin to its name. His topographical writing is supremely attentive, unsensational, and always on the look-out for possible sources of pleasure, whether it be in watching the yellow flanks and feathery crowns of winter reeds in the dykes, or in collecting the names of bungalows along the seafront: Windy Cot, Thistledome, Ecnamor (which, he points out helpfully, is 'romance' written backwards).[10] Romance is not lacking on Romney Marsh. Piper describes with some zest the extent of the smuggling that has gone on here. 'Empty but lidded stone coffins at Ivychurch and elsewhere' he says, 'are pointed out as former hiding-places for liquor, as well as for the corpses of men who had been murdered.'[11]

Piper devoted most of his Romney book to an illustrated gazetteer of the marshland churches he never tired of exploring. Five of his Romney church drawings from this time are included in the exhibition, as well as some of those from the return visits he made again and again in the 1960s, 70s, and 80s. Old Romney Church was bound to lure him, having one of the 'best and least spoiled Georgian interiors in the country'.[12] He painted it in greys and yellows with tiny rich flashes of colour; he inked in the Chinese-style chancel gate and showed the oval text plates, characteristic of Marsh churches, up in the shadows over the chancel arch (cat 49). Notwithstanding the compelling lidded coffins inside Ivychurch, Piper focused his attentions on the exterior, enjoying the texture of the walls (cat 48). 'Owing to the pitting and scoring of the stonework by weather', he writes, 'this church takes on the mood of the day in its appearance, looking dark on a grey day and pale and silvery on a clear one'.[13] So changeful a building rewarded all the attention one could give and Piper painted it in many moods.

Though Pevsner's commission for the Romney Guide suggested that collaboration between the two men might be possible, there is no doubt that they were competitors. Pevsner's monumental series 'The Buildings of England' began to come out, county by county, in the 1950s, providing an almost exhaustive architectural record which the Shell Guides could not hope to rival. Piper had been involved with Shell Guides since the mid-1930s when John Betjeman asked him to write a volume on Oxfordshire, and the making of guide books had been an integral part of his life ever since. His *Oxon* was published in 1938, he researched *Shropshire* with Betjeman in 1939 and saw it through to publication after the war, and (again with Betjeman) became general editor of the series in 1962. On Betjeman's retirement in 1967, Piper was left in sole charge of an enormous project which was very different from Pevsner's but which offered its own distinctive vision of England.

When Pennethorne Hughes, who had been writing the *Kent* guide, died shortly after completing his first draft, Piper stepped in and completed the gazetteer entries as well as contributing more than seventy photographs – of churches, beaches, effigies, local weatherboarding, oast houses and hopfields. The hopfields are among the most striking of his images. The back endpapers show the hop poles in winter, rayed out in their bare rows stretching into the distance, a strange, disorienting landscape of verticals. There is also a photograph of 'hop pole stringing' near Goudhurst. Here again, the poles are bare, but now we know that planting is imminent because the wires are stretched between them. There is a simultaneous clarity and complexity to the structure which might have impressed Moholy-Nagy or Naum Gabo. But in these photographs by Piper an abstract, diagrammatic quality works in conjunction with the ever-present sense of place as he catches the texture of the soil and the overcast sky.

One of the distinctive features of the Shell Guides was the attention paid to monuments. Several of the 1930s guides, including *Oxon*, had included sections devoted to them. These were contributed by Katherine Esdaile, whose research into the history of English monuments was part of a wider re-awakening to the forgotten history of English craftsmanship. Baroque and Georgian sculpture was profoundly unfashionable when Esdaile and the Shell writers first started to explore it in the 1930s, but their work formed the basis for a revival. Piper's 1947 painting of the Waldershare monument (cat 44) was one of many baroque subjects he chose in the effort to get people looking again at things they had been taught to ignore. Emphasising the chiaroscuro, he enjoyed the overdone effects at Waldershare, where the monument to Sir Henry Furness was so large that it seemed almost to burst out of the small country church that tried to contain it.

While he paid attention to the many kinds of art to be found in churches, Piper campaigned to ensure that new art for churches kept being made. He joined an influential circle of people whose aim was to renew that close relationship between art and church which had, for centuries, been a source of experiment and originality in English culture. If churches became changeless museums, he thought, they would lose their power. Piper's interest in church art brought him on many occasions down to Sussex, not least because the bishop of Chichester, George Bell, was among the most active sponsors of modern artists. In a 1942 article for *Studio* magazine Bell argued that 'ancient churches cannot in fact be preserved if they are regarded as ancient records. They must serve a living purpose.' Throughout English history artists had contributed to the fabric of their churches: 'why should not the present age make its contribution?'[14] It was Bishop

Bell who had commissioned the Bloomsbury artists Duncan Grant and Vanessa Bell to decorate the walls of Berwick church. And in 1943 Bell hosted at Chichester a landmark exhibition called 'The Artist and the Church'. The curator, working in collaboration with CEMA, was John Piper.[15]

George Bell's work at Chichester was continued by his friend Walter Hussey, who became Dean there in 1955. In 1963 Hussey asked John Piper to make a work of art which would hang behind the high altar, lift the mood of the sanctuary, and serve as a focal point for the whole cathedral. In response, Piper designed a spectacular tapestry which, seen from a distance, seems to radiate light. His contemporary abstract imagery was framed and supported, quite literally, by the sixteenth-century wooden reredos screen which was already there, and which was in turn made newly visible. The ancient and modern elements were dependent on each other. The colours were bright and radically so, but only as bright as the jewel colours of medieval stained glass when the light comes through.[16]

When he wrote a short book about stained glass in 1968, Piper argued that artists must work in their own contemporary idiom rather than producing timid archaisms. He laid down a challenge to those with the power to commission church art: 'Good artists can be trusted: so clergy, be bolder!'[17] He was certainly bold with the Chichester tapestry, and his stained glass designs, too, were often full of modern character while honouring the long tradition in which he was working. At St Mary's Lamberhurst his *Annunciation to the Shepherds* (cat 101-102) used the expressive distortion he had learned from early medieval art and which he had fused with the modernist language of Picasso and Chagall. The whole window seems to sing out with exclamations as huge hands are thrust out and bodies bend in amazement. Predictably, there were complaints about the angel. Piper had exaggerated the stylised haloes so often found in pre-Renaissance painting and given his angel a circular head. But why should an angel not be all at once a sun and a full moon, a diver and an astronaut, winging down through a glassy cosmos?

There was a posthumous coda to Piper's relationship with Sussex. In 1982 he designed a stained glass window which took its inspiration from an Elizabethan wall-painting at

Shulbrede Priory near Liphook. Shulbrede was mostly in ruins but the south-west corner had survived and been turned into a private house. Inside, beside the fireplace in what was once the Prior's chamber, a nativity scene decorated a wattle-and-daub partition. Its existence was enticingly reported in the old *Highways and Byways* guide to Sussex by E.V. Lucas, part of the series of guides which Piper loved as a boy. Lucas writes about Shulbrede as a marvellous secret:

> As it is now in private occupation and is not shown to strangers, I have not seen it; but of old many persons journeyed thither, attracted by the quaint mural paintings, in the Prior's room, of domestic animals uttering speech. 'Christus natus est,' crows the cock. 'Quando? Quando?' the duck inquires. 'In hac nocte,' says the raven. 'Ubi? Ubi?' asks the cow, and the lamb satisfies her: 'Bethlehem, Bethlehem.'[18]

The apocryphal idea that the animals became articulate on Christmas night has something of the child's dream about it. And an extra part of the charm here is the use of Latin, the language of scholarship, to mimic the familiar sounds of farm animals. Piper translated the scene into a design for a window. He did not quite have room to include a cow, so he chose an owl instead to ask 'Ubi?Ubi?' answered by the lamb who bleets 'Bethlehem!' The window was made by David Wasley and exhibited, but then sat for years in Piper's studio. After Piper's death, Myfanwy decided to find a home for it and install the window in memory of her husband. She chose Iffley Church in Oxfordshire, not far from their home in Fawley and one of the best-preserved Romanesque churches in England.[19] The walls are inhabited by sculpted animals who guard the doors and frame the arches. So Piper's farmyard was appropriate. This scene which Myfanwy chose as a memorial linked death with new life, and it linked the Pipers' lives in Oxfordshire with their long appreciation of Sussex.

Dr Alexandra Harris is a lecturer at the University of Liverpool. She is author of *Romantic Moderns: English Writers, Artists & the Imagination From Virginia Woolf to John Piper* and editor of *Modernism on Sea: Art and Culture at the British Seaside*.

Notes:

1. Piper to Vera and John Russell, *Sunday Times*, 22 March 1964, and quoted by John Russell in his introduction to *John Piper* (Tate, 1983), 16.
2. For biographical detail here and throughout I am indebted to Frances Spalding's landmark biography *John Piper, Myfanwy Piper: Lives in Art* (Oxford University Press, 2009).
3. See John Piper, 'Fully Licensed', *Architectural Review*, 87 (1940), 87-100. He was the first modern commentator to write seriously about the aesthetics of pubs.
4. Piper, 'Abstraction on the Beach', *XXe Siècle*, 1 (1938), 41. On Piper's relationship with the coast, and his transitions between landscape and abstraction, see the exhibition catalogue *John Piper in the 1930s: Abstraction on the Beach* with text by Frances Spalding and David Fraser Jenkins (Merrell, 2003).
5. Piper, J. 'The Nautical Style' (1938), reprinted in *Buildings and Prospects* (Architectural Press, 1948), 11.
6. 'The Nautical Style', in *Buildings and Prospects*, 18.
7. Piper, J. 'Towers in the Fens' (1940), *Architectural Review*, November 1940, 131-4 (131).
8. Piper, J. 'Seaton Delaval', *Orion: A Miscellany*, 1 (1945), 43-7 (44).
9. Piper, J. introduction to an exhibition at the Buchholz Gallery in New York, 1948, reprinted in *John Piper* (Tate, 1983), 39.
10. Piper, J. *Romney Marsh* (Penguin, 1950), 15.
11. ibid, 12.
12. ibid, 32.
13. ibid, 27.
14. Bell, G. 'The Church and the Artist', *Studio*, 124 (1942), 81-92 (83, 86).
15. For more on the exhibition see Spalding, *Lives in Art*, 237-8.
16. On the tapestry see Spalding, *Lives in Art*, 400-403 and, putting the work at Chichester in the context of a wider revival, see Walter Hussey, *Patron of Art: The Revival of a Great Tradition among Modern Artists* (Weidenfeld & Nicolson, 1985).
17. Piper, J. *Stained Glass: Art or Anti-Art?* (Studio Vista, 1968), 39
18. Lucas, E.V. *Highways and Byways in Sussex* (1904; Macmillan, 1921), 11
19. I am most grateful to Stephen Laird for setting me right about the history of this window

1939

Julian Freeman

1939 was John Piper's annus mirabilis. It hadn't been planned: it simply worked out that way. By the end of the year Piper was established in the pantheon of modern British art, having in the process created a core oeuvre in which, in relatively few works, he had formed the technical, visual and philosophical bases of almost everything for which he is now best-known. In the process, he gained an influential patron, in the person of Sir Osbert Sitwell. Just as we might seek a reflection of the Munich Crisis of 1938 in the often achingly acute cantos of Louis MacNeice's *Autumn Journal*, it is to the magnificent, melancholy iridescence of Piper's paintings, watercolours and prints of the second half of 1939 that we have come to refer for a reflection of the first autumn of the Second World War.

By the end of 1938 Piper had relinquished total abstraction, to create formal semi-abstract landscape and topographical works: by 1939 he was executing these in a range of media, often involving visual experimentation, laced with elements of the Picturesque, and combined with an increasingly refined sense of place, and with his own brand of Romanticism. That this was so is incontrovertible: the works are there. Piper's first summer season at Hafod, Dyfed, and an early Autumn visit to Stourhead, Wiltshire, called forth strong, Cotmanesque works of almost theatrical formality, intensely engaged with the landscape parks and houses that were his preferred subjects: all contain a clear sense of a visual and emotional restiveness that would gain greater presence within the next few years when Piper visited the Sitwells at Renishaw. Clearly, the man was on a roll, but there is little seminal evidence to clarify the different speeds and trajectories by which such matter became form, and, here, conjecture may be key.

Anthony West's contention that between 1937 and 1941 Piper underwent a personal, critical revaluation of Turner assumes significance: his assessment of Turner in *British Romantic Artists* (1942) falls short of a declared epiphany, but clearly suggests that, during this period, Piper was discovering a simple but profound truth: "Turner's plan, as it developed, was to become more proficient than anyone else alive at any manner of painting he thought important…" (Piper 1942). As early as 1939, there exist features of Piper's work in Kent and Sussex that represent this notion, for example, at Hamsey, near Lewes, where the results of a sunny day spent recording the simplest of subjects, the plainest of interiors, in watercolour and in photographic format, convey an engagement with the experience in colour and tonal contrast that, in both media, easily beat pictorial convention to the line.

In nearby Brighton, Piper's research with John Betjeman in mid-1939 for the *Shell Guide to Shropshire* (held over because of the war until 1951) had resulted in a voyage of discovery, for neither man knew the county: strangeness proved to be a major stimulus, a quality carried over into the preparations for the 13 *Brighton Aquatints* (1938-1939). In its totality, and in its individual prints, this compelling collection of seemingly disparate topographical images is a modern masterpiece, partly – surely - because Piper was well aware that his decision to use the outmoded medium for a project with more than one meaning might invite serious discussion of its potential as a polemical statement for many conservational reasons; partly because of his mastery of process and medium; partly because, having almost inadvertently arrived at a position of creative integrity, he was able to receive the accolades he justly deserved to secure his artistic authority, and move on.

Dr Julian Freeman is an art historian, curator and critic. Acting Course Leader for Access to Higher Education at Sussex Coast College, Hastings, he is also a Visiting Lecturer to the University of Brighton's School of Historical & Critical Studies, and a member of the Editorial Board of *Cassone*, the online art magazine. His book *British Art: a walk round the rusty pier* was published in 2006 by Southbank.

John Piper at Scotney Castle

Emma Slocombe

In 1945 the architectural historian Christopher Hussey made a review for an exhibition that would instigate a remarkable meeting of minds. The review in *Country Life* was for John Piper's exhibition, The Sitwell Country. The works exhibited were poignant views of landscapes, country houses and architectural ruins, arising mainly from a commission from Sir Osbert Sitwell to illustrate his autobiography. Hussey celebrated Piper as the contemporary successor to the principles of 'the picturesque' as practised by landscape artists of the 18th and early 19th centuries such as Samuel Palmer, John Sell Cotman and the Reverend William Gilpin. According to Hussey, Piper's art was '…helping us to see, to feel with all our faculties, the visual significance to-day of things worth seeing'.[1] Admiration was mutual, for almost two decades earlier John Piper had discovered Hussey's seminal 1927 text *The Picturesque*[2]. For Piper, it validated his belief in the possibility of uniting modern abstraction with the English landscape tradition.

Both architectural historian and artist possessed a deeply felt connection to the English landscape and its architecture and a shared anxiety over the survival of special or ancient places as the twentieth century progressed. Their ensuing correspondence documents a warm friendship where professional discussion gives way to a more personal affection, which was also shared by their wives, Betty Hussey and Myfanwy Piper. The couples spent weekends together, the Husseys recording their first stay with the Pipers at Fawley Bottom in their country house scrap book. The page includes an informal portrait of Piper leaning over his garden gate and is autographed by the Pipers. Writing a letter of thanks on April 16th 1946, the tone is of fond humour, 'The Husseys always wanted to know the Pipers, and they thought they must be an awfully nice family, but were dumbfounded to find they were even nicer, more amusing and talented than they thought possible'.[3]

Looking from the Library of the New House at Scotney Castle, across the gardens towards the ruins of Old Castle the young Christopher Hussey discovered the designed landscape that later inspired *The Picturesque*. That Piper returned to the architectural source of the book that so influenced his early ideas has a romantic charm consistent with his outlook. The Old Castle, with its surviving medieval tower rising above ruined ivy clad walls and reflected in the waters of the moat below captured Piper's imagination. His dark toned photographs begin to break down the building into distinct geometric parts, compositions he revisited in his watercolour sketches and mixed media works. In the spirit of Piper's Shell Guides, Hussey later selected one of these photographs for the cover of his *Guide to Scotney Castle* (1956).

Working from a photograph in Nathaniel Lloyd's *A History of the English Country House* (1949), Piper also completed a commission to realise the Entrance Front of the New House, using rich ochres and reds to bring out the warmth of the stone. The Husseys later hung the work over fireplace in the Hall, flanked by one of the views of the Old Castle, connecting artwork to place in the heart of the building's welcome. It was an act that symbolised the two men's meeting of mind, spirit and aesthetic sensibility. On learning of Christopher Hussey's death in 1970, Piper wrote 'I don't know how we will go on without him'.[4]

1. Hussey, C. 'The Twilight of the Great House' *Country Life* January 26 1945, 153
2. Spalding, F. *John Piper, Mytanwy Piper: Lives in Art* (Oxford University Press, 2009) 133-134
3. Hussey, B. Letter to John and Myfanwy Piper, 16 April 1946 (Tate Archives)
4. Piper, J. Letter to Betty Hussey, 24 March 1970 (Scotney Castle Collection, National Trust)

Emma Slocombe is a curator with National Trust based in the South East. She is the principle curatorial consultant for Scotney Castle and other major properties including Knole and Sissinghurst Castle.

Piper's Kent and East Sussex Shell Guides

David Heathcote

John Piper saw art as life; everything he did was grist to the mill. From his early teens he was an inveterate traveller and made annotated sketchbooks that were a kind of autotravelography. Piper was concerned only with the process of creation and in Piper's finished works there is the sense that whatever the subject or medium they are a work in progress. With his travel books he was no different indeed he saw the process of editing as another medium. Piper's travel books, from his sketchbooks to his last Shell Guide are all one interrelated artwork.

With *Oxon* (1938), Piper's first Shell Guide, he hybridised his sketchbook method adding more photography to create what became a model for the series. In the same year his essay 'The Nautical Style' for the *Architectural Review* used an interest in objets trouves and surrealism, aesthetics normally reserved for modern art, as a tool to coalesce a group of disparate seaside environments, including Dungeness, into a distinctive English style. Both works are early demonstrations of the reflective interplay between artistic method, aesthetics and subject that make Piper's books so rich.

Frequently in his early publications he used Kent and Sussex as a sounding board for ideas. In his *Brighton Aquatints*, 1939 he played with the idea of a method of image making that approximated to the Regency spirit. Piper's hommage was reinforced in a Proustian elegy to Brighton by 'Bosie', Lord Alfred Douglas. In *British Romantic Artists* (1942) he used a neglected period of art history to conceptualise his new appreciation of the landscape. Here again there was reference to Kent in his consideration of Samuel Palmer's Shoreham. In 1950 he published *Romney Marsh*, a miniature version of his *Brighton Aquatints* and a response to his own *British Romantic Artists*; a landscape artist's guide to a remote part of Kent, simultaneously nostalgic, romantic and contemporary. It was a dry run for the new Shell Guides that began with Shropshire 1951.

Under Piper's influence Shell Guides became richly illustrated with photographs, many his, and in recognition of his contribution Piper was made assistant editor in 1959 and assumed full editorship of the series in 1967. As Editor Piper set about making the guides more modern, more illustrated, more detailed and embraced editing becoming a creator at arm's length. His style was to deny his presence using anodyne modernist designs and dropping in the use of (his) illustrations; his contributors became his medium.

An early beneficiary of his editorship was the Shell Guide to *Kent* by Pennethorne Hughes who died after submitting his manuscript leaving Piper to complete the text. Looking carefully from Piper's own artwork and earlier writing across to Pennethorne Hughes' *Kent*, Piper's eye and mind are most visible in the photographs chosen for the guide. Often his own, these photographs recreate views Piper had created or admired in others' work or are preparatory images for later work. An image of hop poles 'near Goudhurst' became Piper's ink drawing *Hopfields at Ospringe*. The photograph of Fairfield Church in floods by Douglas Weaver exactly mirrors his own painting of it in *Romney Marsh*. When Hughes fails to celebrate Samuel Palmer's residence at Shoreham, Piper inserts his own photograph *Samuel Palmer Country in Winter, Shoreham* recreating Palmer's view in his *Harvest Moon* featured in *British Romantic Artists*.

W.S. Mitchell's *East Sussex* text was old fashioned for Piper's guides. To leaven it he chose sparkling images to play against the text. *Brighton Pavilion* by Edward Piper has the same point of view as John's Pavilion in *Brighton Aquatints*, even the tonal values are similar showing the lengths John's editorial hand extended. Elsewhere he illustrates churches he felt underplayed in Mitchell's text like St Bartholomew's which Piper reveals in all its Byzantine splendour, unsurprisingly it had also featured in *Brighton Aquatints*.

Piper used his long knowledge of Kent and East Sussex to discreetly improve his authors' views of the county. He 'edited in' his remembrance of the essence of place, not one view, but a feeling having a number of visual expressions. This is the special quality of the authorial voice behind Piper's Shell Guides.

Dr David Heathcote is a freelance historian, writer, curator, broadcaster and lecturer. His book *A Shell Eye on England. The Shell County Guides 1934-1984* was published in 2010.

'A Gift of Smiling Colour'
Stephen Laird

Typical works from the last 15 years of John Piper's career are mixed media drawings combining gouache, watercolour, ink, pencil and crayon. Most of the late pictures feature English or Welsh churches and castles, their weathered profiles set against dramatic skies. The well-wrought picture surfaces carry a range of glowing colours, with objects and moods evoked by the combination of a draughtsman's precision and quick, gestural strokes of a pen or brush. In the later 1980s Piper renewed (after 30 years) a particular focus on flowers and vegetation. The artist's health was beginning to fail but the two Sissinghurst images shown here (cat 79-80) offer a personal vision of the irrepressible vitality of nature.

Piper's popularity during this period was bolstered by the production of high quality 'limited edition' prints derived from his pictures, most of them screenprints made by Chris Prater at Kelpra Studio. Piper's approach to art seems to have been re-invigorated by the successful realisation of these prints and by his understanding of the craft behind the printing process - he was evidently thrilled by the printer's 'parallels' or 'interpretations' of his works.[1]

Screenprinting involves pushing inks onto paper through a succession of photographically produced (or sometimes hand cut) stencils, leaving layers of dense, overlapping colour on the printed sheet. *Petham, near Canterbury* 1977 (cat 73), *Ruckinge Church* (cat 74) and *Romney Marsh Dyke* (cat 76) both 1978 and the Sissinghurst pictures are clearly the work of an artist who has developed a strong empathy with the creative possibilities (and constraints) of screenprinting: like the prints, these originals derive their power from the layered application of a restricted range of expressive, opaque colours. The story of the creation of the prints and of their reception by critics is an interesting one. Pat Gilmour argued that Piper's late prints are essentially photographic reproductions, but Rigby Graham (at the other extreme) has claimed that they are 'brighter, more intense, less restrained' and 'very different' in comparison with Piper's originals.[2]

Some editions including Ivychurch 1983 (cat 78) and the smaller prints of Scotney Castle 1982 (cat 72) were made by photo-etching Piper's images onto nylon-backed copper printing plates before adding the colour areas to the plates by hand. These were done by Nigel Oxley, also at Kelpra Studio. Each Scotney Castle etching was printed in eleven colours from two plates (one for shadows, the other for colour highlights).[3] A certain translucency and a uniform but grainy surface texture is the result. For the larger Scotney Castle print 1976 (cat 71), Piper worked upon a lithographic transfer medium from which the printing plates (one per colour) were made.

David Fraser Jenkins observes that Piper's late work has the marks of the 'accumulated impacts' of the challenges and interests of the artist's earlier career, including his work in stained glass (where he used radiant colours expressively and harmoniously) and his fondness for British architecture and topography. Piper's ultimate legacy, 'a gift of smiling colour'[4] endures in both the originals and the prints.

1. Essays by John Piper and Orde Levinson in *Quality and Experiment: John Piper - The Complete Graphic Works* (Lund Humphries 1996, and the new edn. 2010).
2. Rigby Graham quotes Gilmour in *Piper in Print*, ed. Hugh Fowler Wright (Artists' Choice Editions, 2010).
3. For the technical details see Nigel Oxley's *Colour Etching* (A&C Black, 2007) and Chris Prater's essay in Geoffrey Elborn (ed.), *To John Piper on His Eightieth Birthday* (Stourton Press, 1983).
4. David Fraser Jenkins' essay in *John Piper in the 1960s & 1970s*, an exhibition catalogue accompanying a show at Agnew's, London (November and December 2007).

Revd Dr Stephen Laird is Chaplain and Lecturer in Religious Studies at Kent University and Vicar of Blean, Canterbury. In his PhD thesis he explored the reflections of Christian sensibilities found in twentieth century British landscape painting. He is a regular contributer to *Art and Christianity*.

Three stained glass commissions in Kent and Sussex

Nicholas Cranfield

'I have not hesitated to make additions that seemed desirable within this context, especially about monuments and stained glass'[1] wrote Piper in 1969 when he and his friend John Betjeman jointly completed the *Shell Guide to Kent* that had been left unfinished by Pennethorne Hughes at his unexpected death.[2]

Stained glass had long been a love of Piper's and it long remained so, although in the 1969 guide only one of his photographs depicted a window.[3] An early photograph of his own studio, taken around 1936,[4] shows two of his large painted sketches of ancient glass alongside his modernist romantic abstracts; he later painted and photographed windows at Waterperry St Mary, in Oxfordshire.[5]

The juxtaposition of ancient glass and his abstract work in the 1936 photograph is informative for Piper's own deeply held view that Christian artists ('sculptors, wall-painters and glass-painters') never indulged in pure abstraction; 'their abstraction', he wrote in 1938, 'such as it is, is always subservient to an end – the Christian end, as it happened'.[6]

The three windows in Kent and Sussex date from 1981 (St Lawrence College, Ramsgate - chapel window) and 1985 (Lamberhurst St Mary and Firle St Peter). In the window at Ramsgate (not in this exhibition) Piper's contribution is a Christ figure based on the Romanesque tympanum of the pilgrimage church at Beaulieu-sur-Dordogne.

The more successful windows, both made by David Wasley, are those for the two parish churches. Sheep feature predominantly in both and their inclusion marks the artist's final return to landscape, a far cry from the abstracted windows (1969-1971) that, for instance, so delight at Totternhoe St Giles, Nettlebed St Bartholomew or at Wellingborough All Hallows, all jointly made with Patrick Reyntiens.

Following the death of the seventh Viscount Gage in 1982, for whom Piper had previously painted three aspects of Firle Place, his daughter (The Hon Lady Cazalet) wrote to Piper (August 19 1983) to commission a window to honour him in the local parish church.[7] The Pipers met the family, and the local Archdeacon, at a party at Firle in January 1984 to discuss this further and a design was shown to the parish in April that year. The final design is called *Homage to William Blake's Book of Job* and depicts the 'Tree of Life' from Revelation xxii, 2. (Locally Firle (or Ferle) is claimed as the Old English for an oak and the Gage family crest is surmounted by a ram.)

The design drew substantially on the *Design for the curtain 'Earth' - scene 1 of the ballet Job* (cat 104), that Piper had designed for the 1948 revival of the 1931 Ninette de Valois ballet that had first been performed at Sadlers' Wells. When the company transferred to the stage of the Royal Opera House after the War it was found that the original Gwendolen Raverat designs were too small and Piper was brought in to design the major revival (20 May 1948).

At Lamberhurst Peter de Rougemont had commissioned a memorial window for his first wife who also died in 1982. Both had been friends of the Pipers and Piper used a design that he had originally prepared for the three light window at Firle; when the Gage family chose to use a different window Piper offered the design to Lamberhurst.

It is based on a carved wooden panel from one of the doors (Holztür) of the Romanesque church of St Maria-im-Kapitol at Köln, dating to c. 1065.[8] The angel, which is also reminiscent of that in his 1973 lithograph *The Annunciation to the Shepherds*, provoked considerable discussion.

Piper drafted a letter to Basil Marshall, the priest in charge at Lamberhurst who was about to retire, in which he offered to 'translate back' the angel as there were mixed views about the angel's face. Peter de Rougemont made it clear, when Piper read him the proposed letter, that he would not sanction any changes and so Piper never sent the letter. On 8 October de Rougemont wrote to the PCC strongly supporting the 'new' angel and in the end this image was accepted.[9]

The common theme of both windows is the localised setting. The sheep also introduced a personal note as Piper had owned a flock of sheep since 1961 when he had bought them when he discovered the difficulty of drawing a sheep's head for the Parable windows in Eton College Chapel (Luke xv, 4 -7) although those at Firle represent the local Southdown breed.

Whether including local referents or working more universally as an abstract artist Piper always saw his work as being subservient to an end, the service of the Church; 'the Christian end, as it happened'.

1. Hughes, P. *Kent A Shell Guide* (1969), p 7.
2. Piper also included 77 of his black and white photographs among the illustrations.
3. The window *Joy Creation and Love* was made by Morris and Co in 1903 for Shoreham St Peter and St Paul from a design by Burne Jones (op.cit, p140). Piper's own first attempt at stained glass was a commission gained for him by Betjeman for Oundle School Chapel in 1953.
4. Jenkins, D. F. (ed.) *John Piper A Painter's Camera* (1987), p 13.
5. Osborne, J. *John Piper and Stained Glass* (1997), illustrated at p 34.
6. Piper, J. 'Abstraction on the Beach' *XXe Siècle* I (1938) p 41.
7. Incorrectly entered as 1987 in Orde Levinson's *Catalogue Raisonné* 2010 p 214.
8. These are now displayed at the west end of the south aisle, indoors.
9. Osborne, J. (op.cit., p 137) inadvertently reprinted the letter to Basil Mitchell as if it was sent. I am grateful to Mr de Rougemont for sending me the original correspondence.

Revd Dr Nicholas Cranfield FSA, former Fellow of Selwyn College, Cambridge currently lives and works in South East London. He has collected works by Piper for 35 years and writes regularly as arts correspondent for the Church Times and other publications.

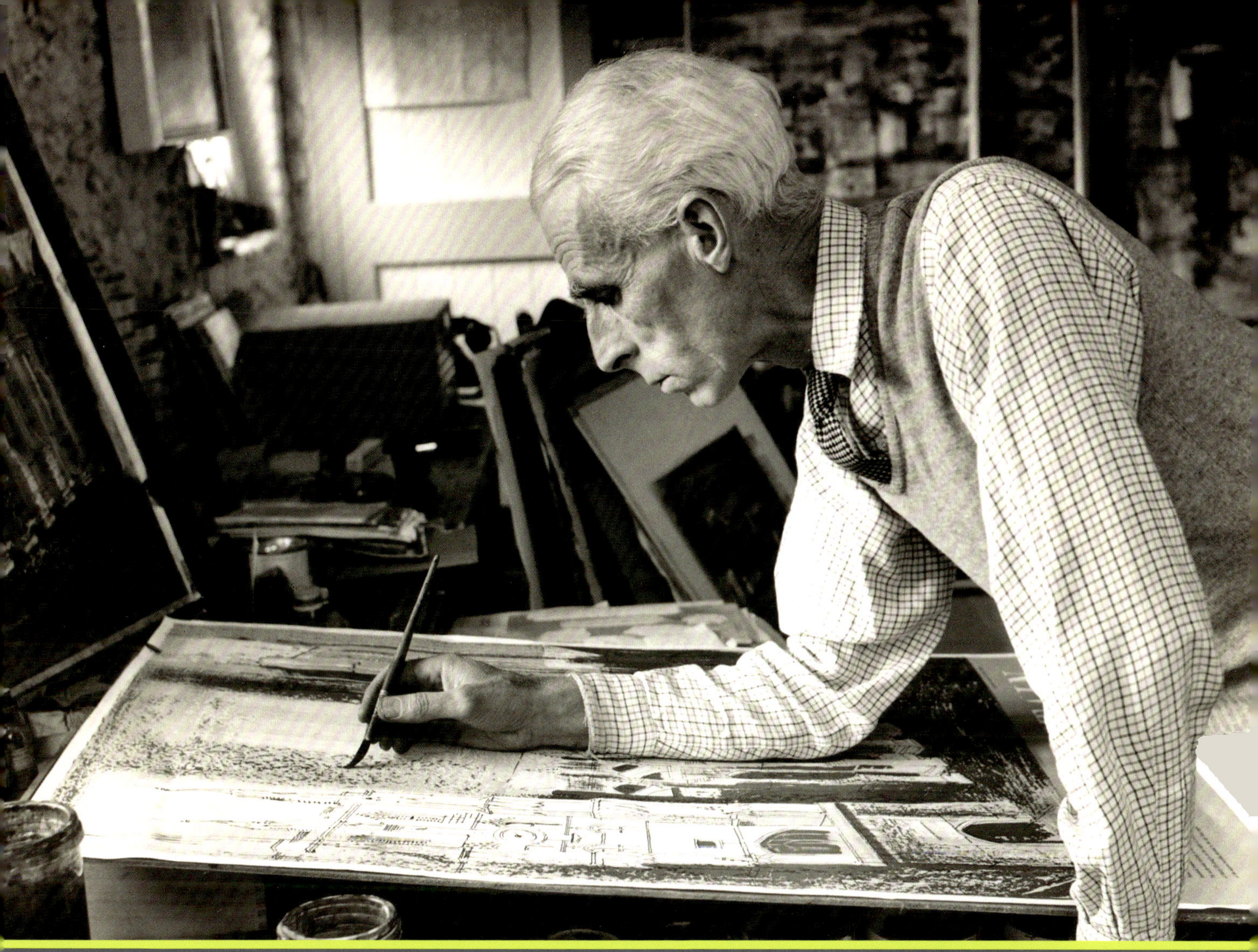

Landscape in Kent & Sussex

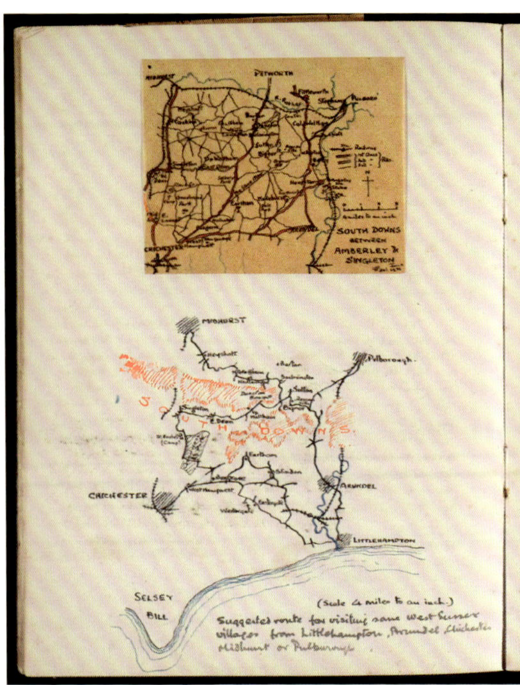

SOME WEST SUSSEX VILLAGES.

There are few sights more pleasing than, when walking on the South Downs, you watch a combe or valley gradually open out as you approach it, and disclose a village or hamlet, with the cottages appearing one by one, huddled round the old grey church. The village will be built towards the foot of the slope of the Downs, which, if you are in western Sussex, will probably be wooded right to the top. Just such a village as this is Bignor, hidden away in a cup of the Downs to the South-west of Pulborough. Bignor was a place of importance in the days of the Romans; for it stands on the Stane Street, their great military highway from Chichester to London, and was the site of a villa, whose pavements have been unearthed in a field near the village.

Mr. Hilaire Belloc, who was born at Slindon on the southern slope of the Downs, has written very

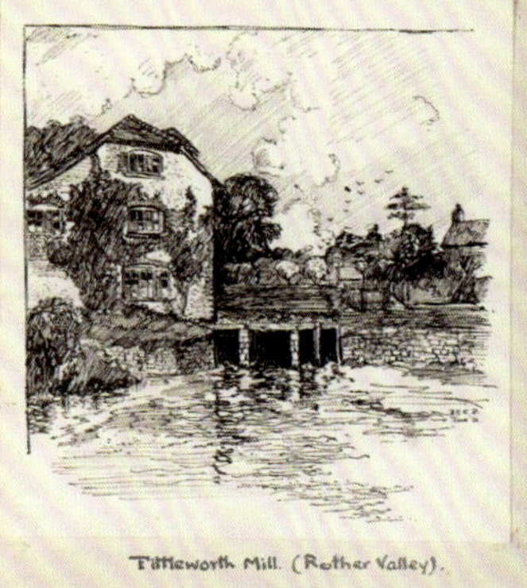

Tittleworth Mill. (Rother Valley).

1. ***Journey books***
1921

Ink
23 x 36 cm

Tate

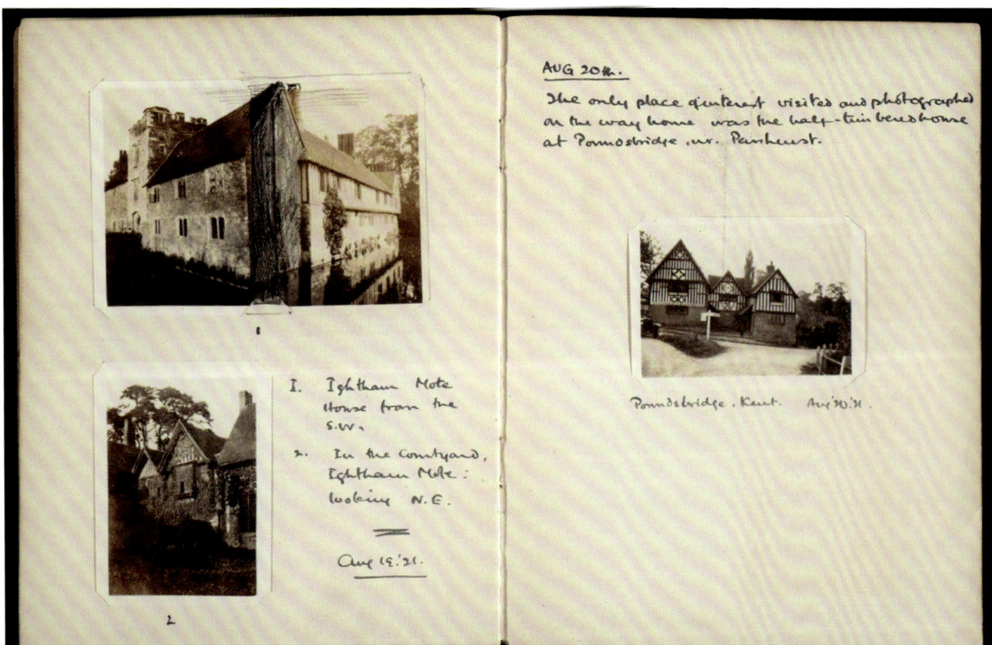

1

2

1. Ightham Mote House from the S.W.
2. In the Courtyard, Ightham Mote: looking N.E.

Aug 19.'21.

AUG 20th.

The only place of interest visited and photographed on the way home was the half-timbered house at Poundsbridge, nr. Penshurst.

Poundsbridge. Kent. Aug 20.'21.

2. ***Journey books***
1921

Ink and photographs
23 x 36 cm

Tate

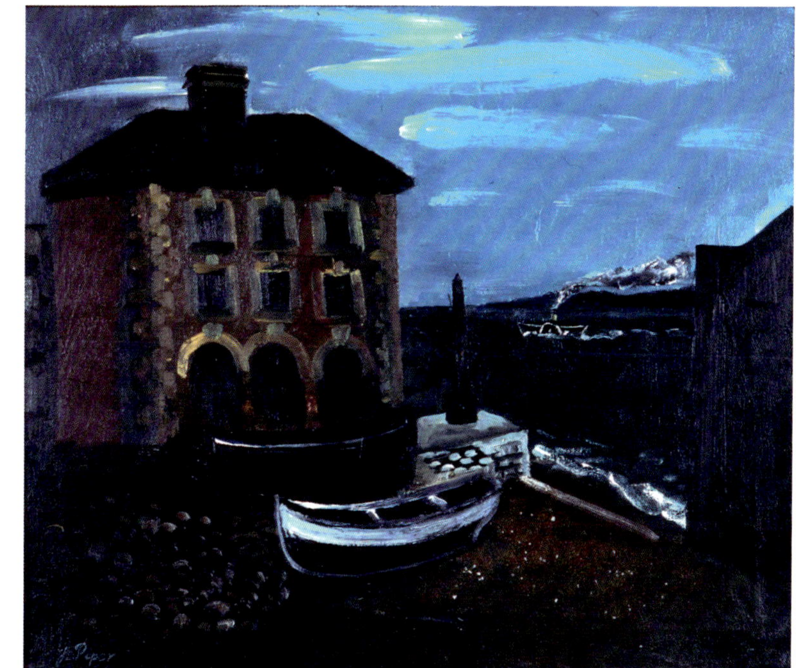

3. ***Custom House***
1930

Oil and sand on canvas
49.5 x 59.1 cm

Private collection

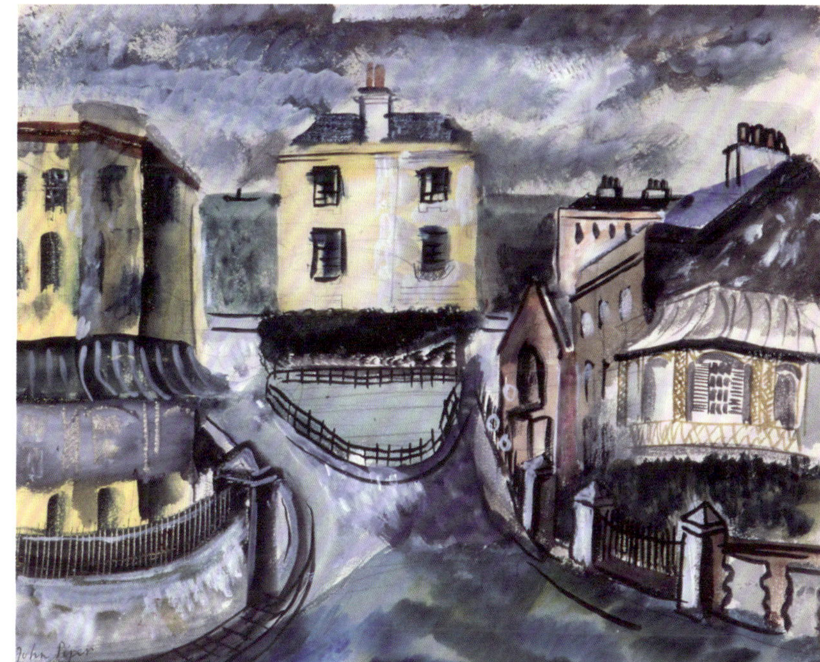

4. ***Apartment houses***
c. 1931

Ink, pencil and watercolour
35.6 x 44.5 cm

Private collection

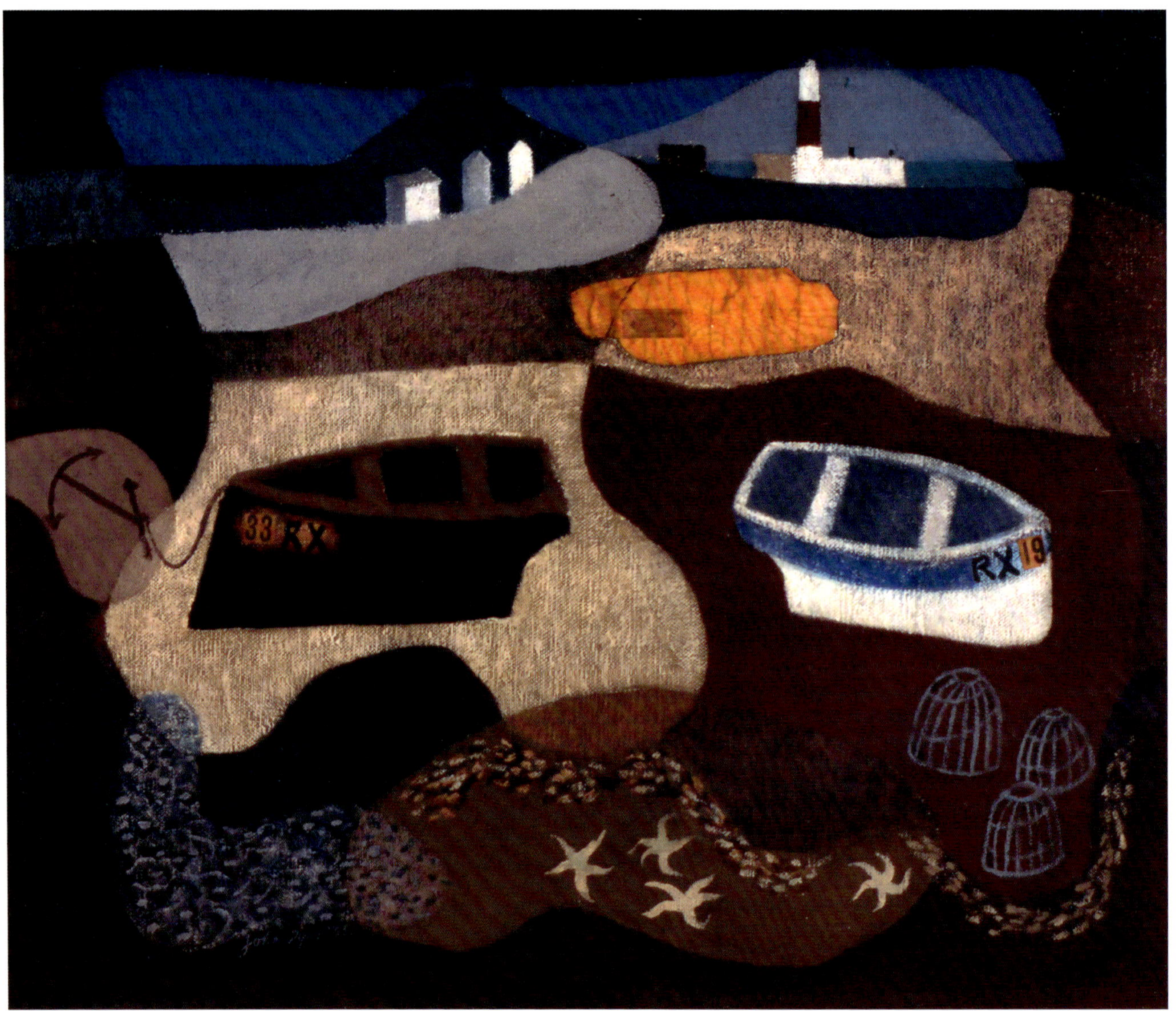

5. ***Foreshore with Boats, south coast***
1933

Oil and collage on canvas
62.2 x 74.9 cm

Private collection

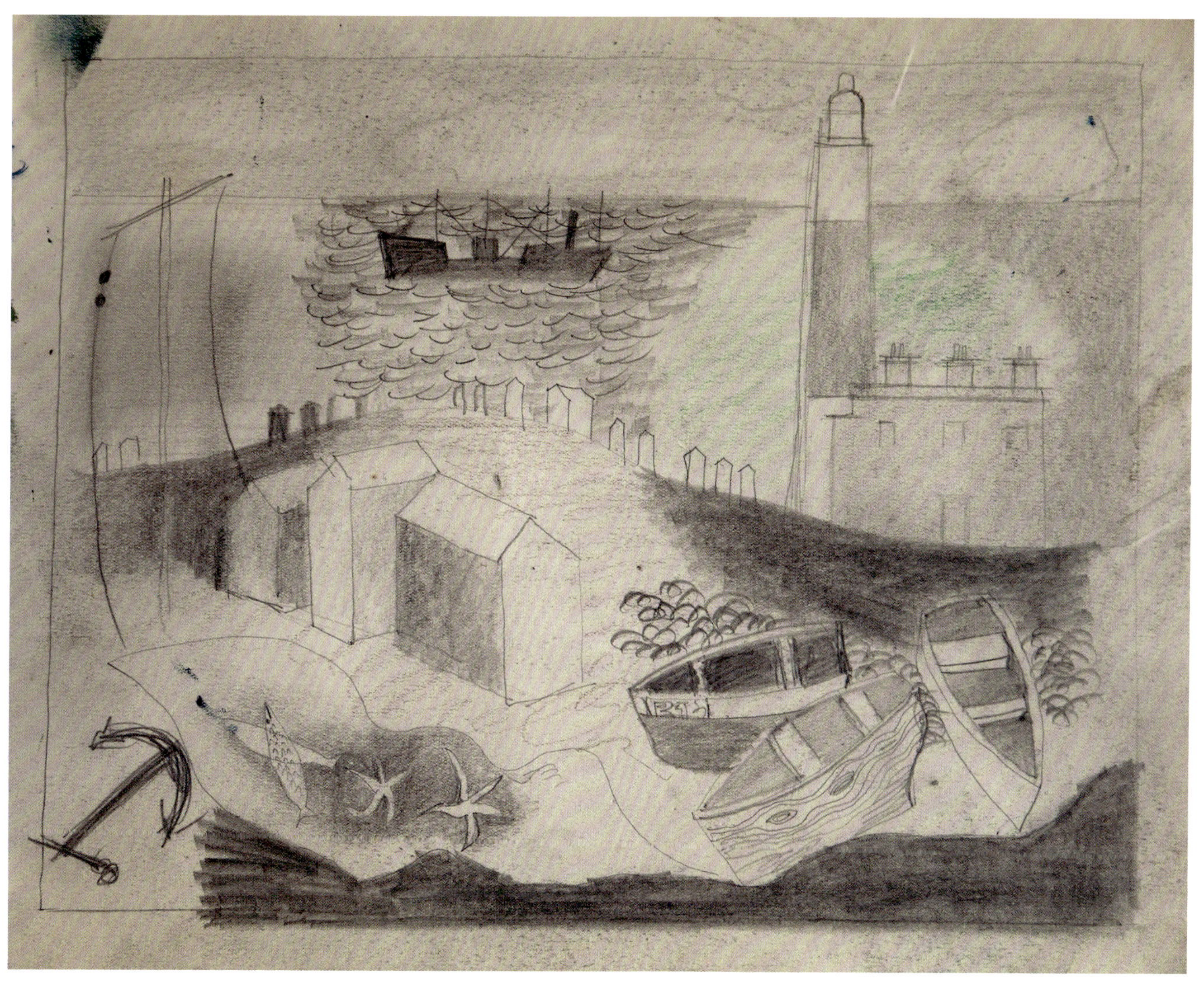

6. ***Sketchbook***
1934

Pencil
17 x 25 cm

Private collection

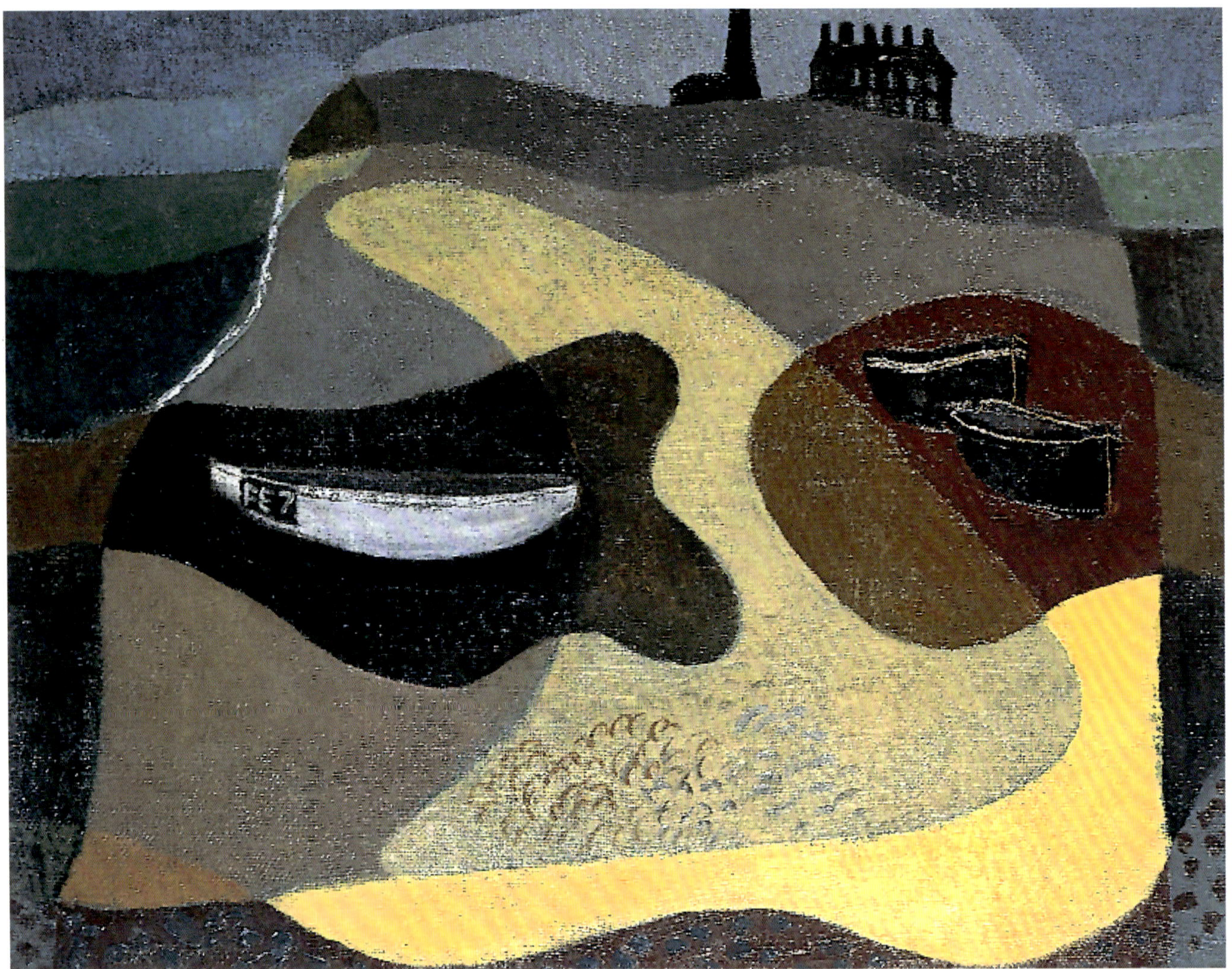

7. ***Boats on Shore***
1933

Oil on canvas
44.4 x 54.4 cm

Kirklees Collection, Huddersfield Art Gallery

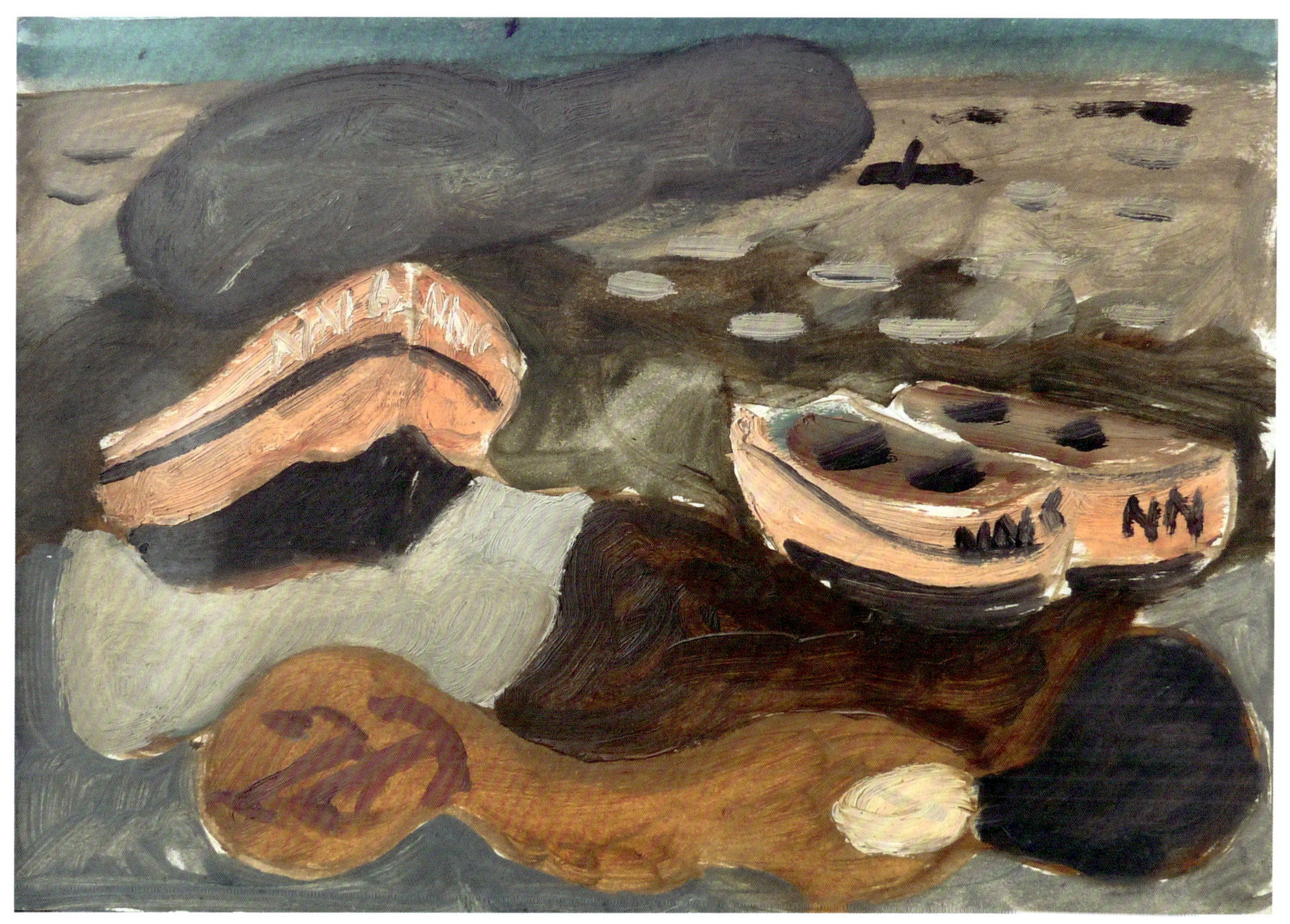

8. ***Sketchbook***
1933

Mixed media
17 x 25 cm

Private collection

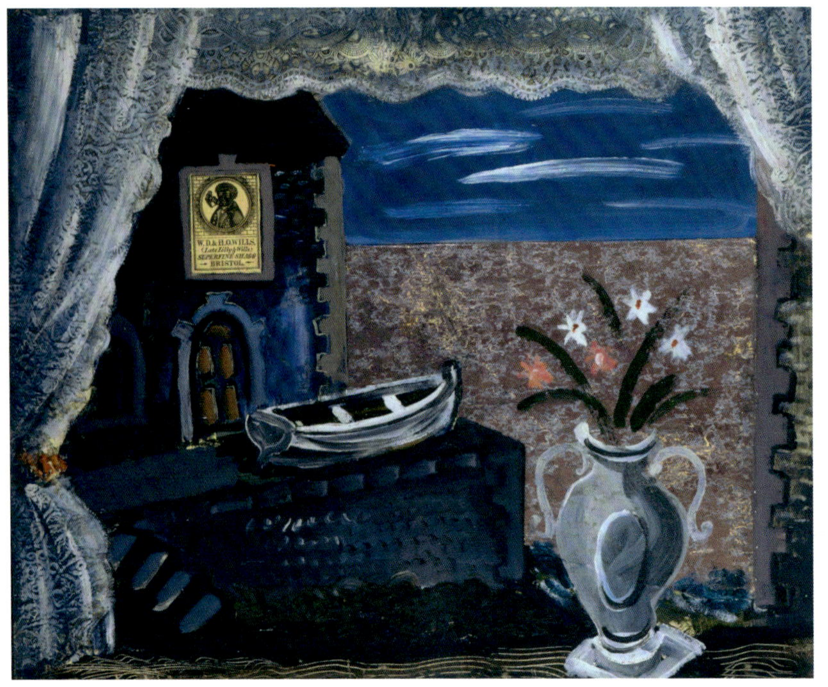

9. ***The Harbour at Night***
1933

Oil and collage
50 x 60.5 cm

Private collection

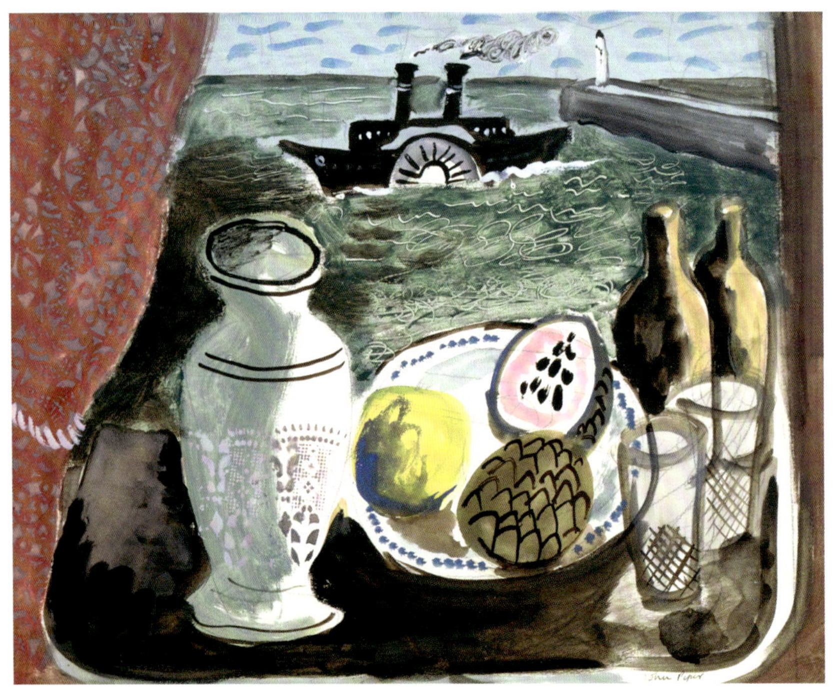

10. ***Still Life with Window, Paddle Steamer and Pier***
1932

Pencil, watercolour and gouache with stencil
37.5 x 47 cm

Courtesy of the Derek Williams Trust, on loan to Amgueddfa Cymru - National Museum Wales since 1984

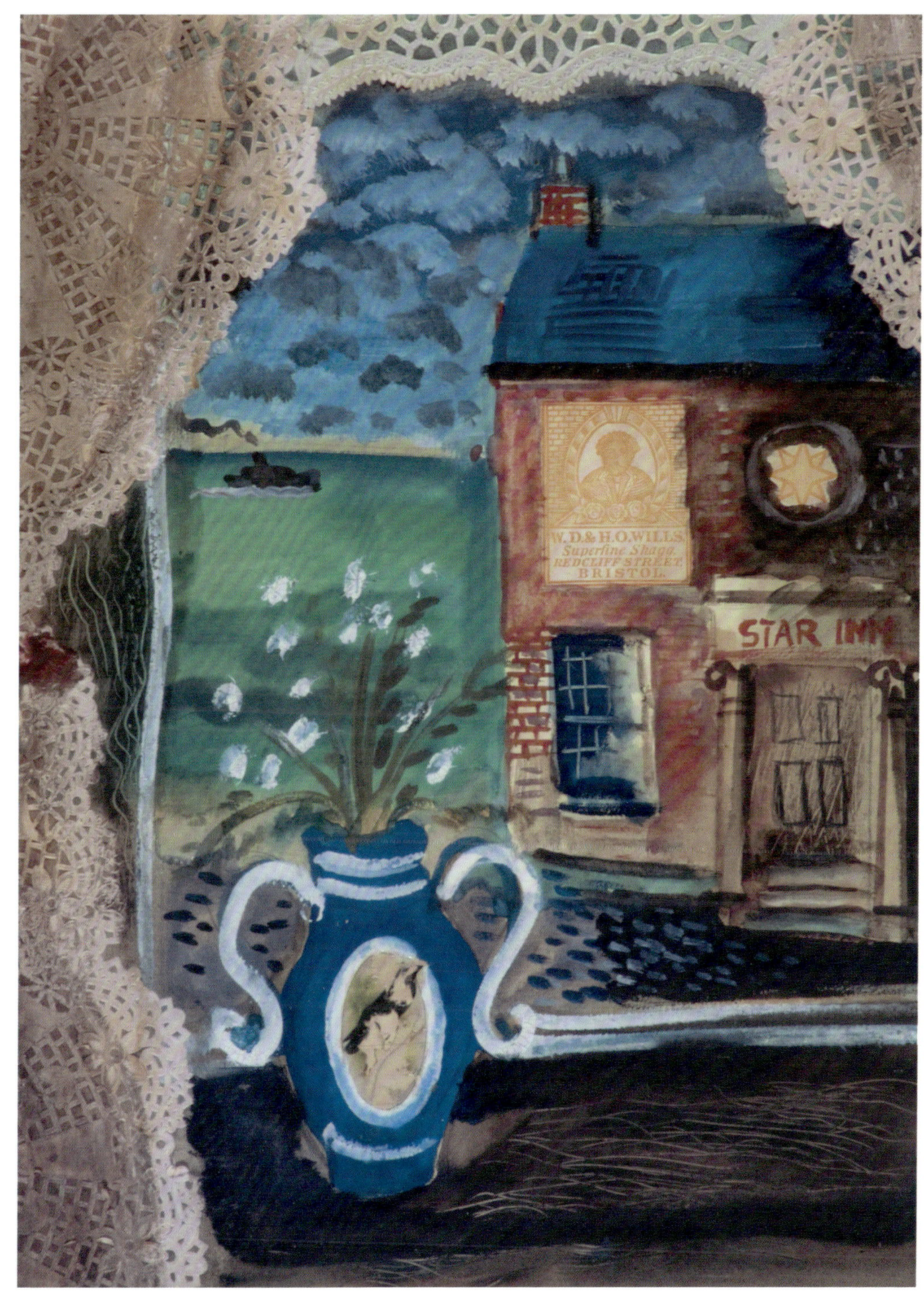

11. ***Star Inn***
1933

Watercolour and collage
46.5 x 33.5 cm

Private collection

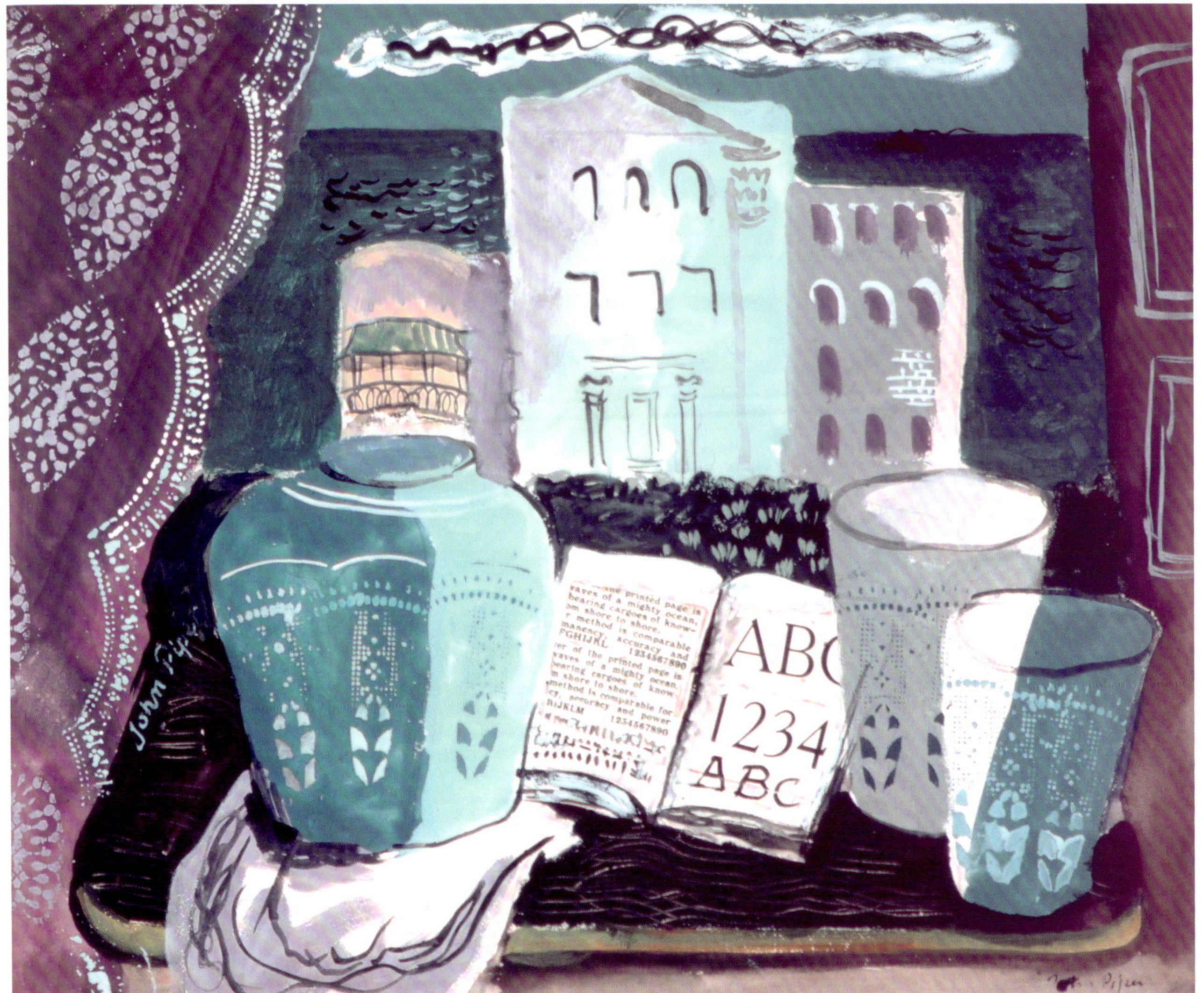

12. ***Houses on the Front***
1932

Watercolour and collage
with stencil
37.5 x 46.3 cm

Private collection

13. ***Beach with Shells***
1933

Pencil, ink, gouache and oil with
collage
49 x 38.1 cm

Victoria & Albert Museum, Given by the Artist

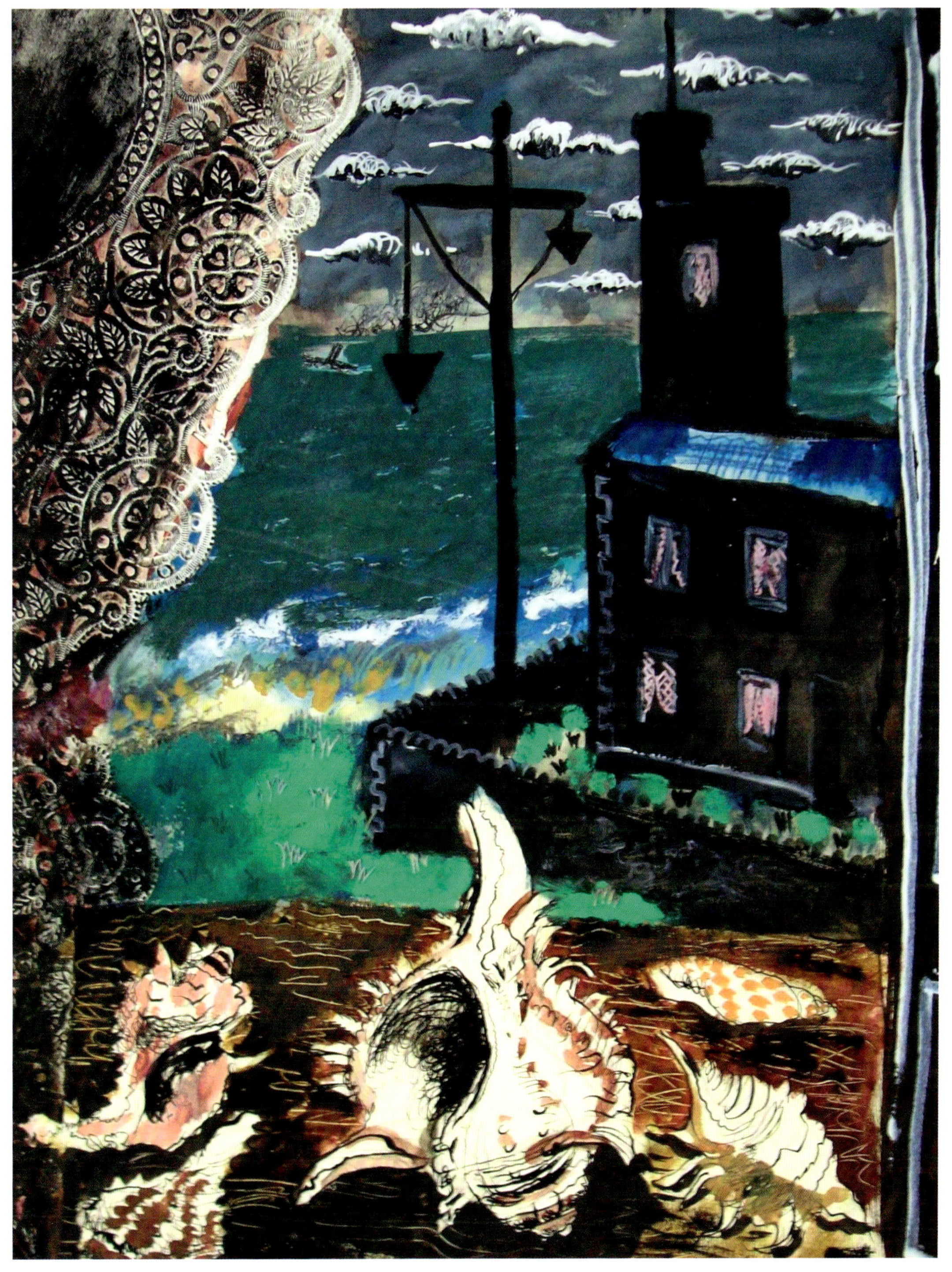

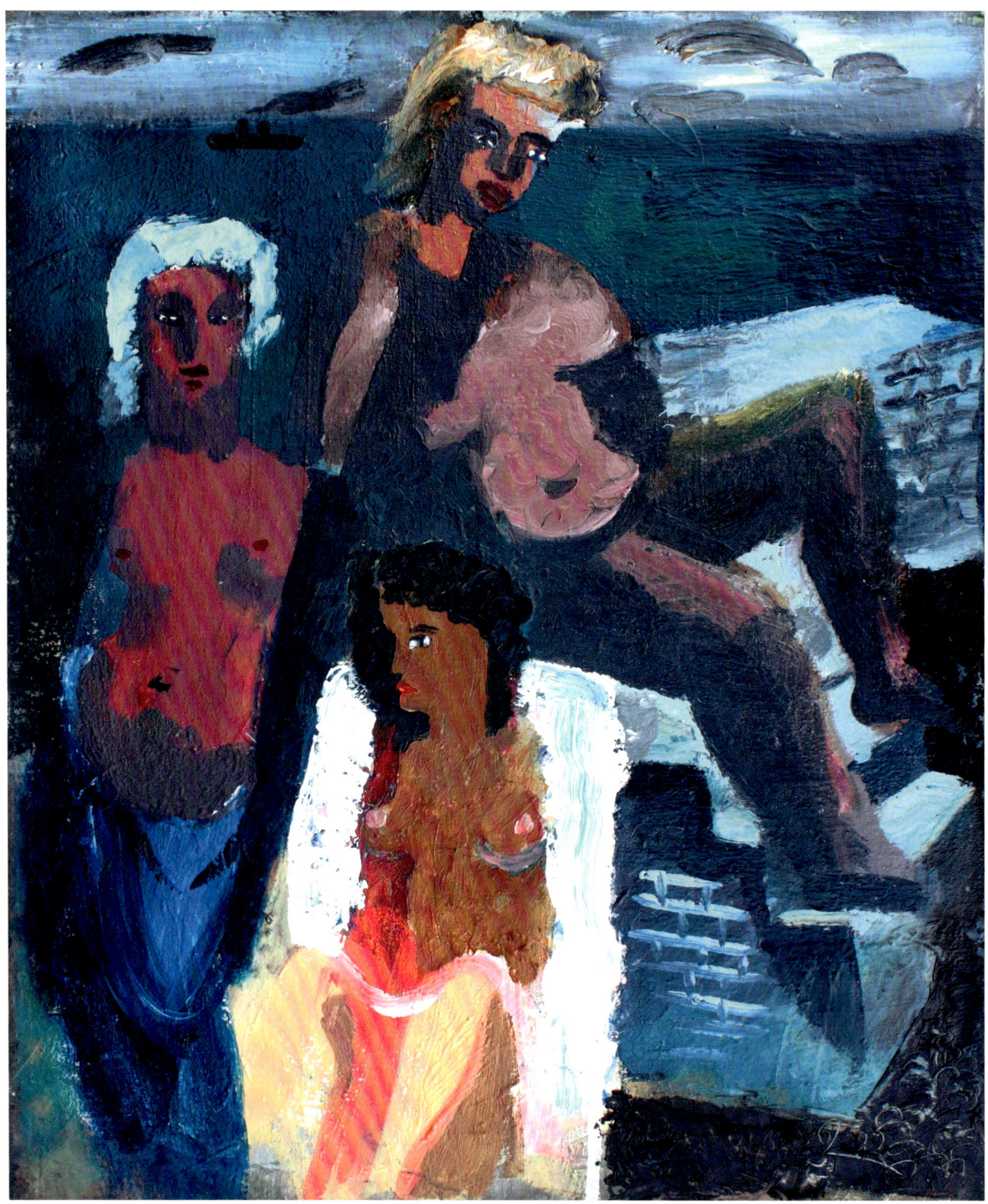

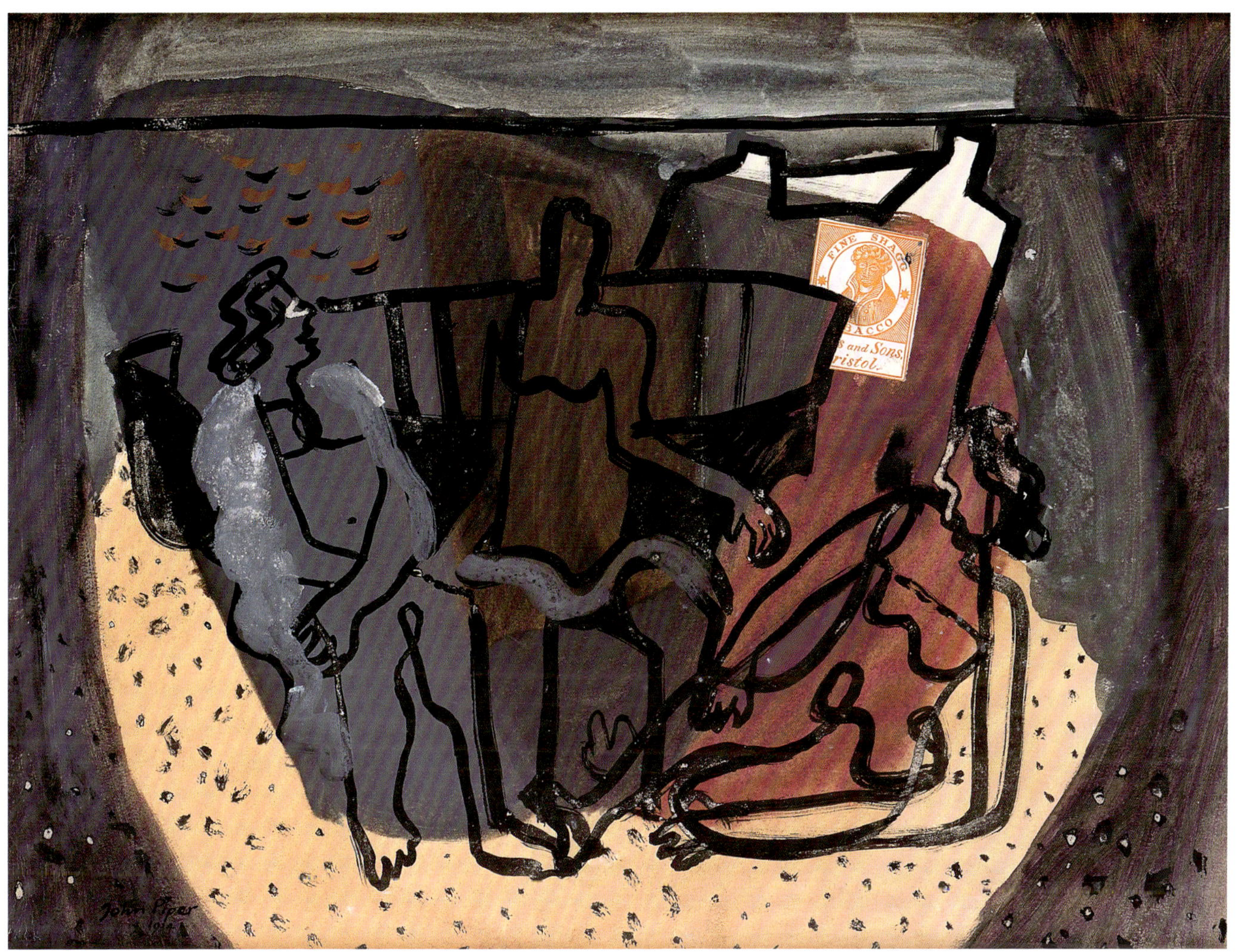

14. ***Dungeness Beach Girls***
1933

Oil on canvas
61 x 50.8 cm

Private collection

15. ***Three Bathers beside the Sea***
1934

Collage and gouache on card
38 x 51 cm

Pallant House Gallery, Chichester (Accepted by HM Government in lieu of Inheritance Tax, Katherine Duff-West Bequest. Allocated to Pallant House Gallery, 2003)

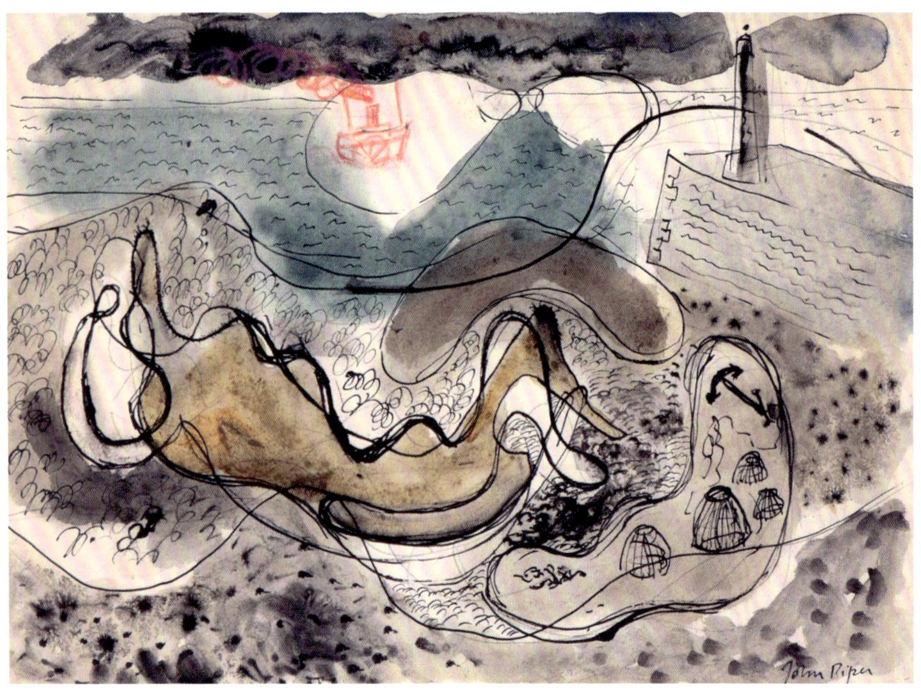

16. ***Beach Scene***
1933

Watercolour, ink
and crayon
28 x 38 cm

Private collection

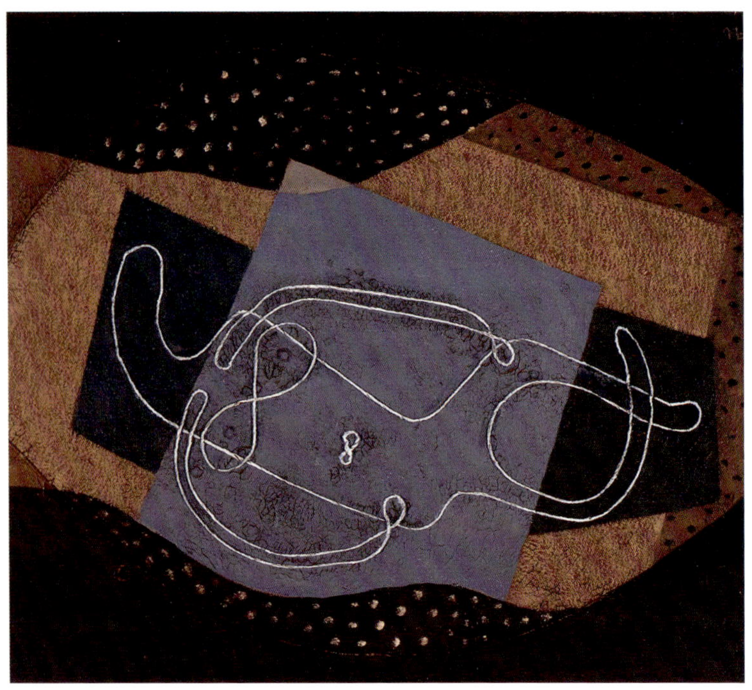

17. ***String Solo***
1934

Mixed media,
oil and string on
canvas
47.5 x 55.9 cm

The River and Rowing
Museum, Henley-on-Thames

18. ***String Figures***
1934

Oil and string on
canvas
68.6 x 55.9 cm

Private collection

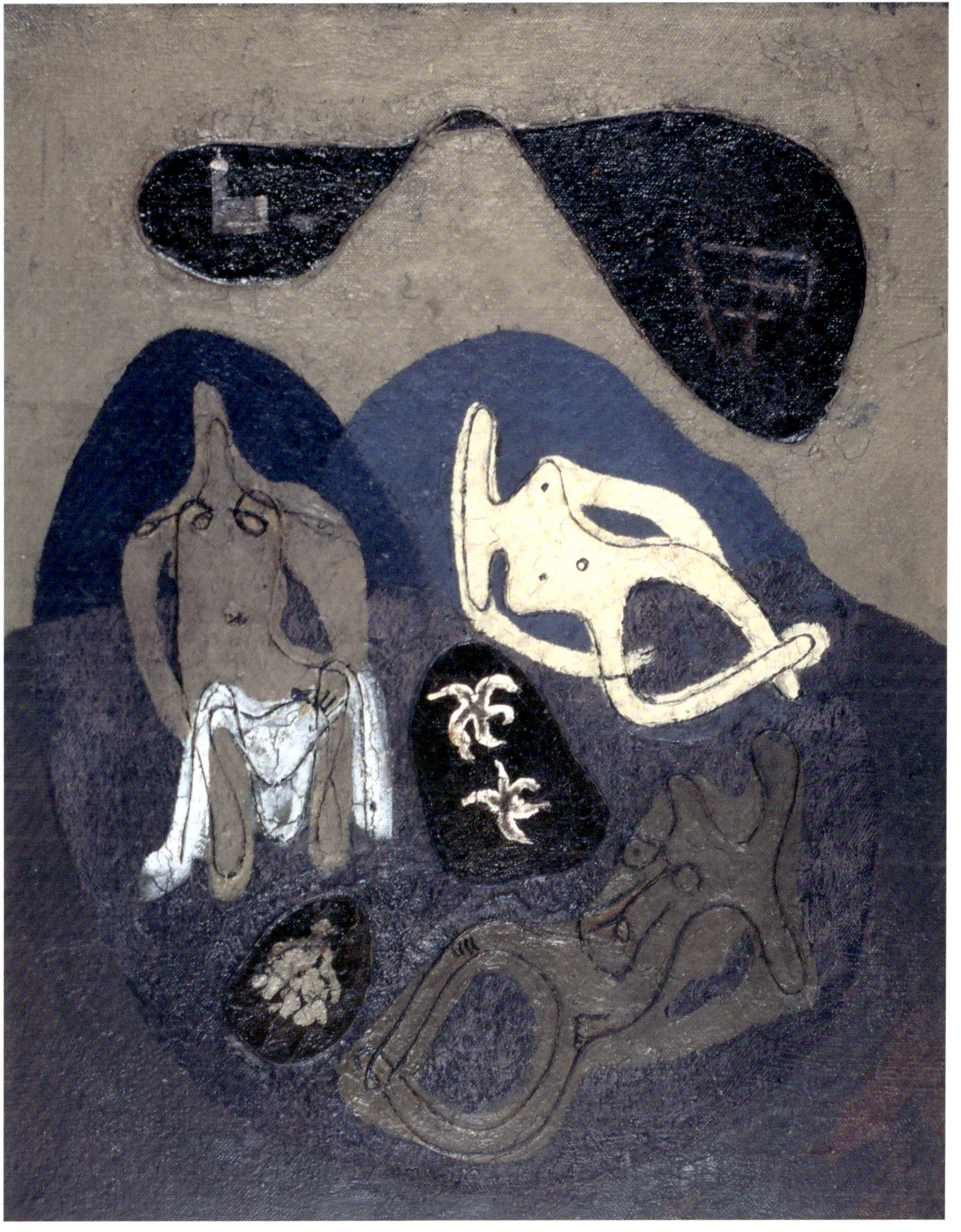

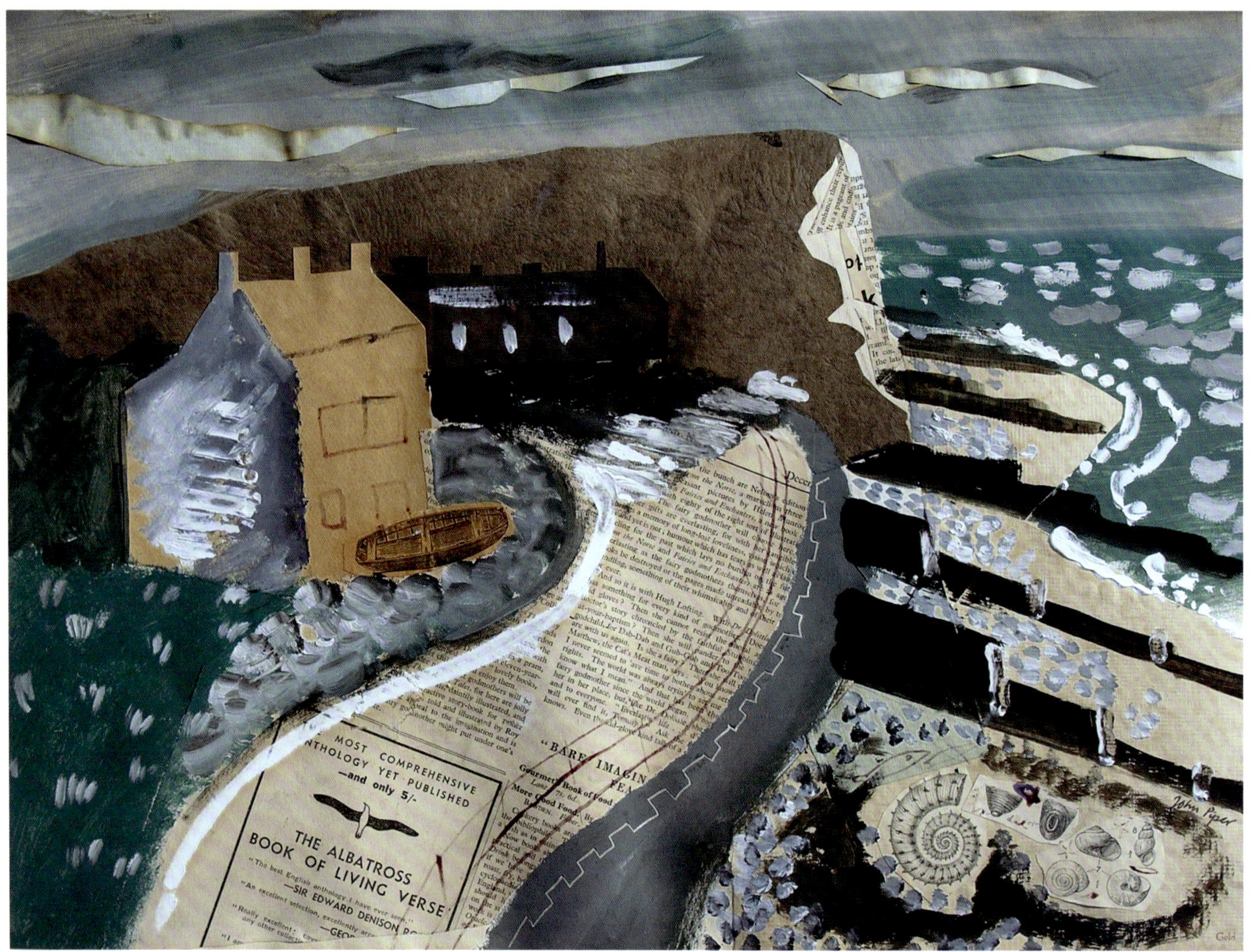

19. ***Seaford Head***
1933

Ink, watercolour and collage
37.5 x 50 cm

Private collection

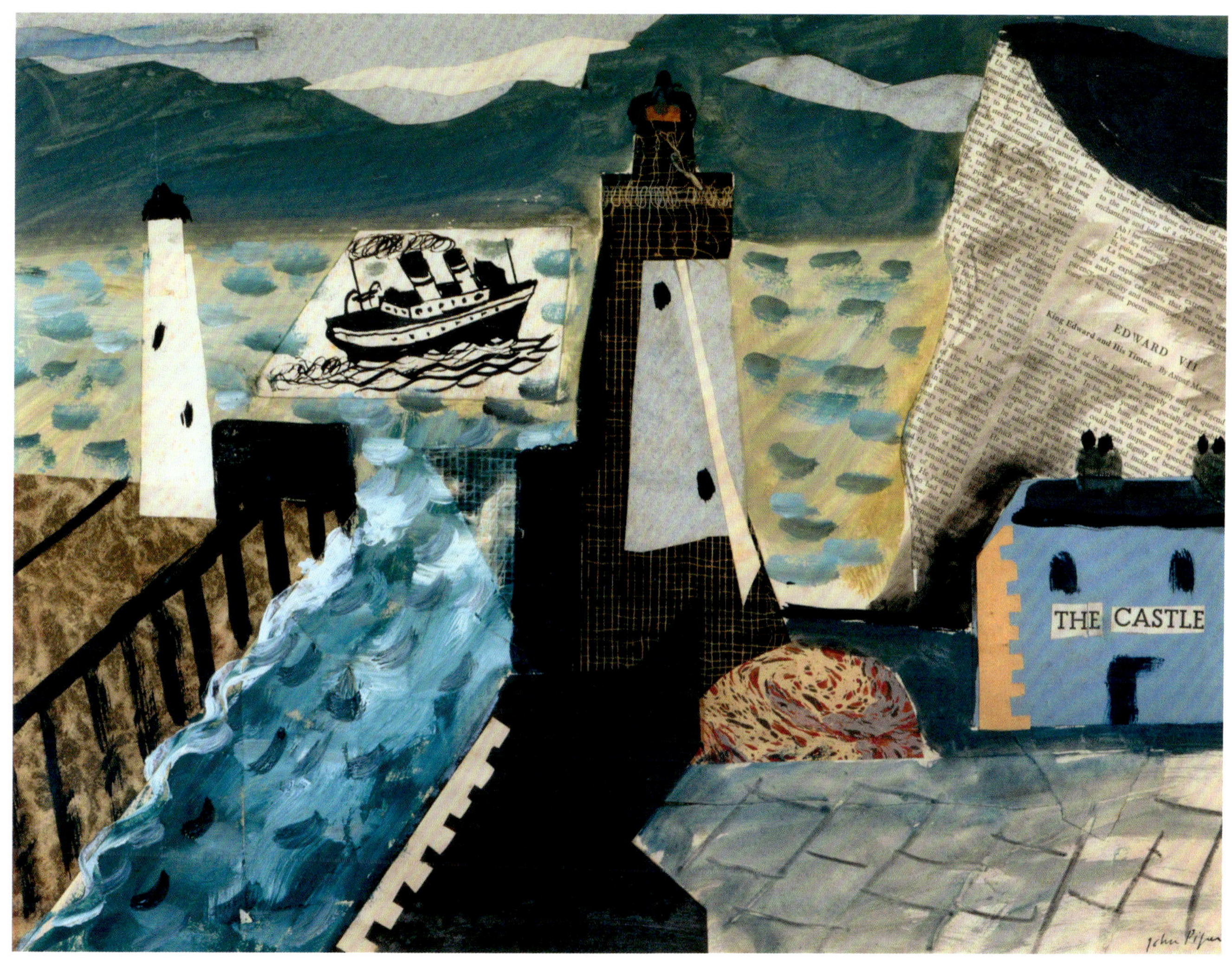

20. ***Newhaven, The Castle***
1934

Ink and oil with collage
37 x 50 cm

Private collection

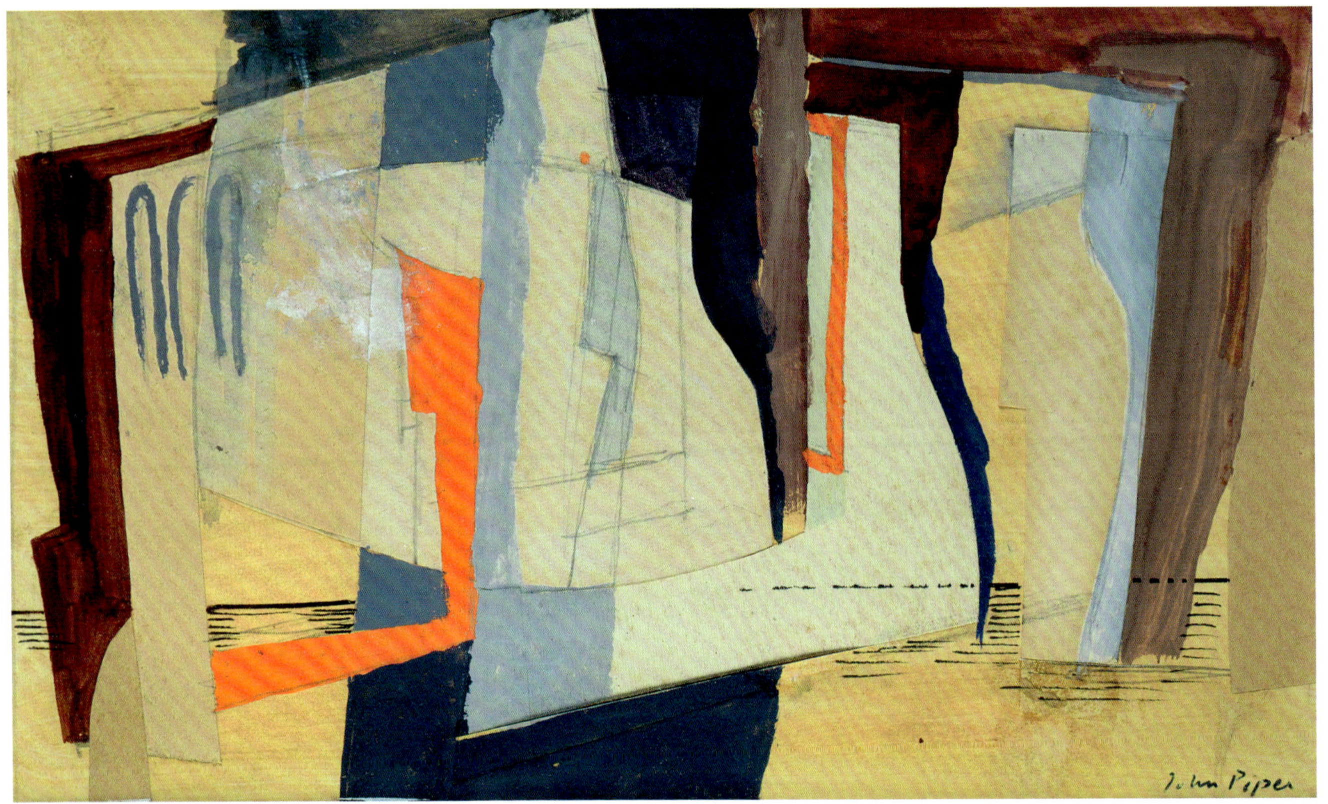

21. ***Abstract***
1935

Ink, watercolour and collage on paper
11.2 x 19 cm

Pallant House Gallery, Chichester (Kearley Bequest, through The Art Fund, 1989)

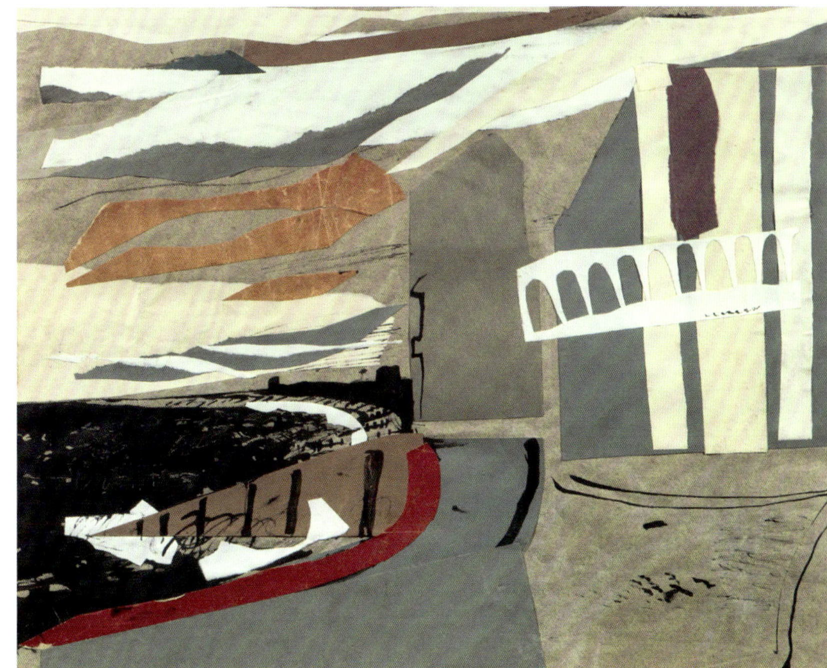

22. ***Littlestone-on-Sea***
1936

Ink and collage
35.9 x 47.6 cm

Tate

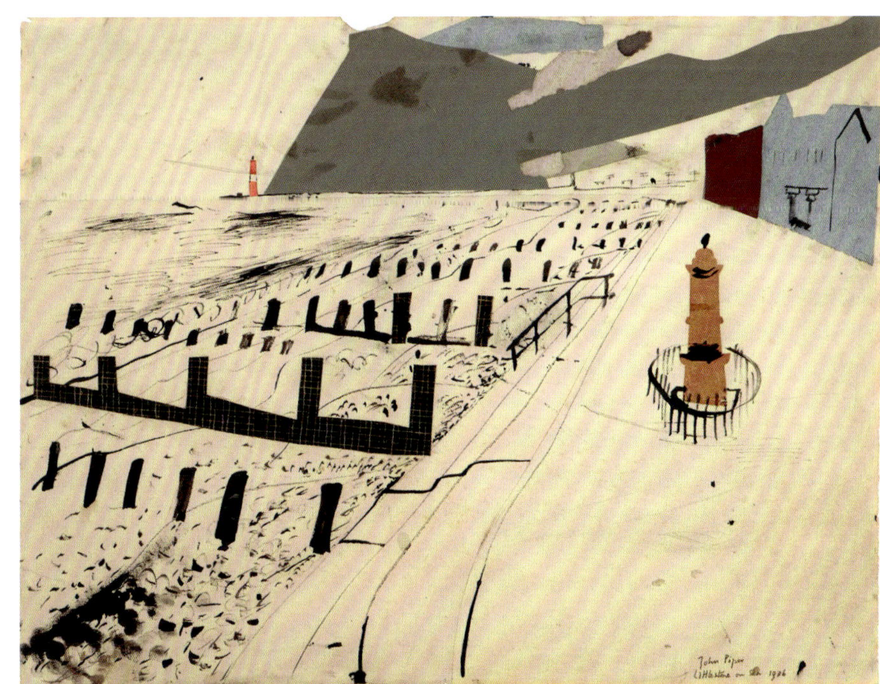

23. ***Littlestone-on-Sea***
1936

Ink and collage
36 x 48 cm

Kettle's Yard, Cambridge

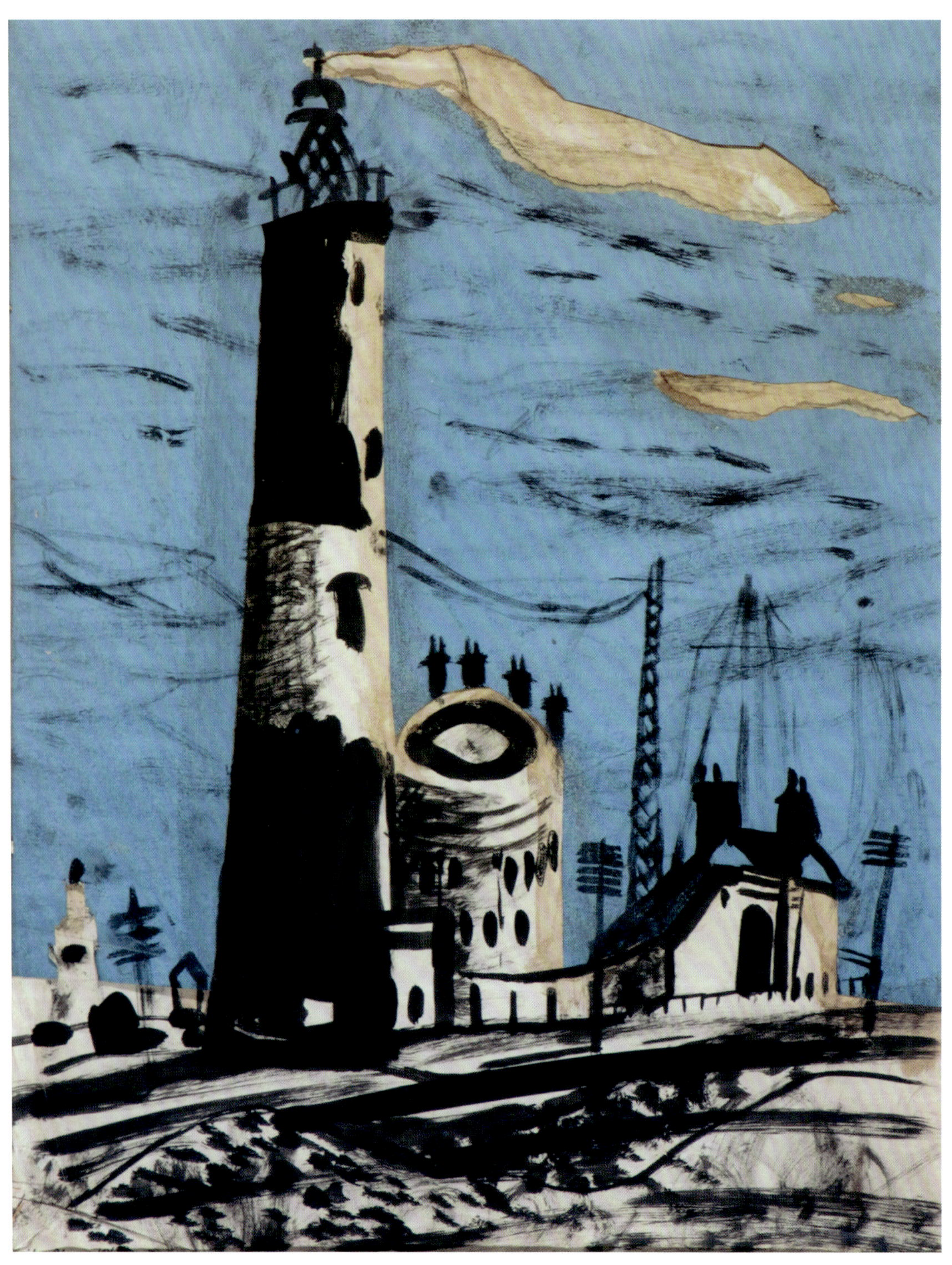

24. ***Lighthouse at Dungeness***
1936

Ink and collage
50.2 x 39 cm

Piper Estate on loan to
Rye Art Gallery, Sussex

25. ***Newhaven***
1937

Ink, gouache and collage
38 x 48 cm

Private collection

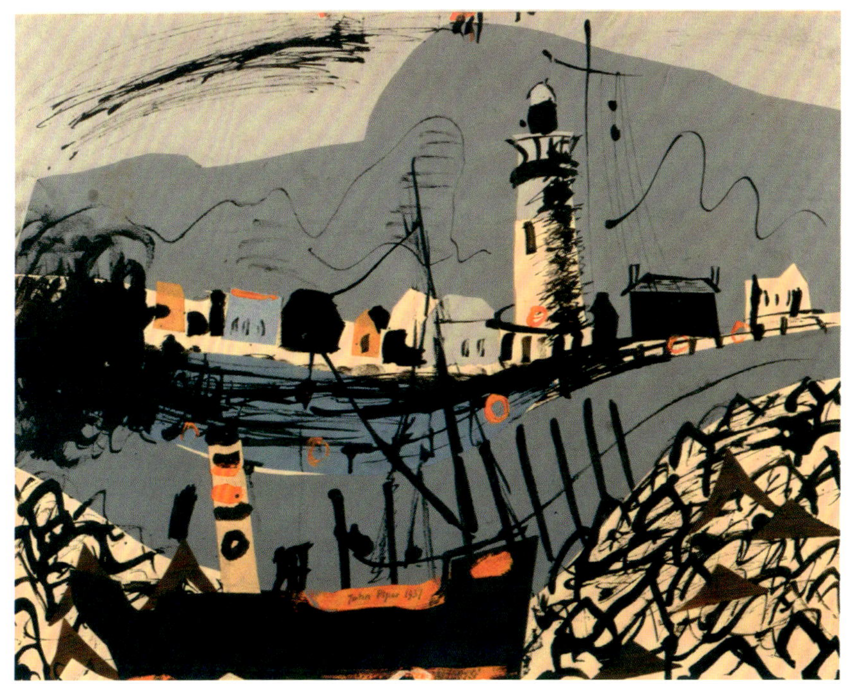

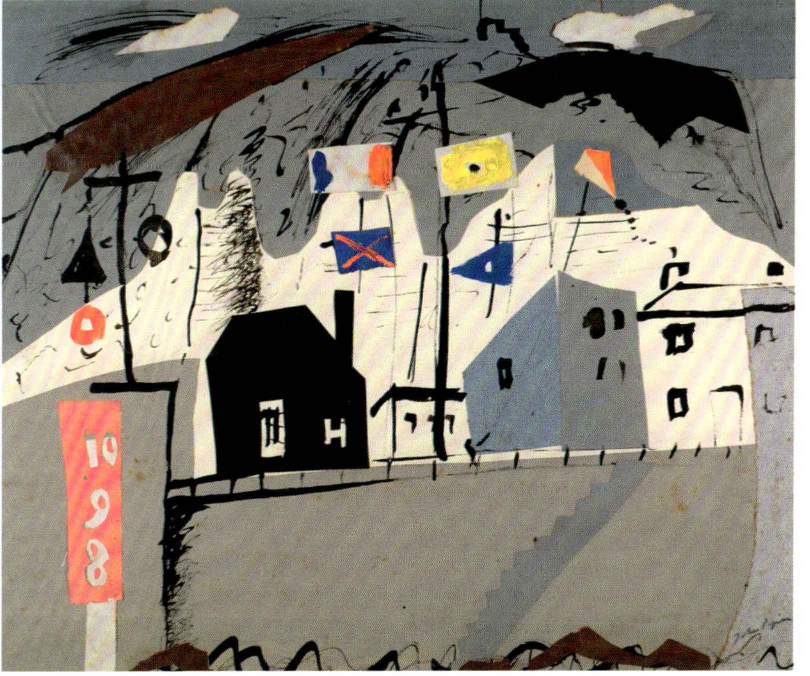

26. ***Newhaven, Sussex***
c. 1936-37

Ink, watercolour, gouache
and collage
39.4 x 48.2 cm

Private collection

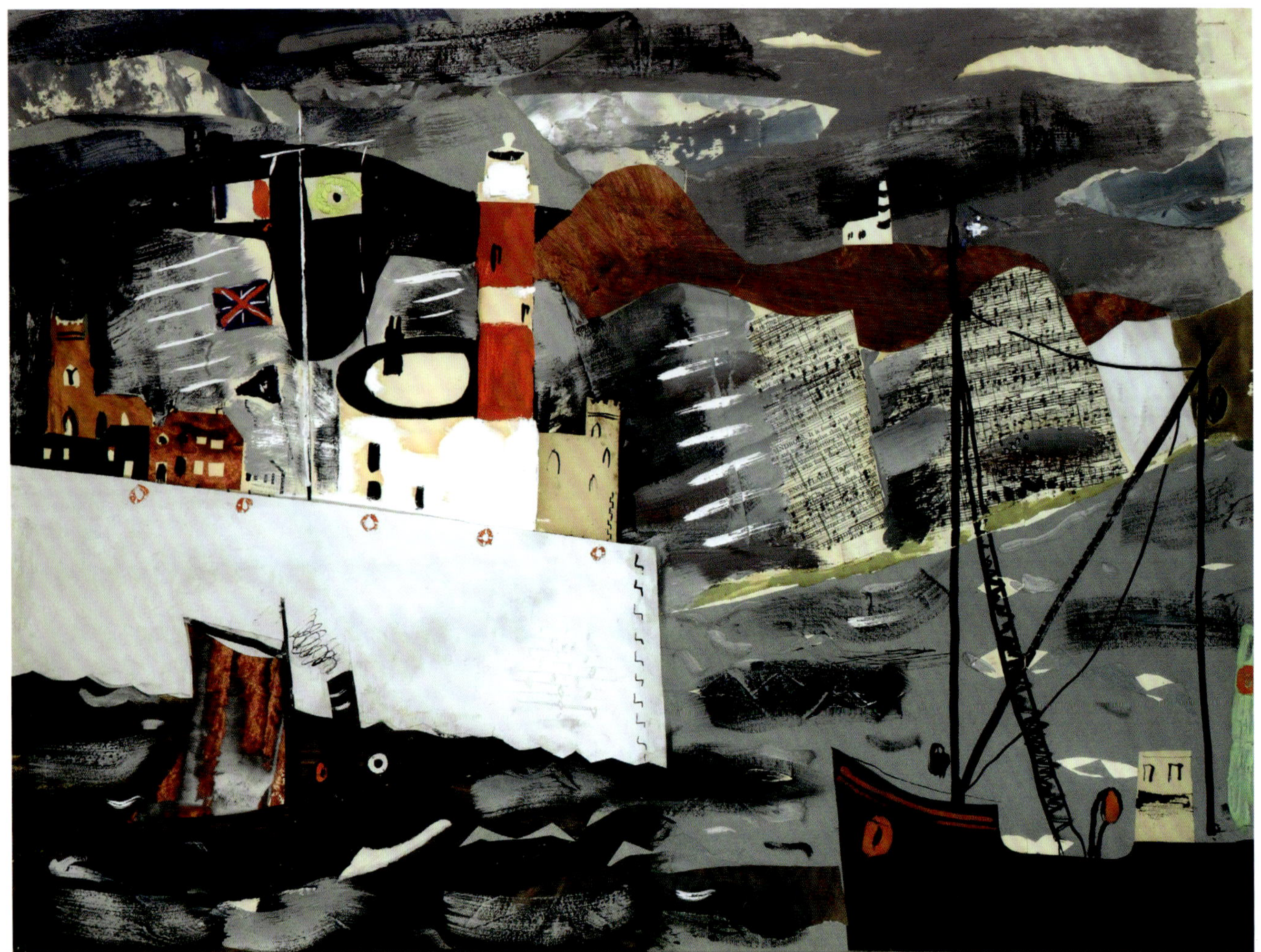

27. ***Harbour Scene, Newhaven***
1936-37

Ink, gouache and collage
60.9 x 81.3 cm

Private collection

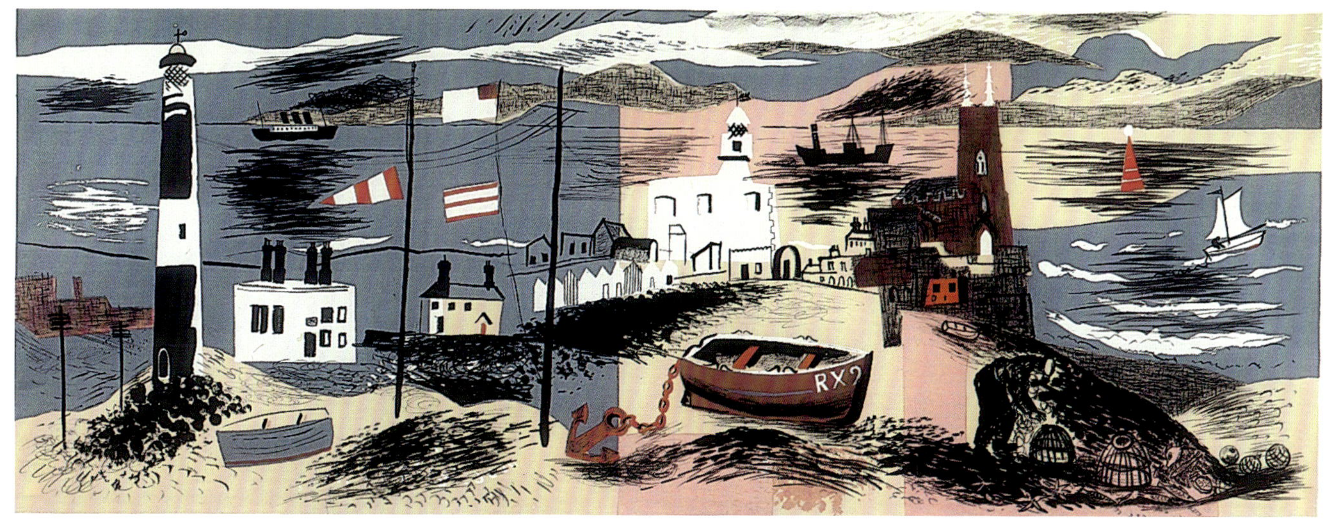

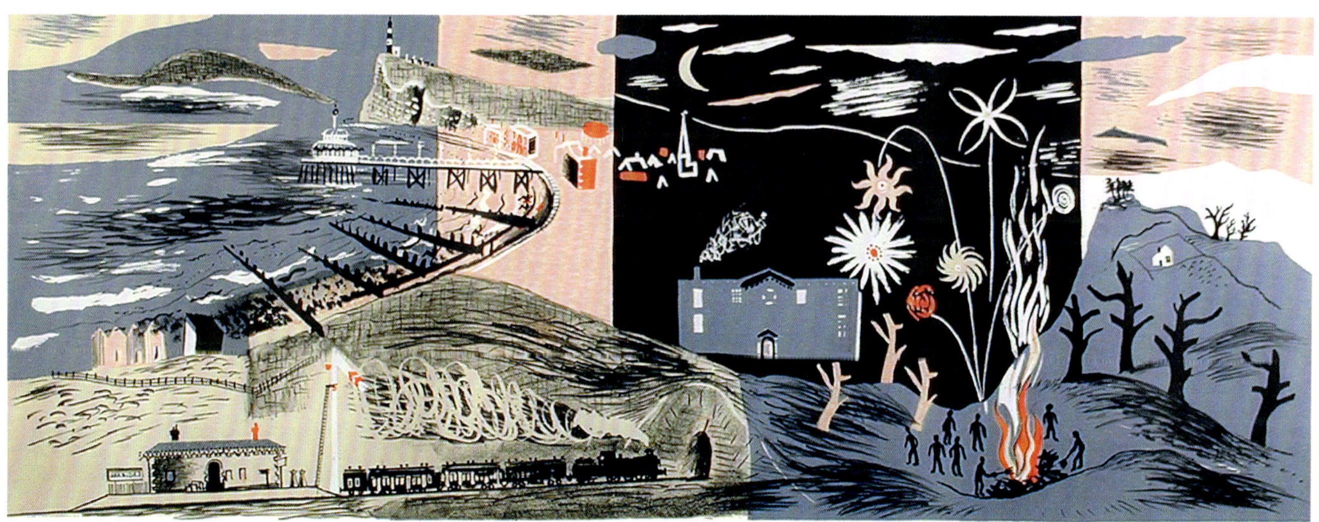

28. ***Nursery Frieze I and II Seaside & Landscape***
1936

Lithograph Levinson 8-9
46 x 122 cm

Private collection

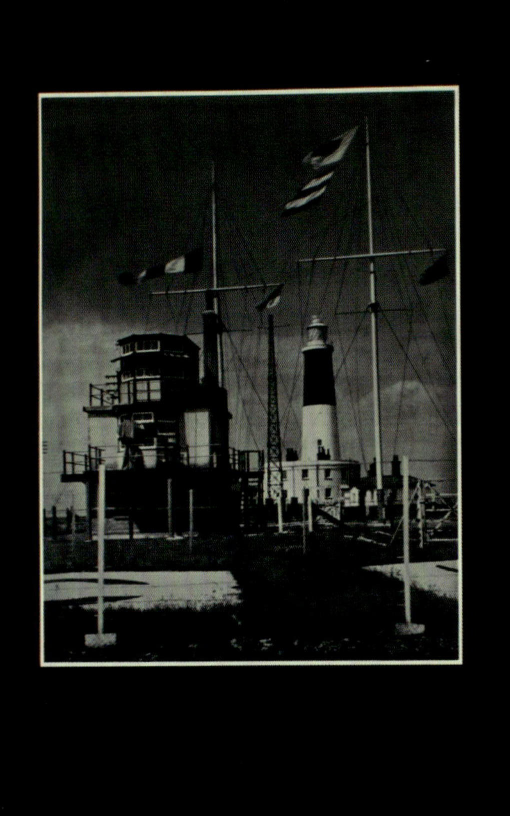

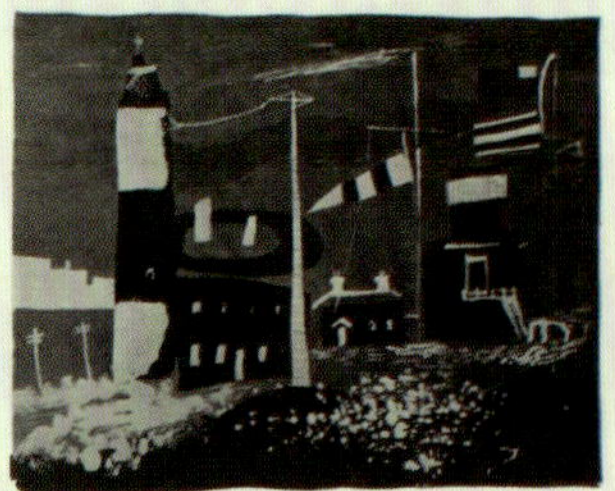

THE NAUTICAL STYLE

By JOHN PIPER

THERE is a clear tradition of sea-coast building—particularly in England, with its intense maritime pride and efficiency. This is a study of the fruits of the tradition, and of its development by generations of maritime builders; of the use they have made of the sea-influence and the frequent misuse that landsmen have made of it.

The tradition has a strong functional bias, and a vital one. This functionalism has two sides. On the coast waves break and salt foam scatters and denudes, gales blow stronger and the rain is more searching. Buildings must be sturdy and close to the earth. But besides that, the coast belongs to the mariner rather than the landsman. To the mariner the sea is a livelihood, but the coast is dwelling place, harbour, menace, shelter and everything else.

Sailor's taste has always played its part in coast building: the lighthouse is an obvious example. It is the most obvious of many functional buildings—the customs house, the lifeboat house with its slipway, the boat-building shed, the harbour itself—but even lighthouse builders have never banished taste altogether from their buildings. This taste is quite undefinable, but it has qualities that can be named. The first is gaiety. In colour, for instance: stripes, spots and a whole simple colour-symbolism belong to it—the gaiety that is reflected in sea shanties and in early naval prints. (And in "Sailors don't care.") The second quality is strength. Since a sailor has to depend on his boat for his life he never forgets, and sometimes exaggerates, the force of the wicked elements when he is building anything at all. The third quality is not so easy to suggest. It is the quality of strong contrasts, more than half functional but partly tasteful, found in the capacity to make a square stone jetty look right in a choppy sea, to put a simple cylindrical tower in the right place on a rounded hill, to cut water and air with sharp edges, to exaggerate the lightness of something that floats on the sea and the weight of something that resists it. Pure functionalism, centuries of trial and error, would never have got so far; would never be quite so right every time. Boat building is certainly the main direct influence on coast building in general, and boat building is by no means purely functional.

Above all these qualities there is a straightforwardness, an absence of *nuance*; but never an absence of romance. The *nuance* romanticist might find the whole nautical tradition harsh and disgusting but for one fact: that the tradition is itself one of contrast—contrast with the subtle colour and changes of colour in waves and in the sky over the sea, the subtle noises and silences of the sea, the exquisitely subtle, shifting, evanescent shapes of waves and sands and pebbles and cliffs. People think of this contrast when they say "I'm going to the sea for a change," or "for a breath of fresh air." (Or "Skegness is so bracing.") It is not simply the sea air that is such fun and such a change, it is the whole gamut of heightened contrasts that the seaside provides, and that is strong enough and infectious enough to make life there seem fuller and gayer.

When sea-coast towns first became resorts these desirable nautical qualities were played on by everyone. Instead of reflecting inland-town building habits builders made the most they could of seaside convictions and seaside quirks, to everyone's immediate delight and to posterity's benefit. People who went to the seaside for a change got it—and it was a matter of more than the presence of the sea, that they were not used to, and the change of air. But for one reason and another (thoughtlessness, insensitiveness, development in too much hurry, for quick money) later builders largely forgot these desirable ways, and began developing the seaside town as if it were an inland town. "Home-from-home" ideas had something to do with it. People wanted a change when they went to the sea, but a change with home comforts; and that meant buildings (or so the builders thought) that looked as much as possible like the houses that visitors lived in all the year round. People also decided that seaside gaiety, when too gay, was "loud." These influences were slow in their effect, because the idiom was deep-rooted and reasonable. But they worked in the end, and the result

On the opposite page (and in the title-piece above): Dungeness, one of the nodal points on the English coast and rich in maritime architecture.

29. ***The Nautical Style***

January 1938

Architectural Review

35 x 28 cm

Private collection

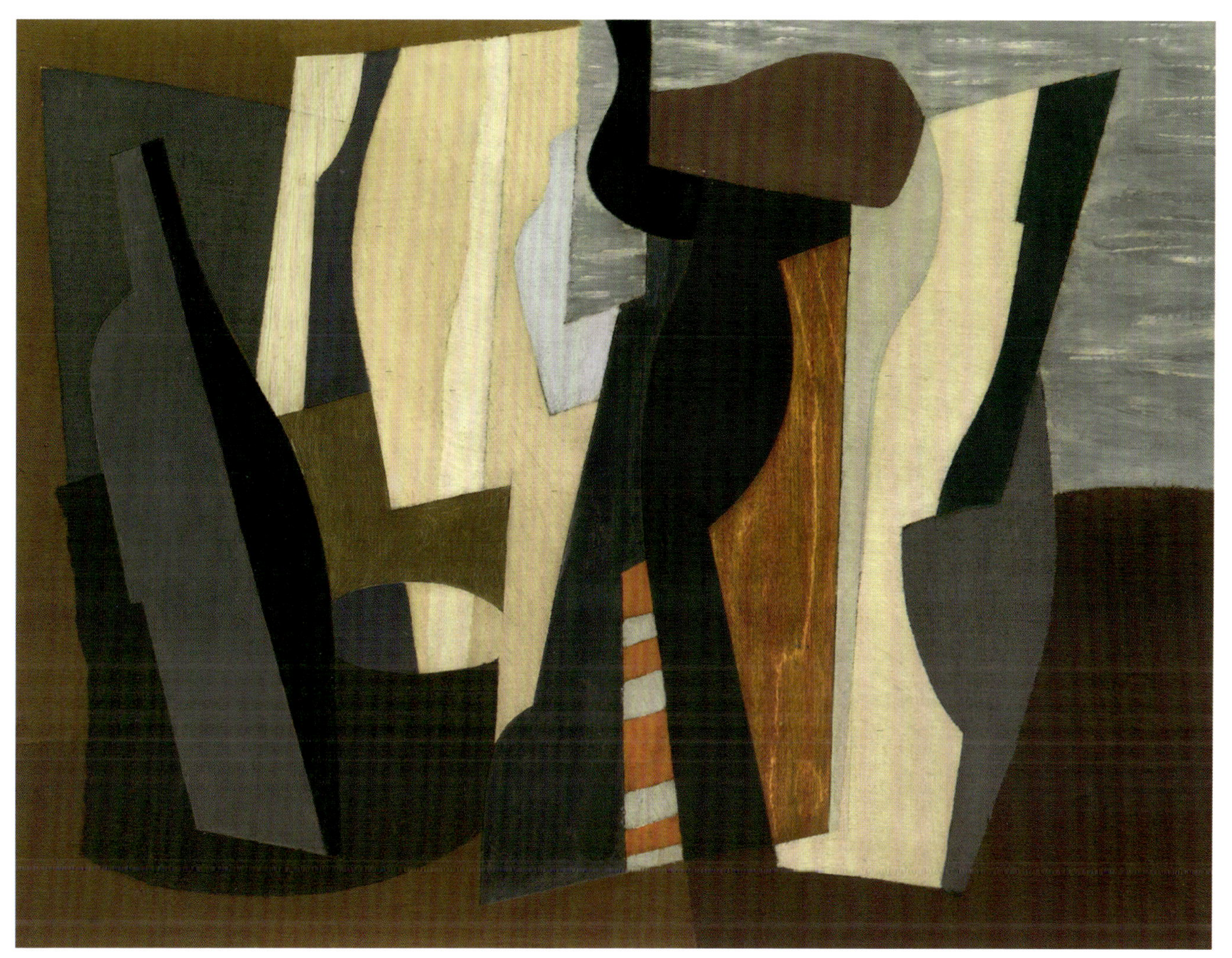

30. ***Sea Buildings***
1938

Oil, pencil and ripolin on canvas laid on panel
30.5 x 40.5 cm

Richard Green Gallery, London

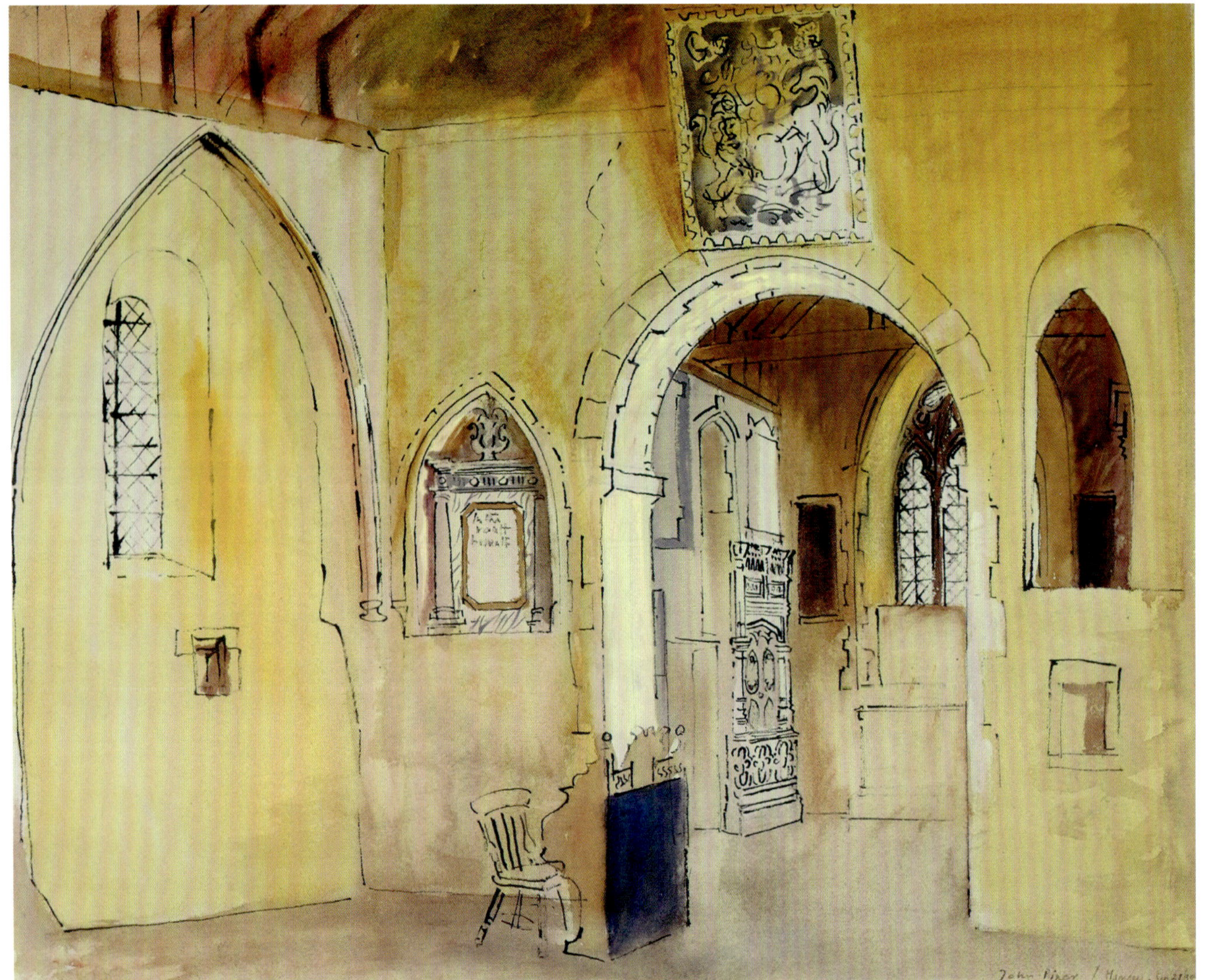

31. ***Hamsey Church, Sussex***
1939

Watercolour
48.3 x 36.8 cm

Derby Museums and Art Gallery

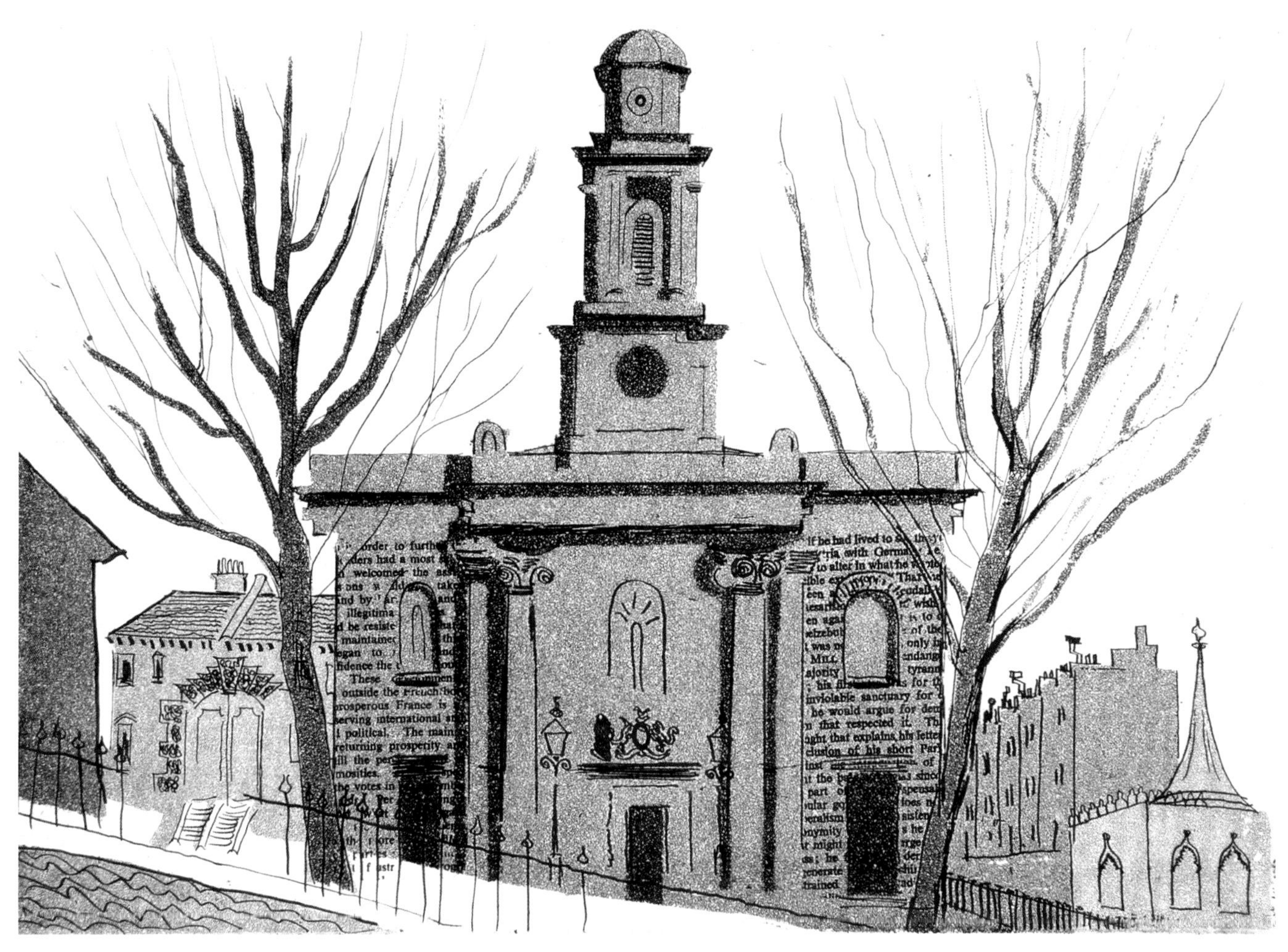

32.

Brighton Aquatints
1939

12 Aquatints - Levinson 12-23 (Levinson 21 illustrated)
19.6 x 27.6 cm

Private collection

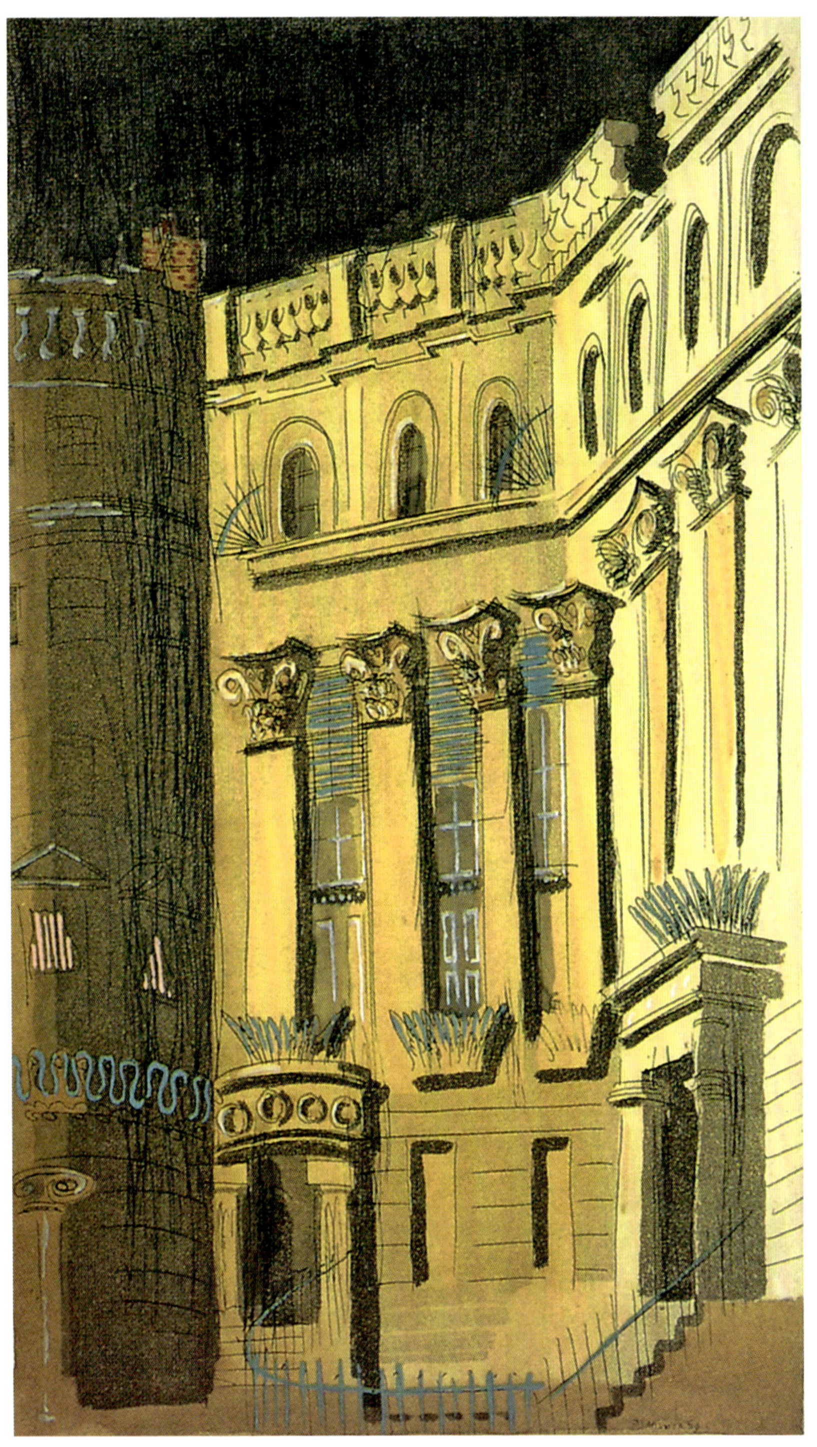

33. ***Brunswick Square***
1939

Aquatint - Levinson 11A
25 x 16 cm

Private collection

34. ***The Royal Pavilion, Brighton***
1939

Ink and wash on paper
39 x 54.5 cm

The Murray Collection

35. ***Brunswick Terrace***
1939

Ink and collage on paper
32 x 56 cm

Private collection

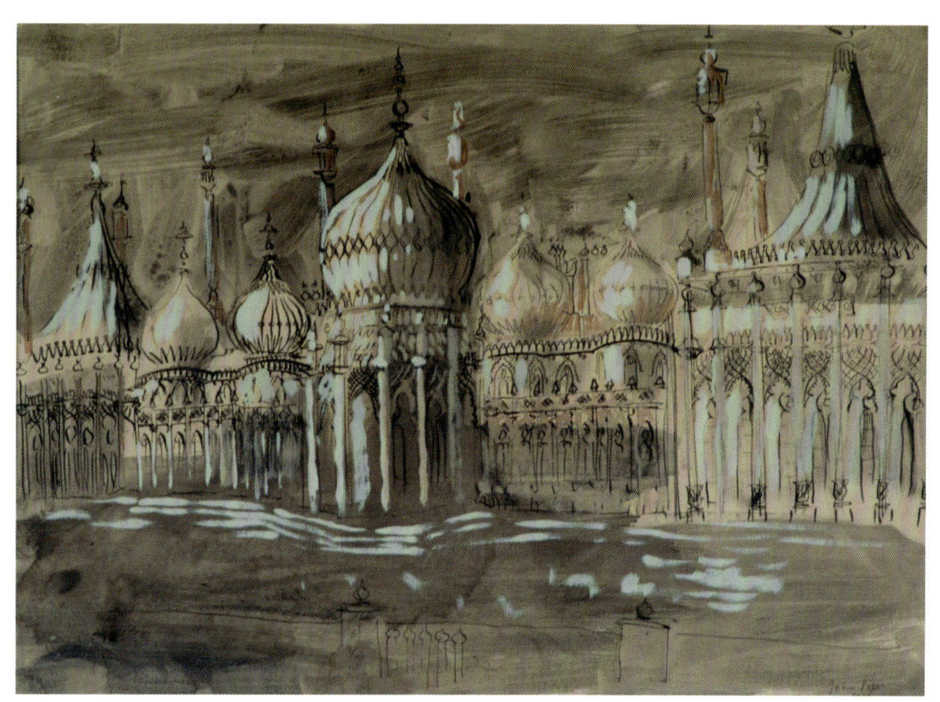

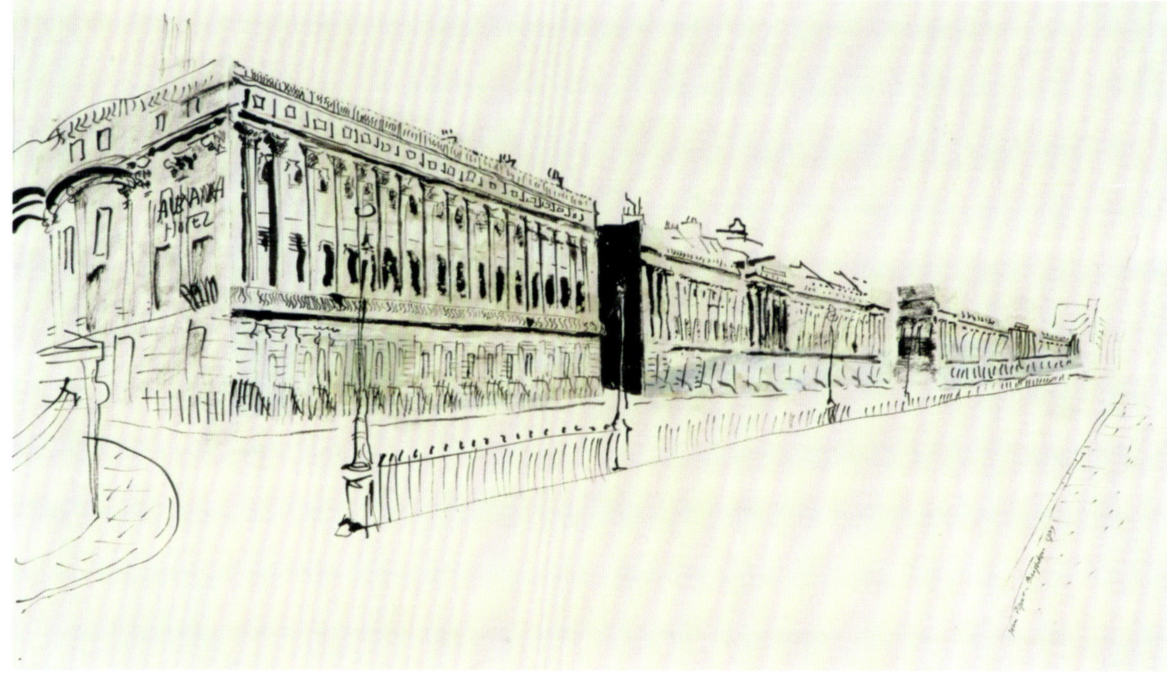

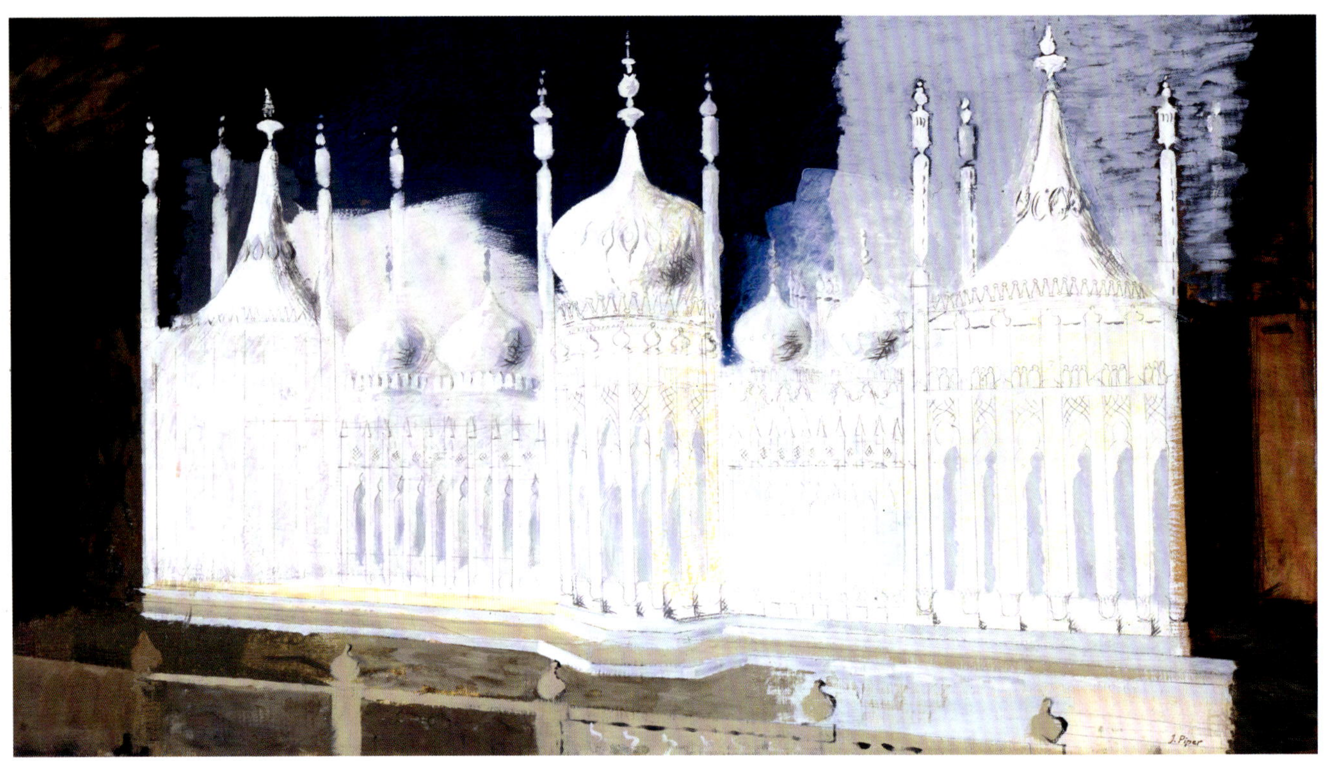

36. ***Brighton Pavilion***
1939

Oil, pencil and collage on board
53 x 96 cm

Private collection

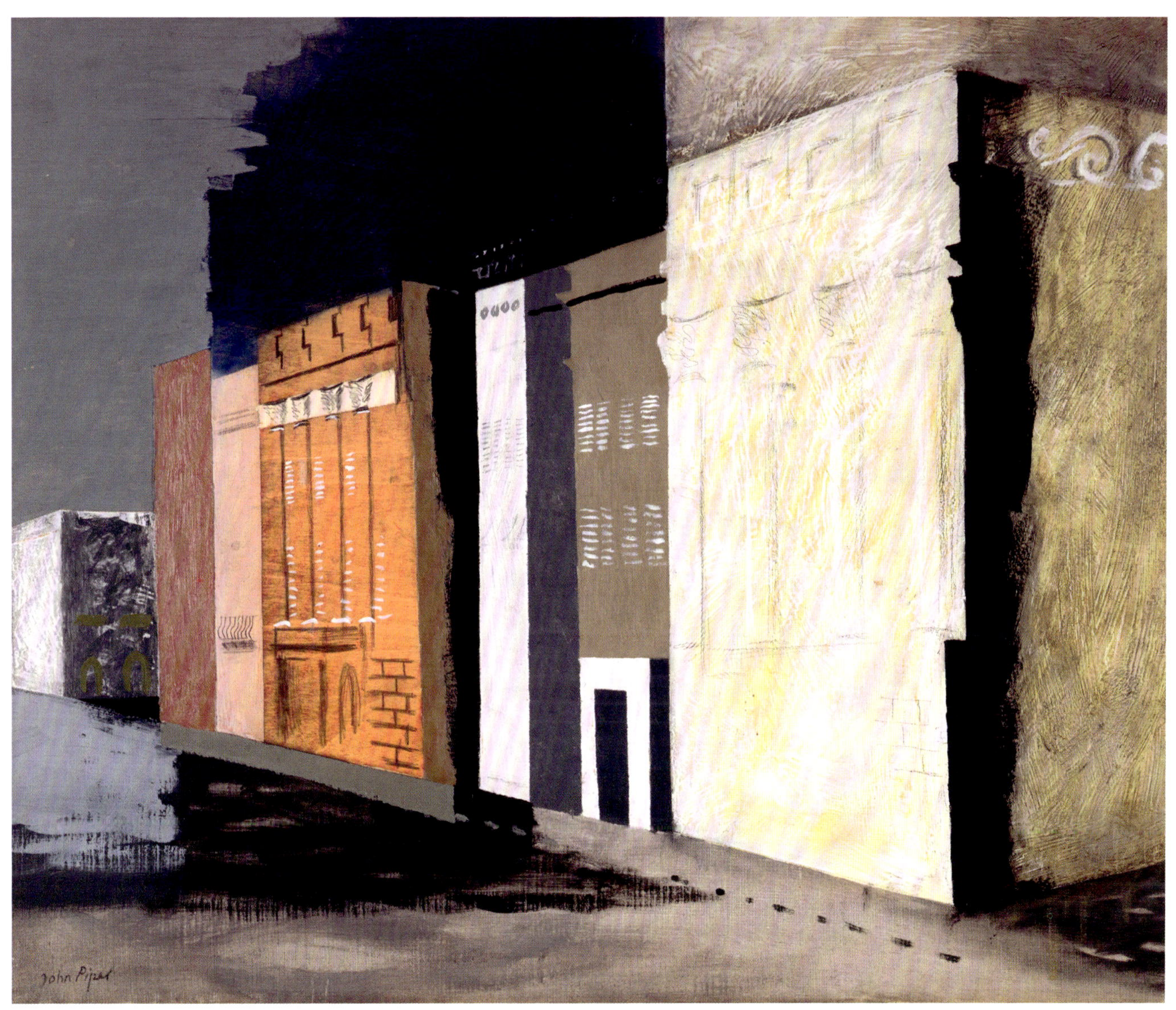

37.

Dead Resort, Kemptown
1939

Oil on canvas
45.7 x 55.9 cm

Leeds Museums & Galleries (Leeds Art Gallery)

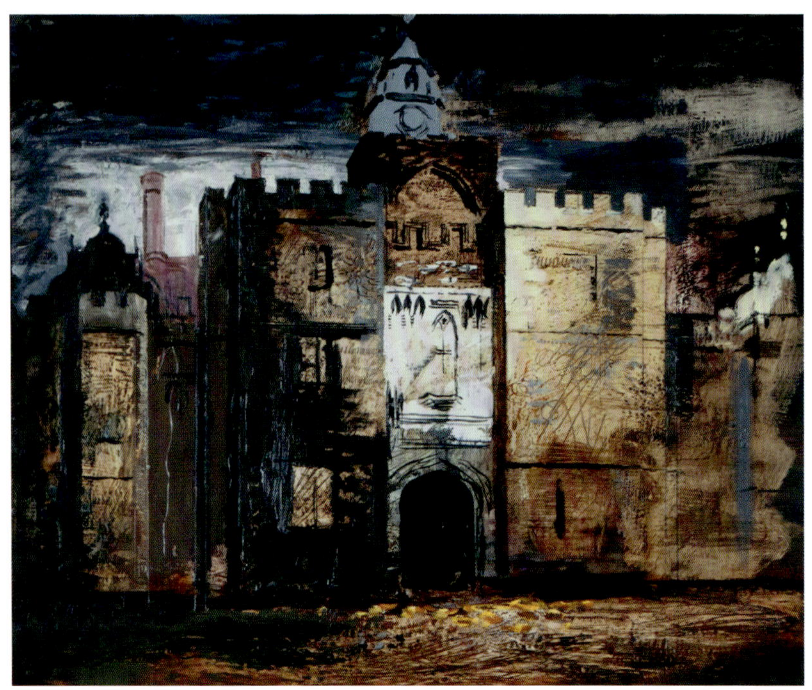

38. ***The Gatehouse, Knole***
c. 1942

Oil on canvas laid on board
63.5 x 50.8 cm

Private collection

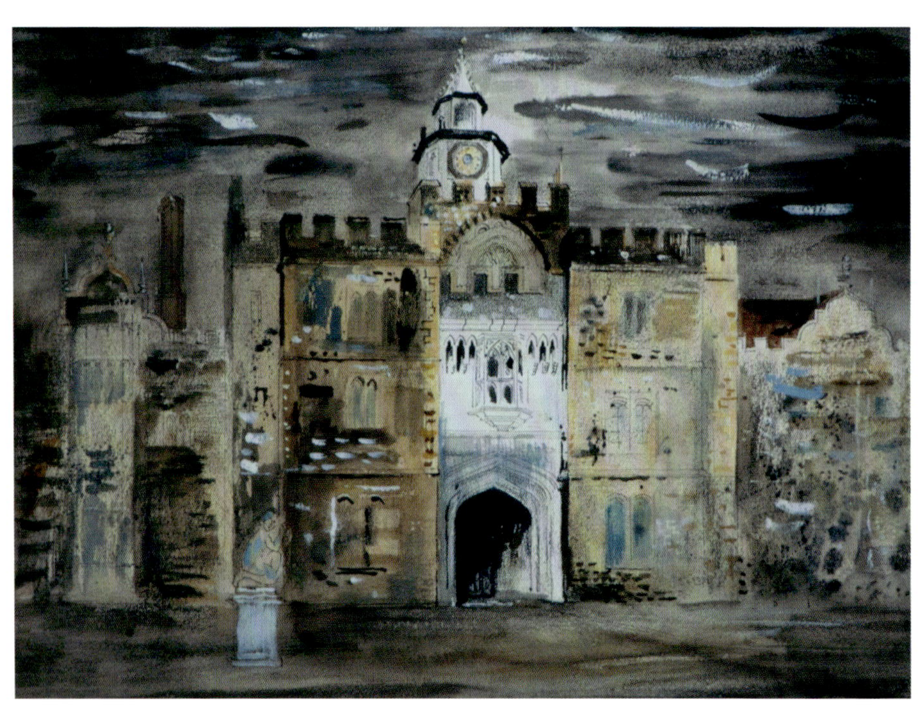

39. ***The Gatehouse, Knole***
c. 1942

Ink and watercolour on paper
37.8 x 52 cm

Private collection

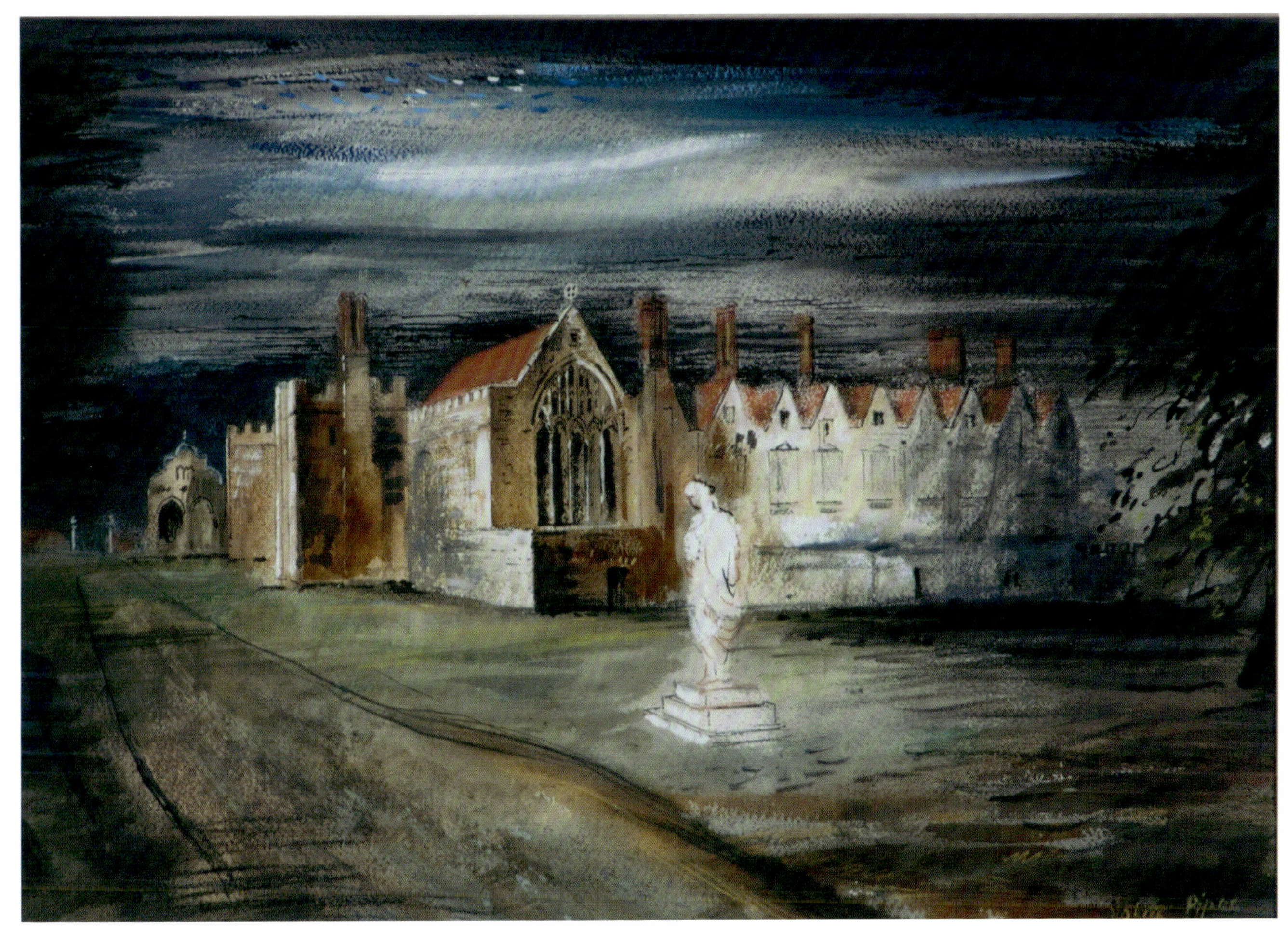

40. ***Knole from the South***
c. 1942

Ink and watercolour on paper
36.5 x 53.5 cm

Private collection

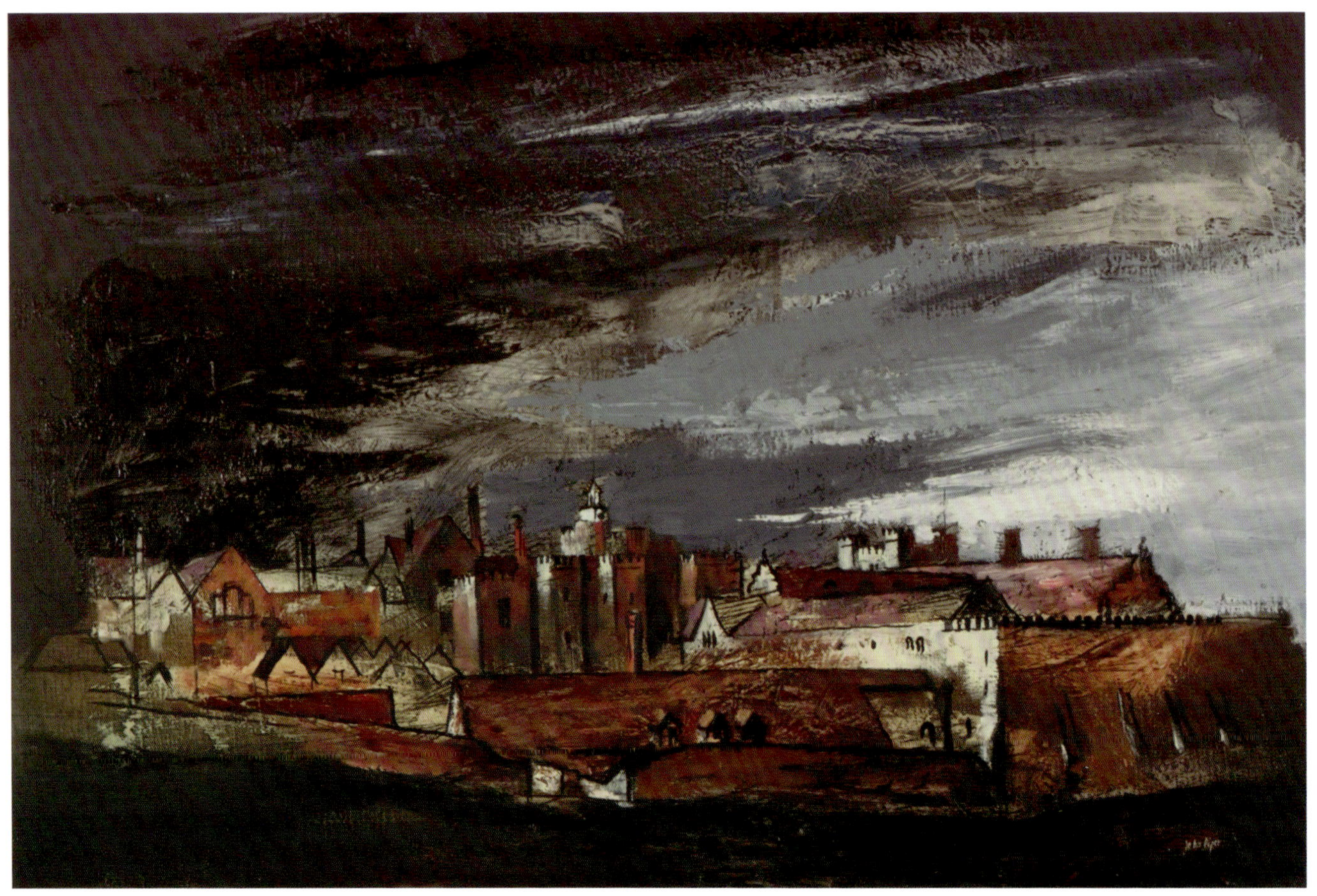

41. ***View of Knole***
c. 1942

Oil on canvas
53.3 x 76.2 cm

The Sackville Collection

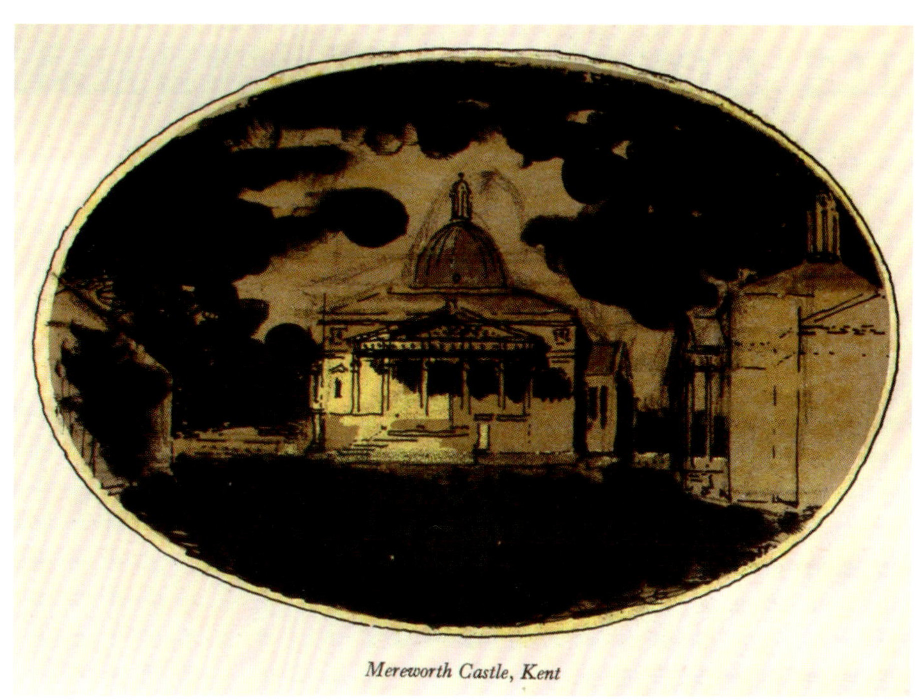

Mereworth Castle, Kent

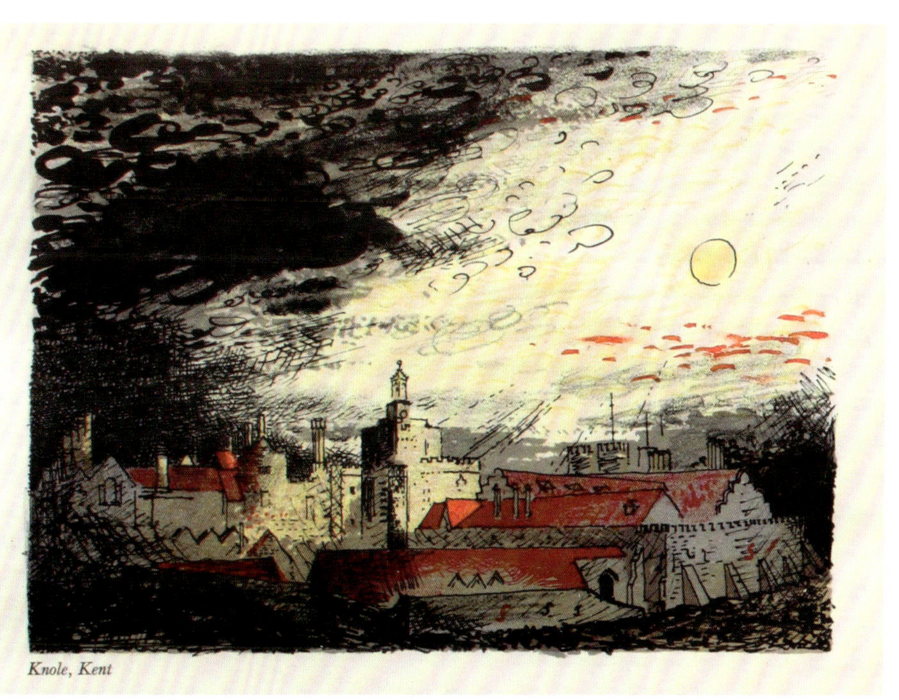

Knole, Kent

42. ***The Colour of English Country Houses***
1944

Autolithographs in International Textiles No. 8 - Levinson 47-57 (Levinson 48 and 52 illustrated)
35 x 24 cm

Private collection

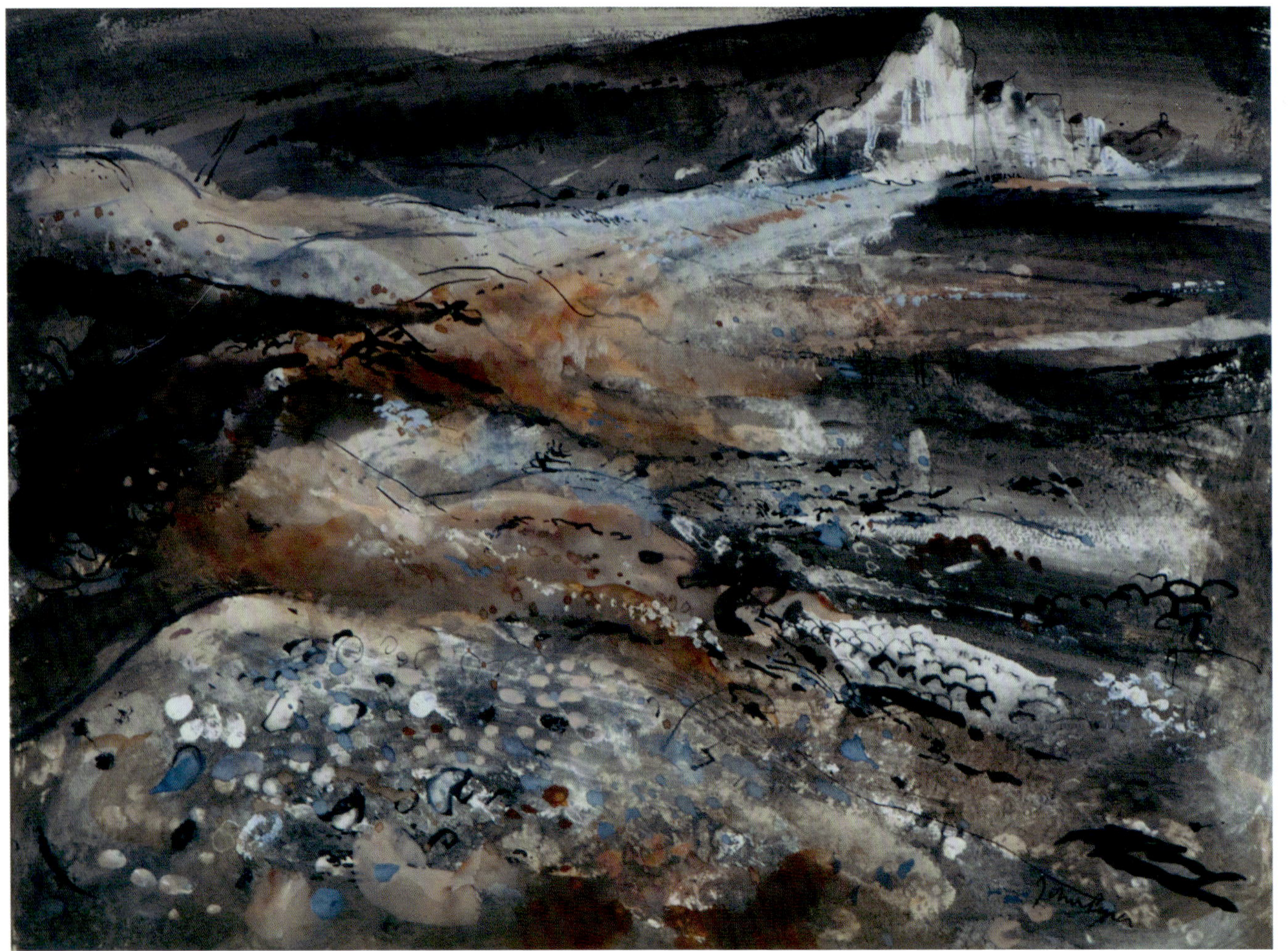

43. ***Cuckmere Haven***
1946

Watercolour on paper
38 x 53 cm

The National Trust, Scotney Castle

44. ***Monument, Waldershare***
1947

Oil on canvas
61 x 45.7 cm

Private collection

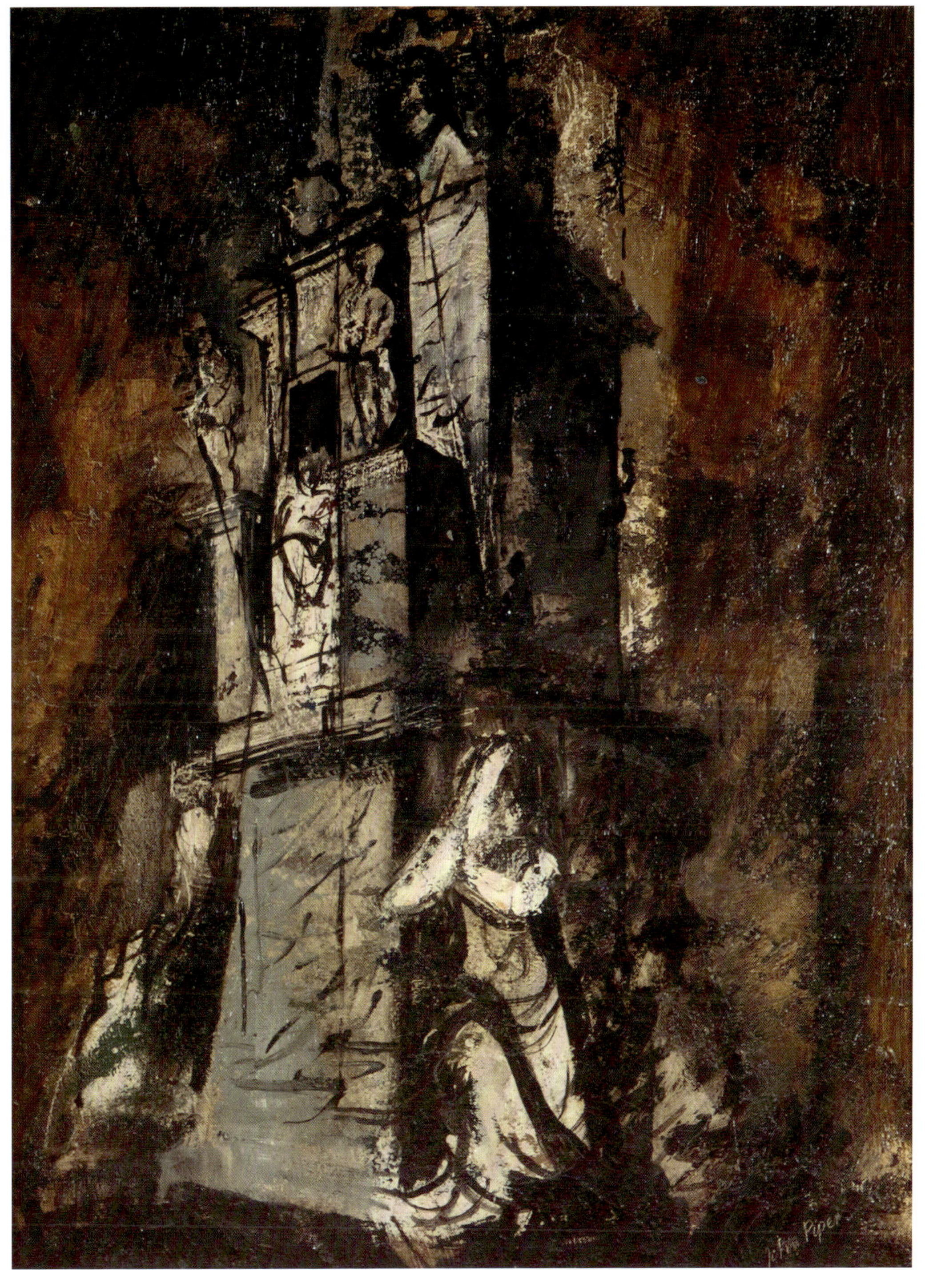
John Piper

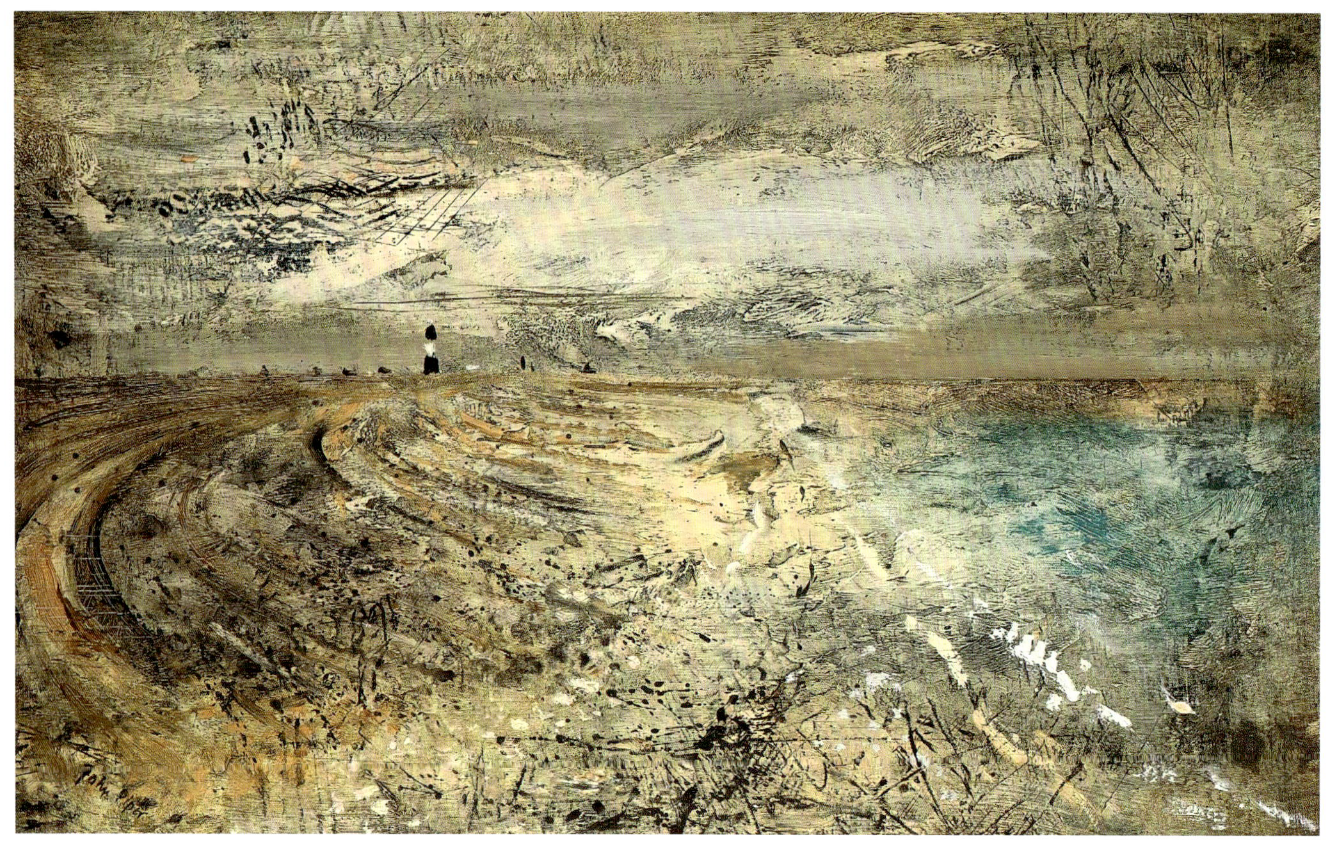

45. ***Dungeness***
1947

Oil on masonite
38 x 61 cm

Private collection

46. ***Dungeness***
1947

Oil on panel
15.2 x 20.3 cm

Private collection

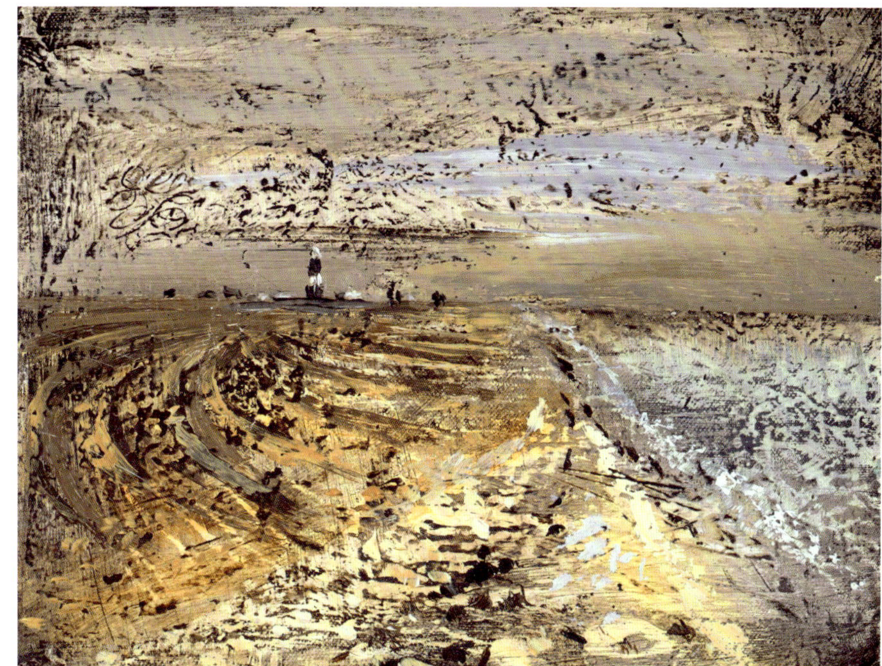

47. ***Dungeness from the Galloways***
1947

Ink and gouache on paper
39 x 49 cm

Private collection

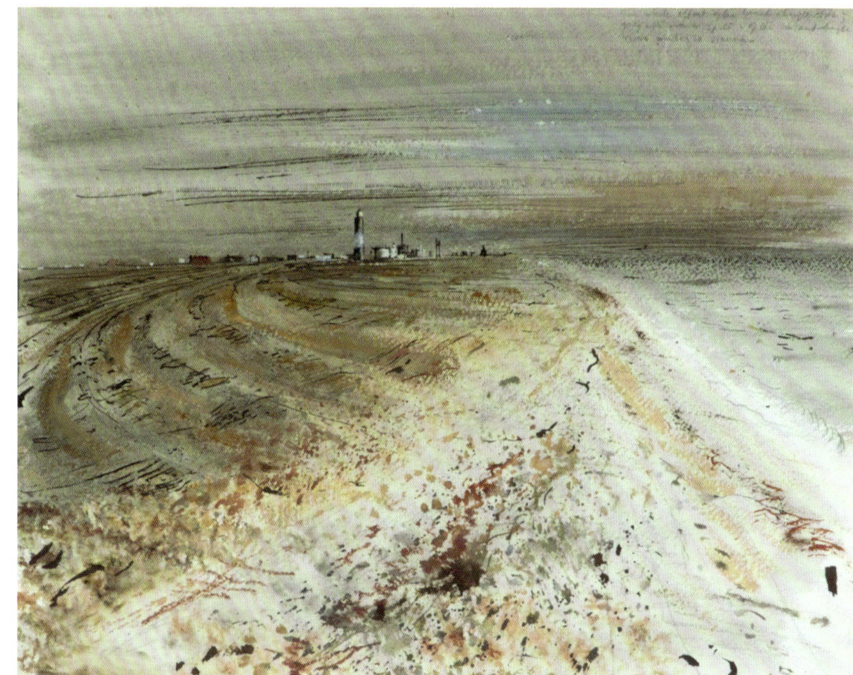

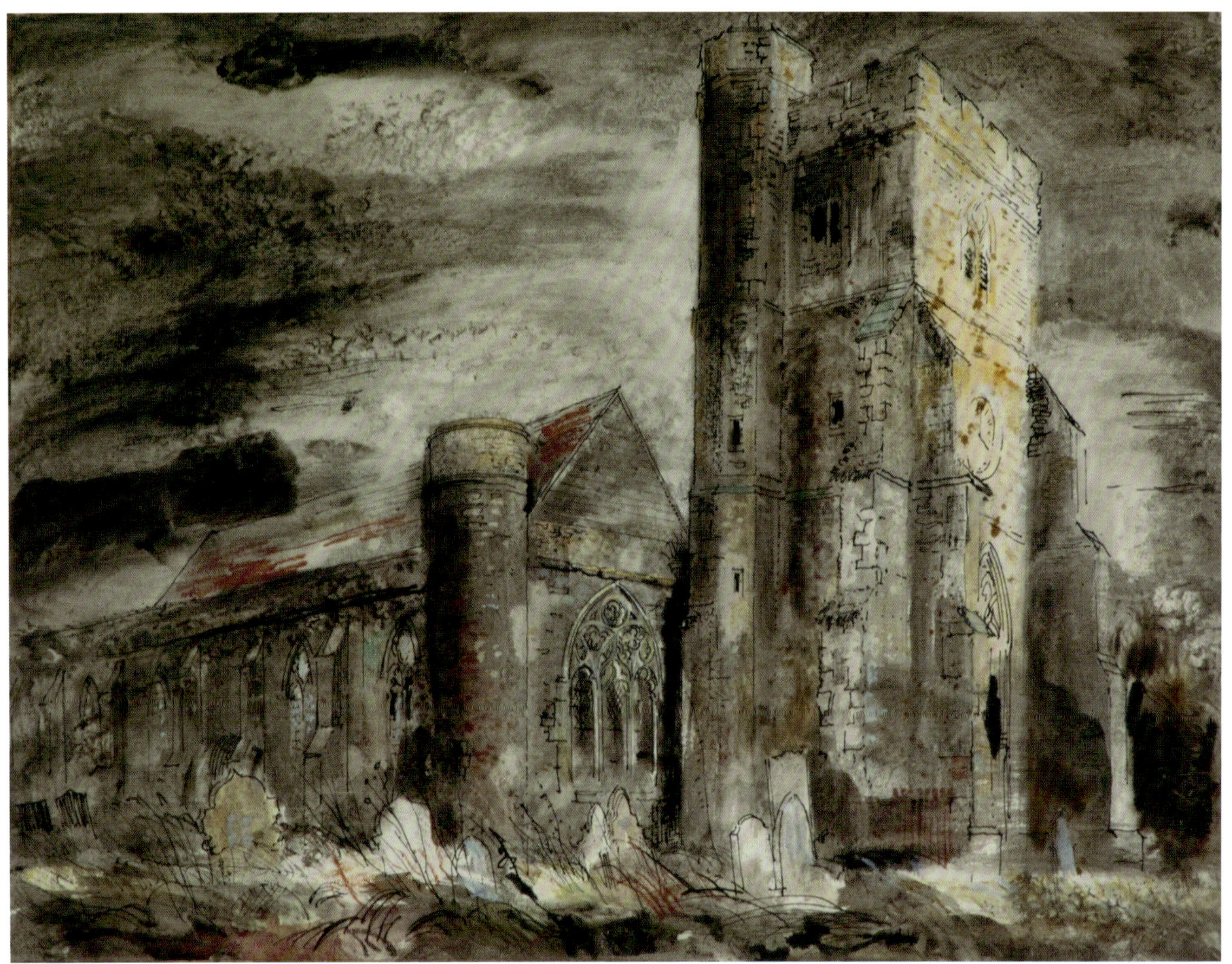

48. ***Ivychurch***
1947

Watercolour, pen and ink
39 x 51 cm

Private collection

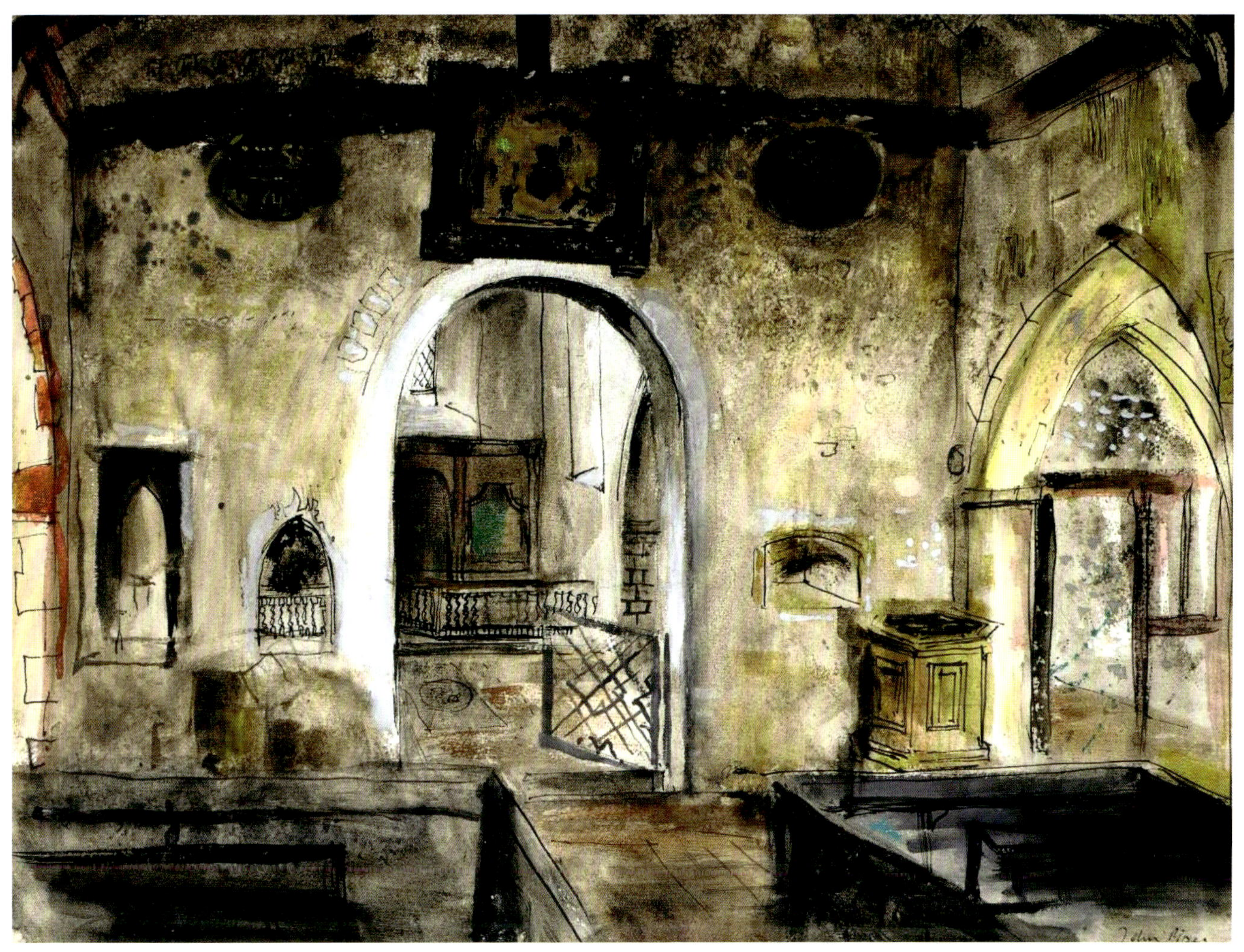

49. ***Old Romney Church, Kent***
1947

Ink and watercolour
37 x 50 cm

Private collection

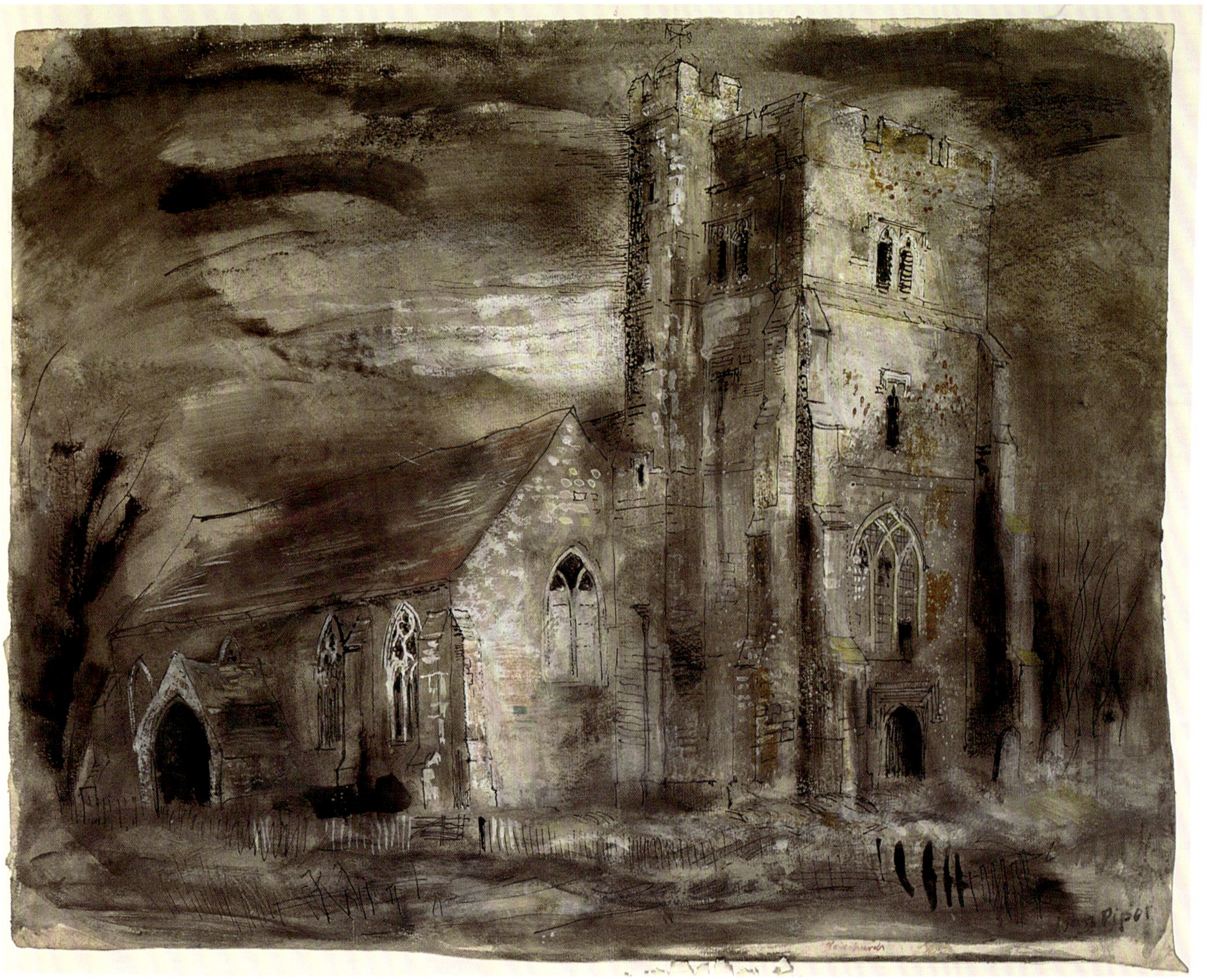

50. ***Newchurch, Romney Marsh***
1947

Ink and watercolour
40.6 x 55.8 cm

Private collection

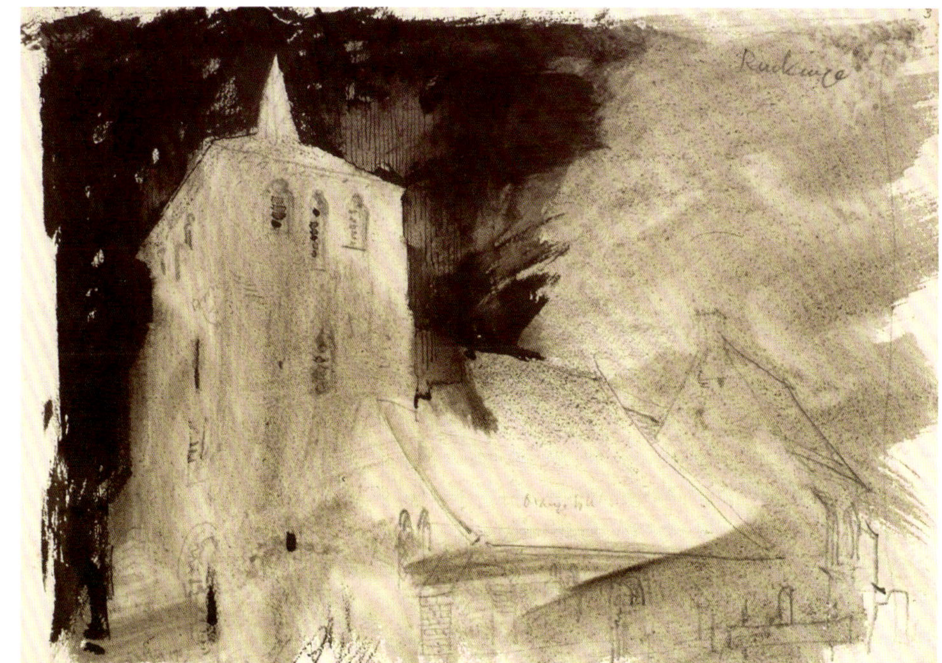

51. ***Ruckinge Church***
1947

Ink on paper

Tate

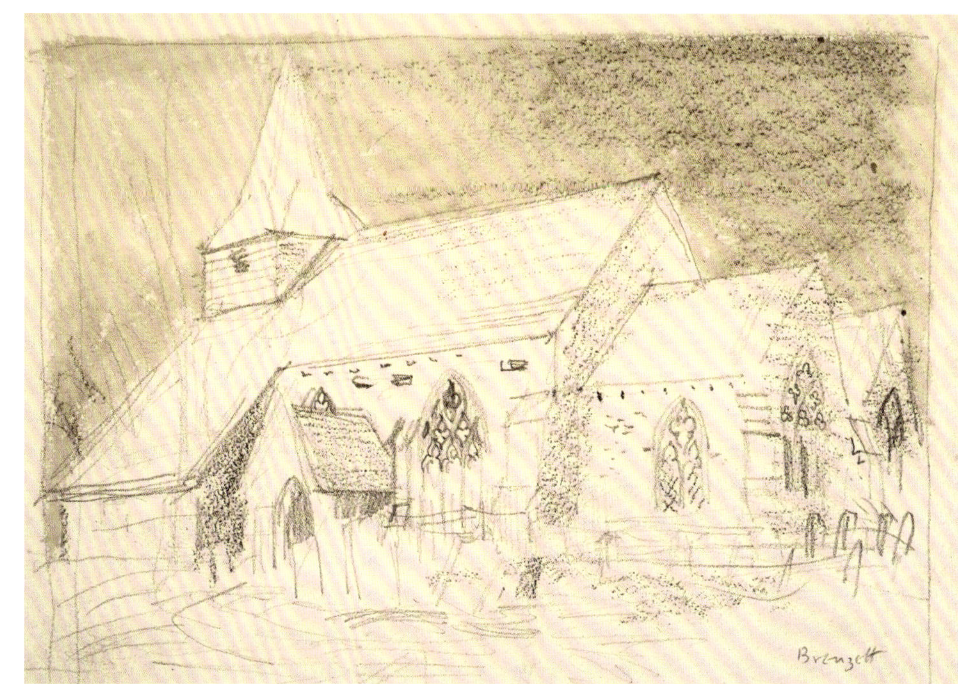

52. ***Brenzett Church***
1947

Pencil on paper

Tate

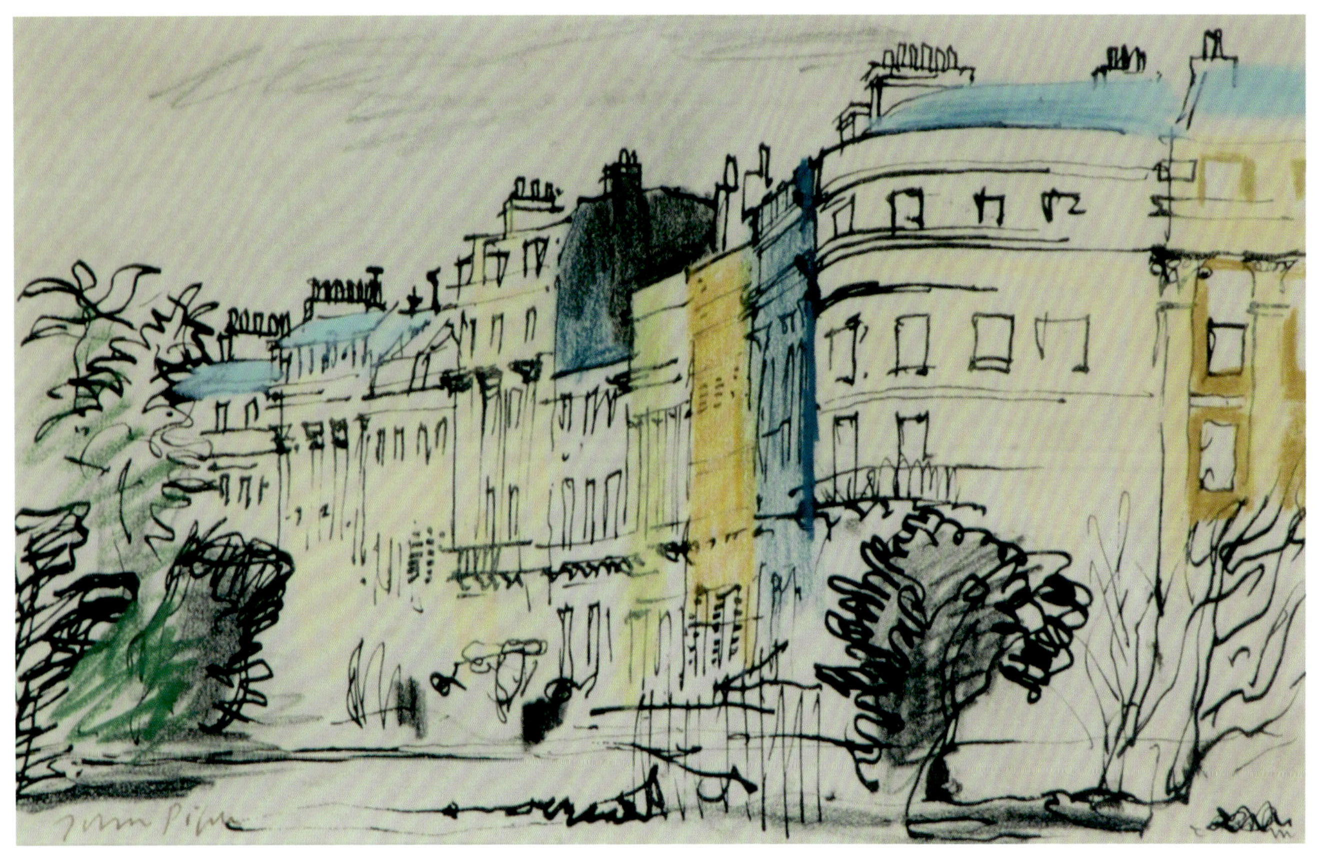

53. ***Houses, Brighton***
1947

Ink and watercolour on paper
10 x 18 cm

Private collection

54. ***Scotney Castle, Kent***
1948

Pen, ink and wash
12.7 x 18.3 cm

Private collection

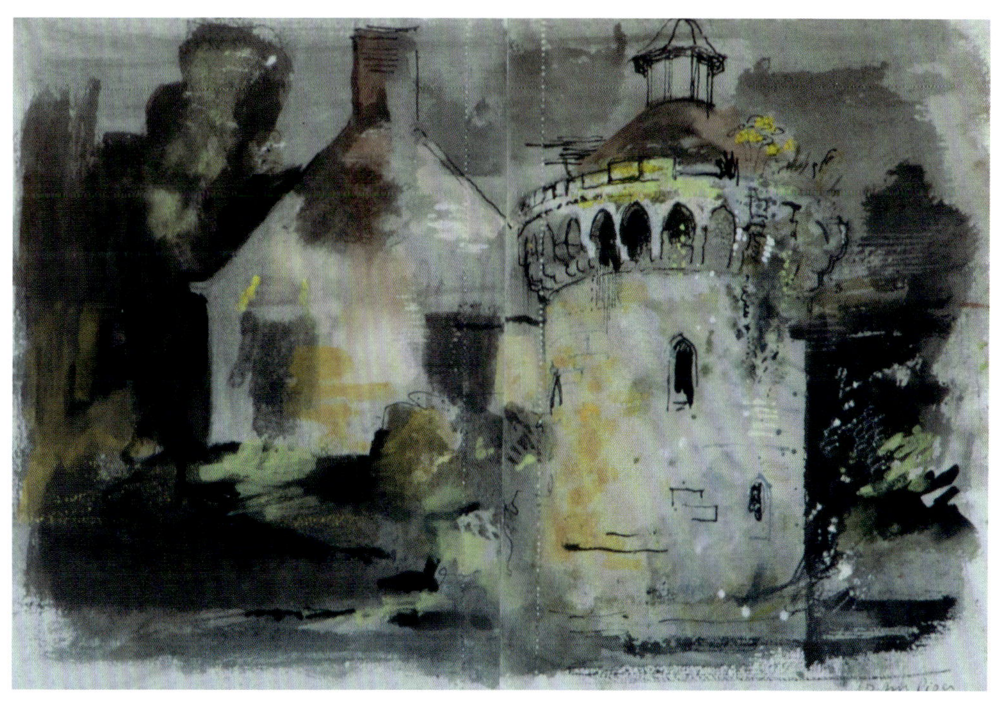

55. 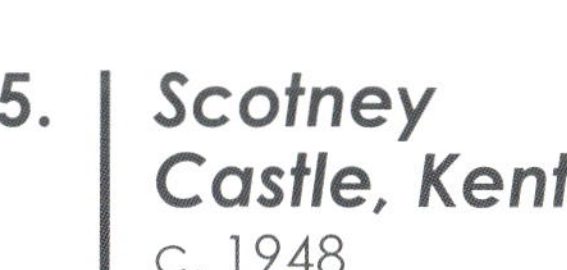
Scotney Castle, Kent
c. 1948

Pen, ink, wash and crayon
19 x 28 cm

Private collection

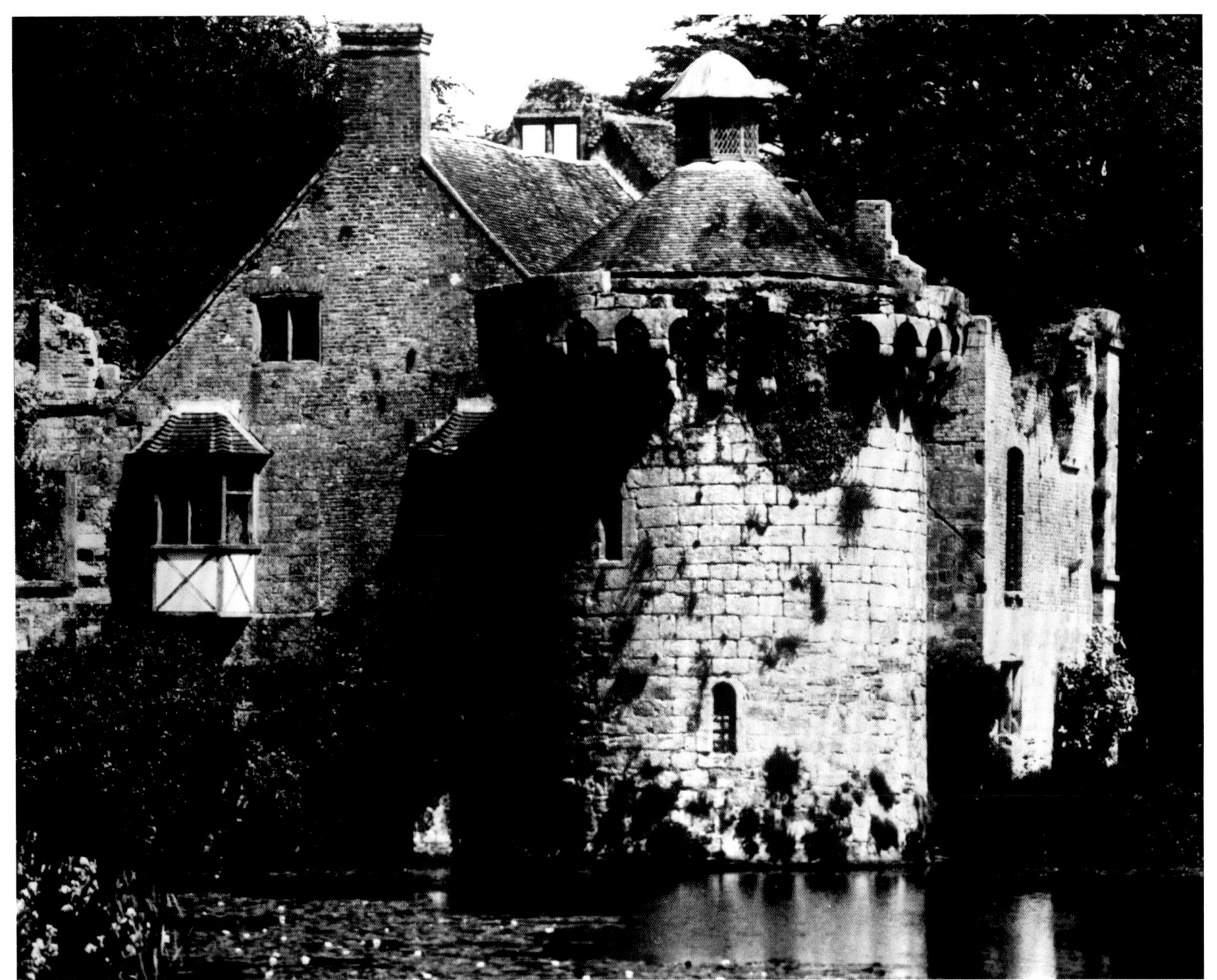

56. ***Photographs of Scotney***
1956

Photographs

Tate

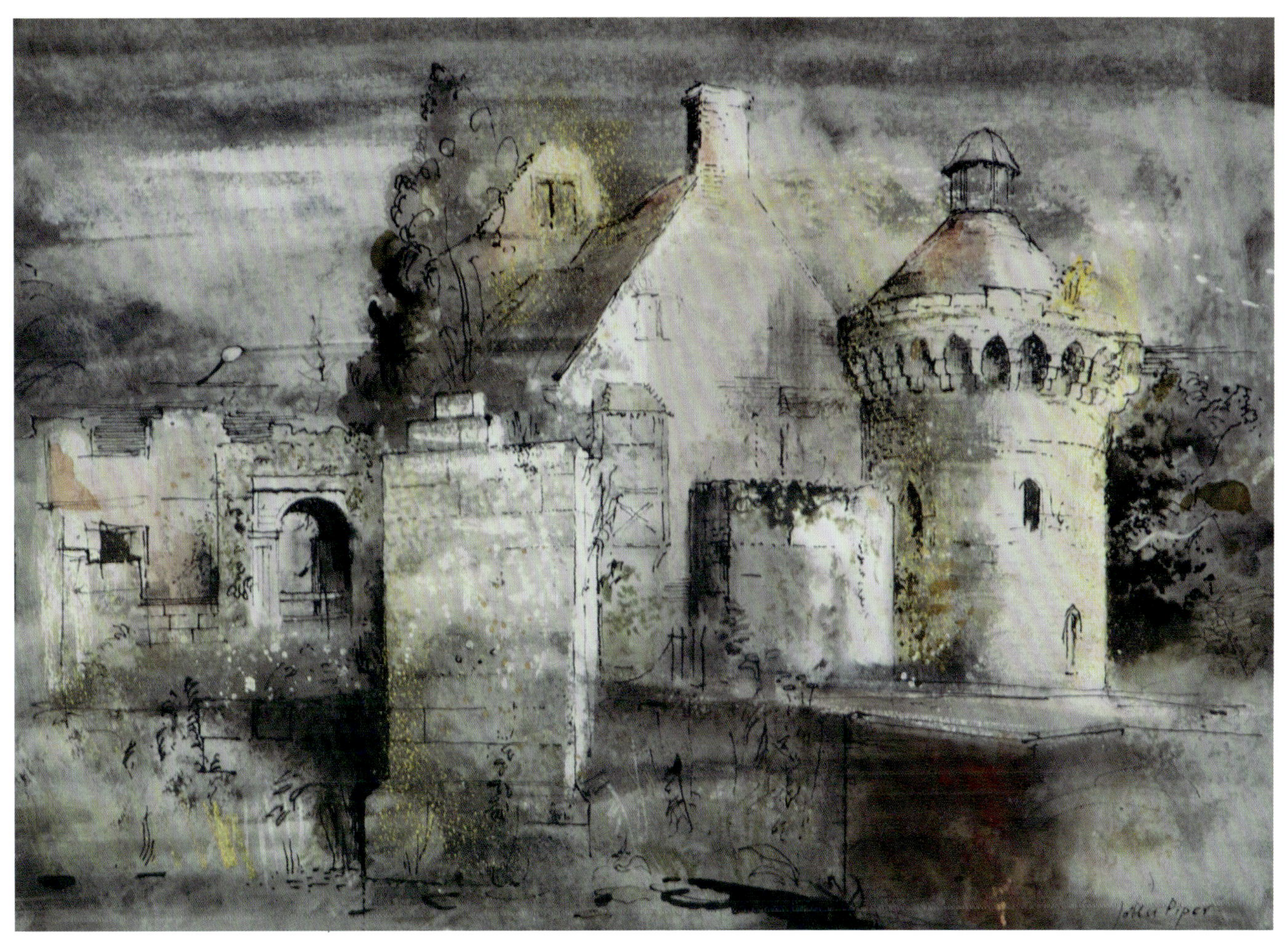

57. ***Scotney Old Castle***
1949

Pen, ink and gouache
36 x 50 cm

The National Trust, Scotney Castle

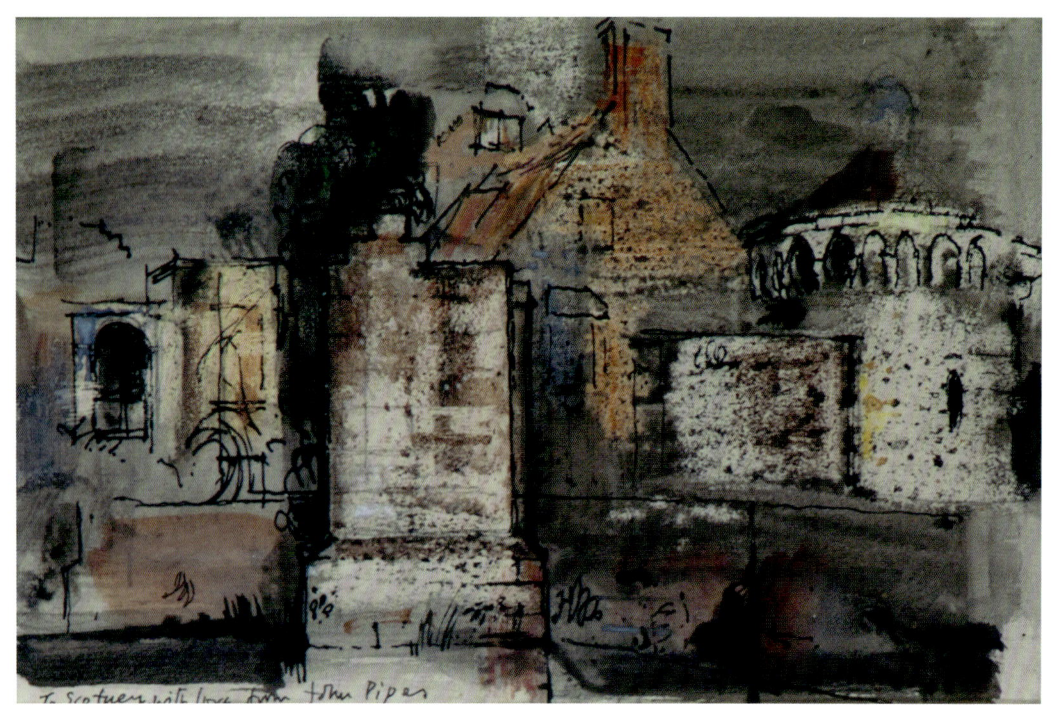

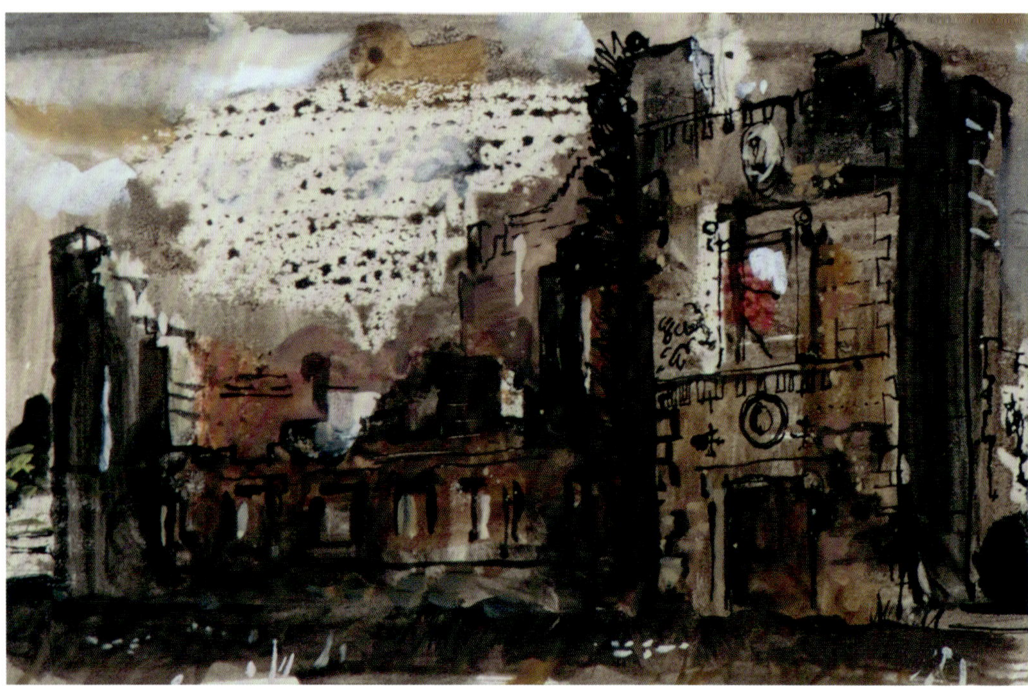

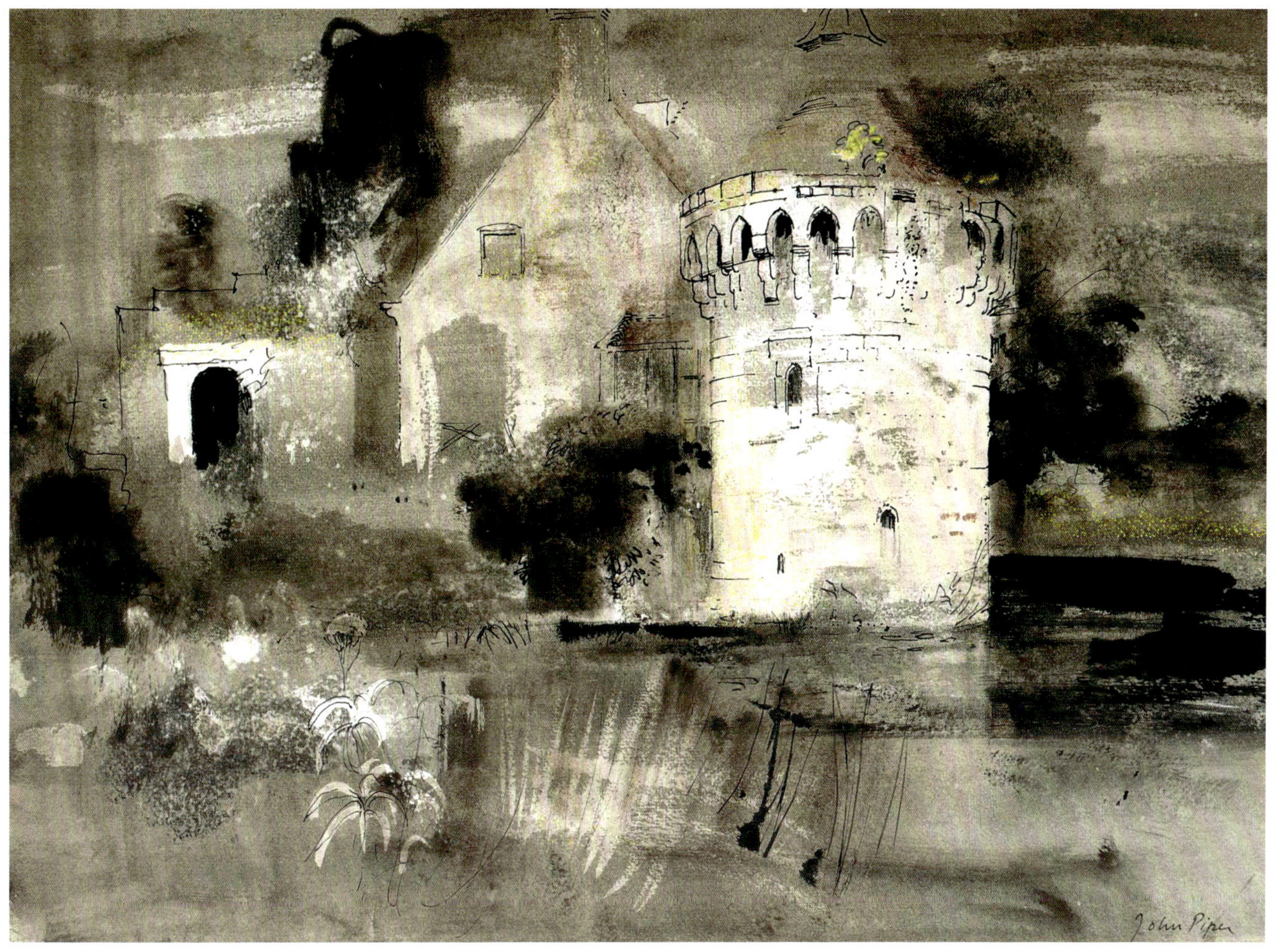

58. ***Two views of Scotney Old Castle***
1949

Watercolour and bodycolour
14.4 x 22 cm each

The National Trust, Scotney Castle

59. ***Scotney Castle, Kent***
1949

Watercolour, wash, pen and ink
36 x 50 cm

Private collection

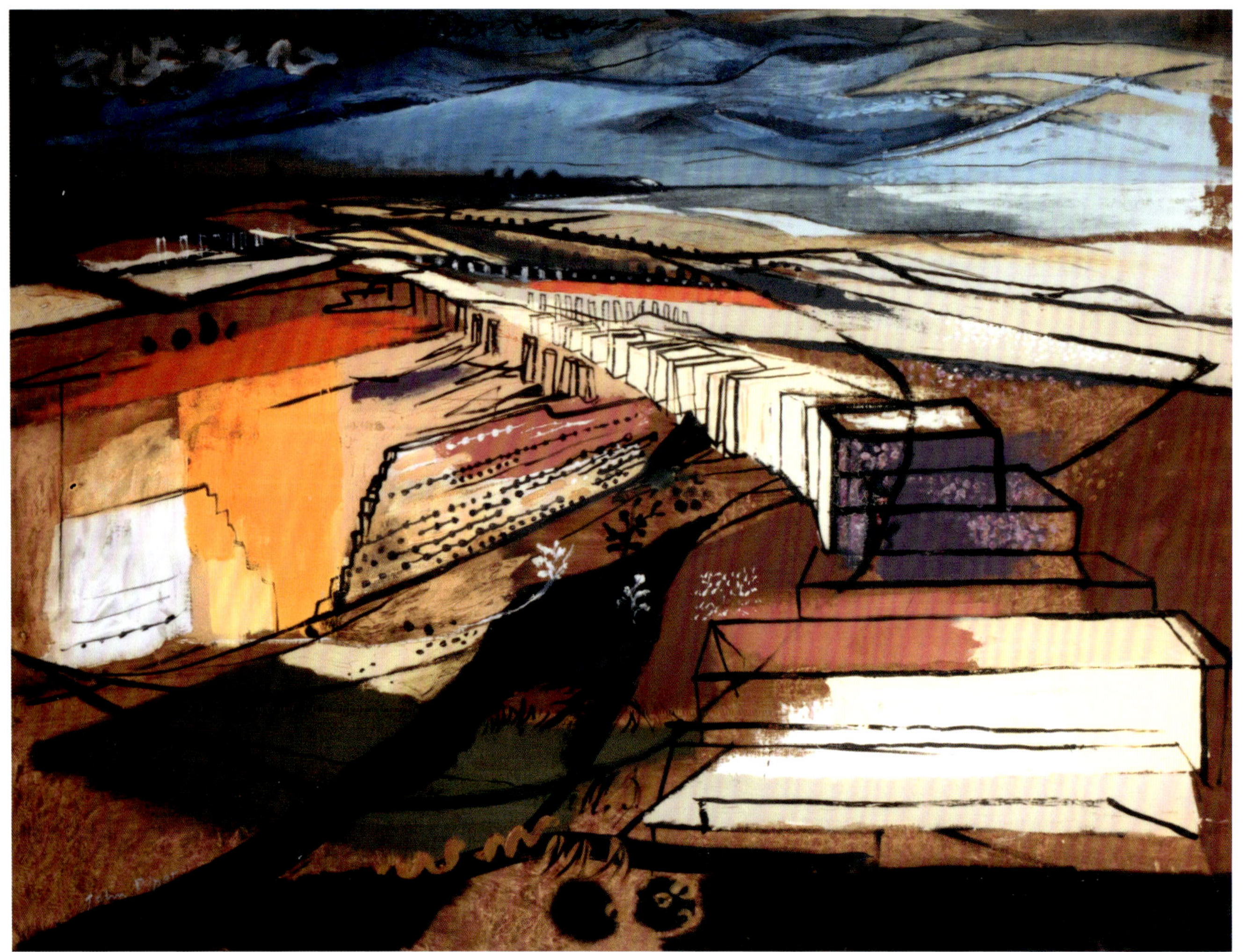

60. ***Clymping***
1953

Oil on canvas
91.4 x 122 cm

Britten—Pears Foundation

61. ***Clymping***
1953

Gouache on paper
61 x 76 cm

Private collection

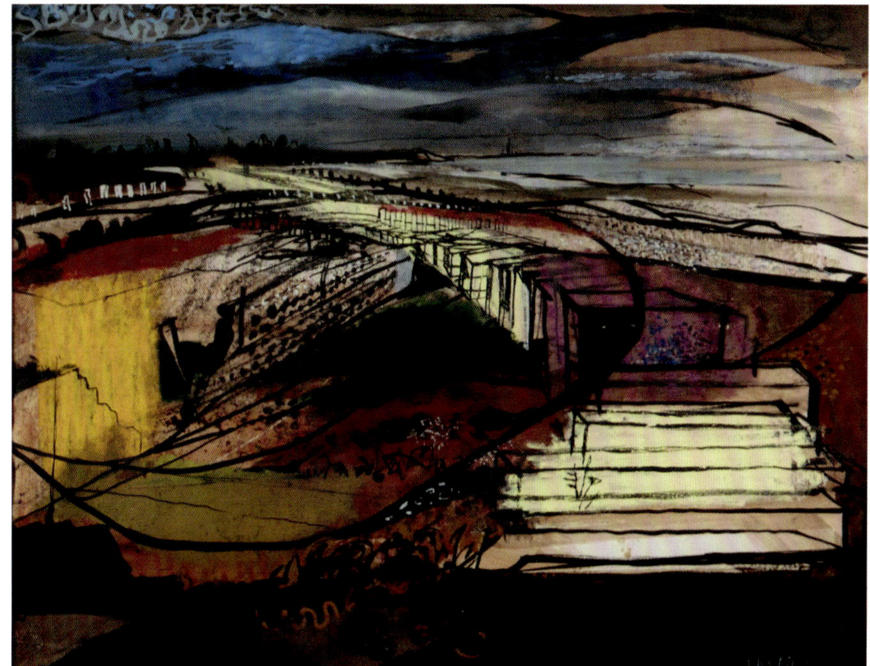

62. ***Clymping Beach***
1953

Lithograph - Levinson 81
40.8 x 56 cm

Private collection

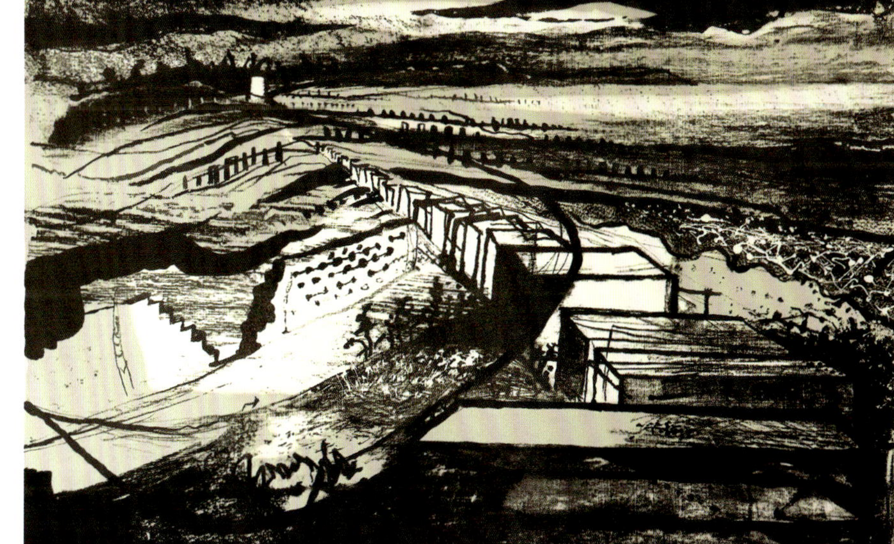

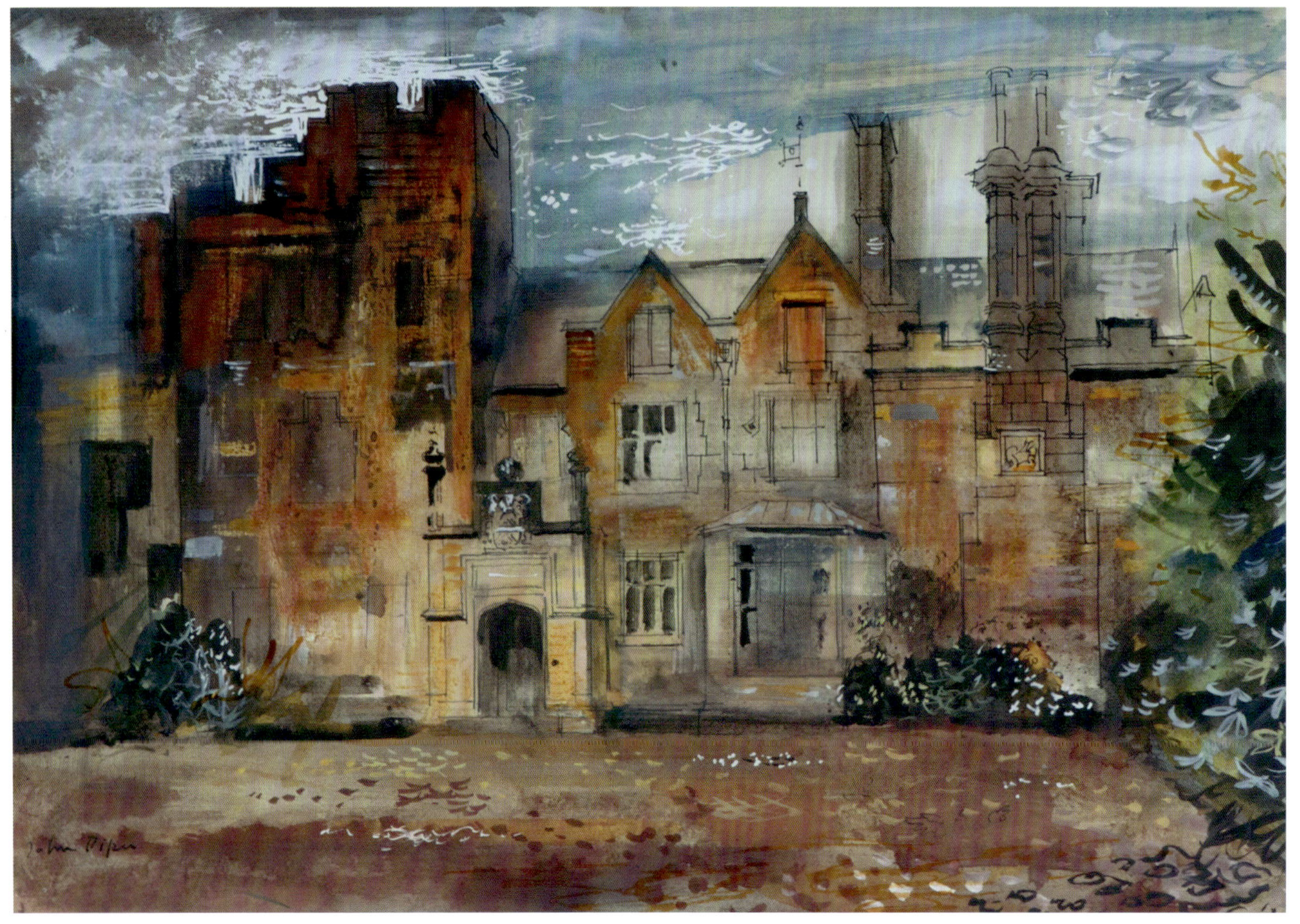

63. ***New Scotney Castle, the Entrance Front***
1956

Pen, ink and watercolour on paper
39 x 55.5 cm

Tne National Trust, Scotney Castle

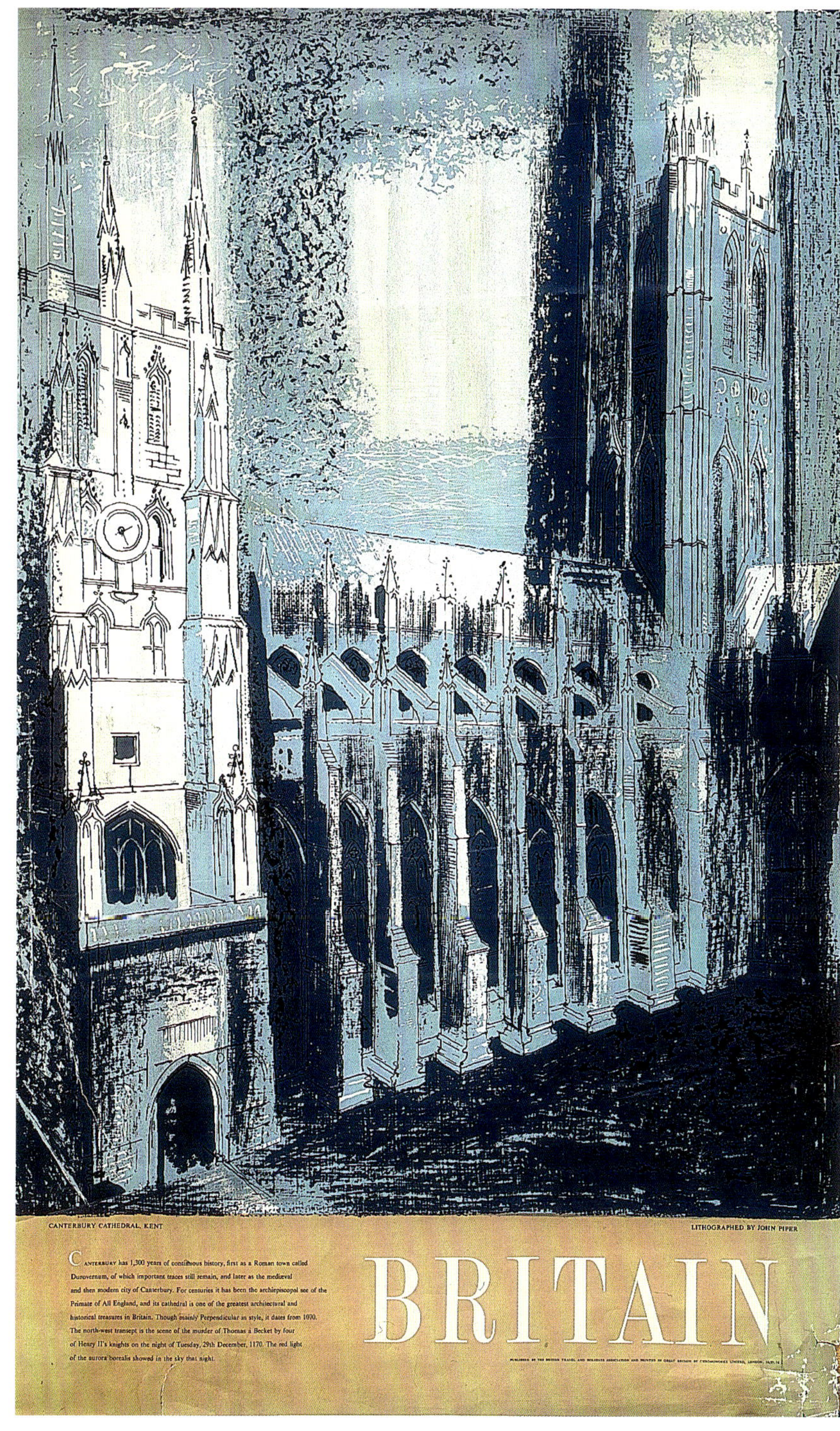

64. ***Canterbury Cathedral***

1956

Autolithograph poster - Levinson 102

99 x 61 cm

Private collection

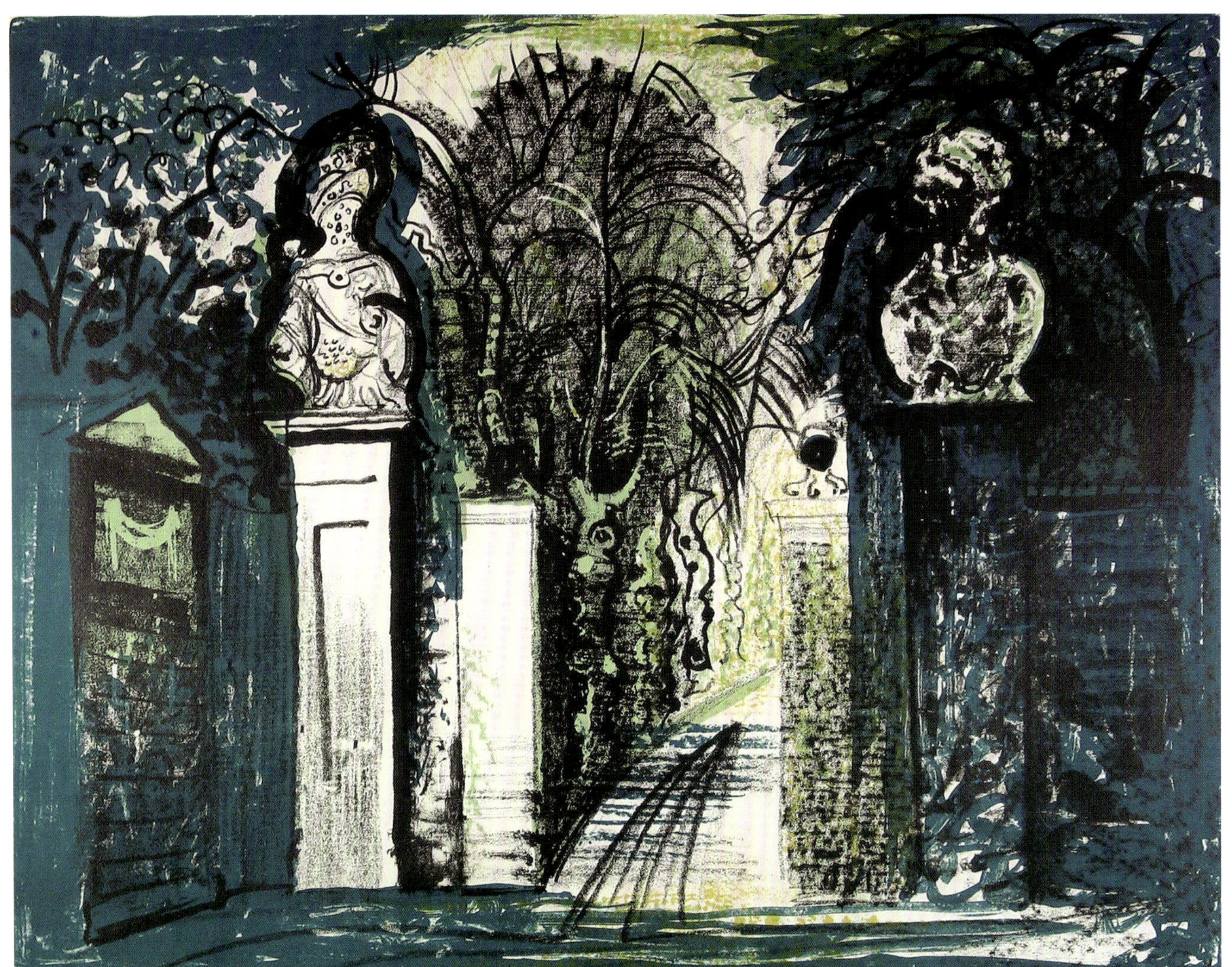

65. ***Petworth Park Gate***
c. 1958

Lithograph - Levinson 105
43.4 x 56.6 cm

Leicester Museums

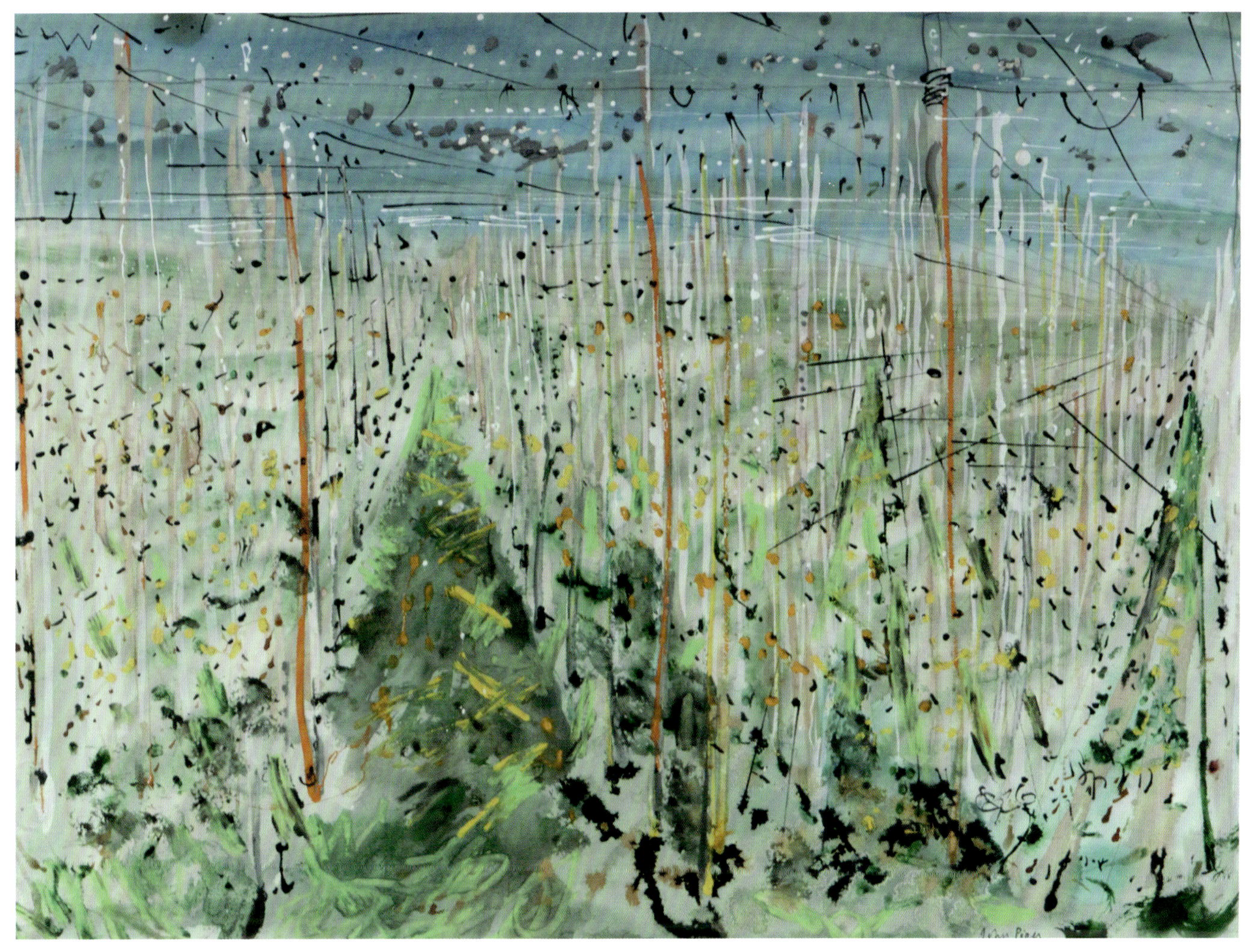

66. ***Hopfields at Ospringe***
1968

Ink on paper
38.1 x 58.4 cm

Private collection

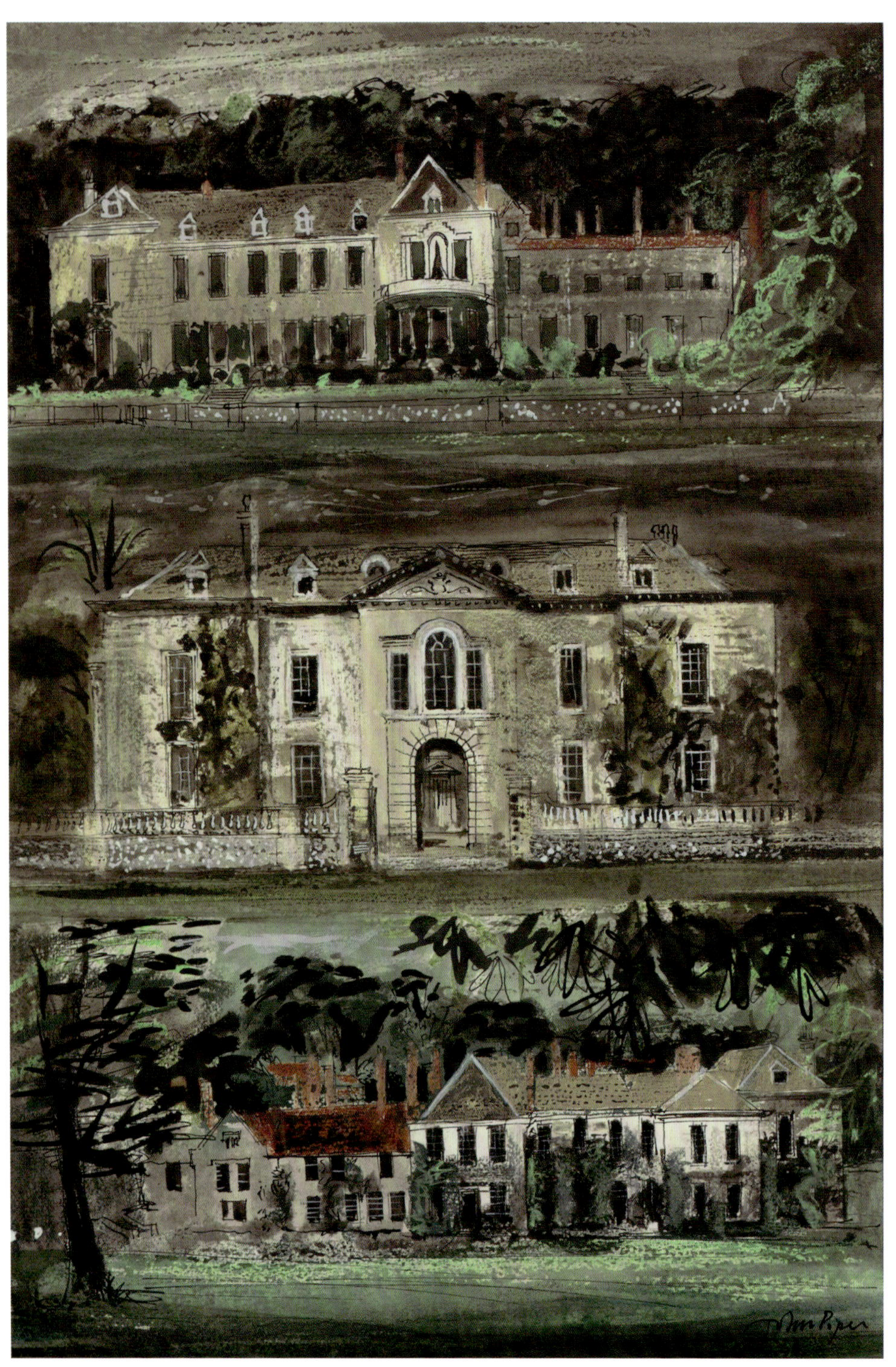

67. ***Three Views of Firle***
c. 1970s

Ink, watercolour and crayon on paper
61 x 40.6 cm

Given to Lord Gage by the family of the late Richard Wainwright

68. ***Chichester Cathedral***
c. 1970s

Watercolour & bodycolour
66 x 76 cm

The Trustees of Stansted Park Foundation

69. ***View of Chichester Cathedral from the Deanery***
1975

Ink, watercolour and crayon on paper
40 x 60 cm

Pallant House Gallery, Chichester (Hussey Bequest, Chichester District Council, 1985)

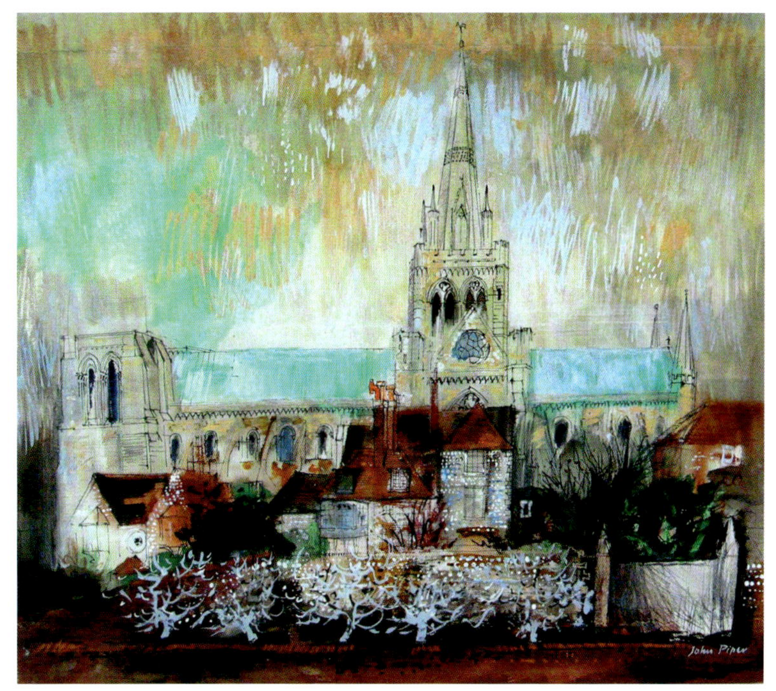

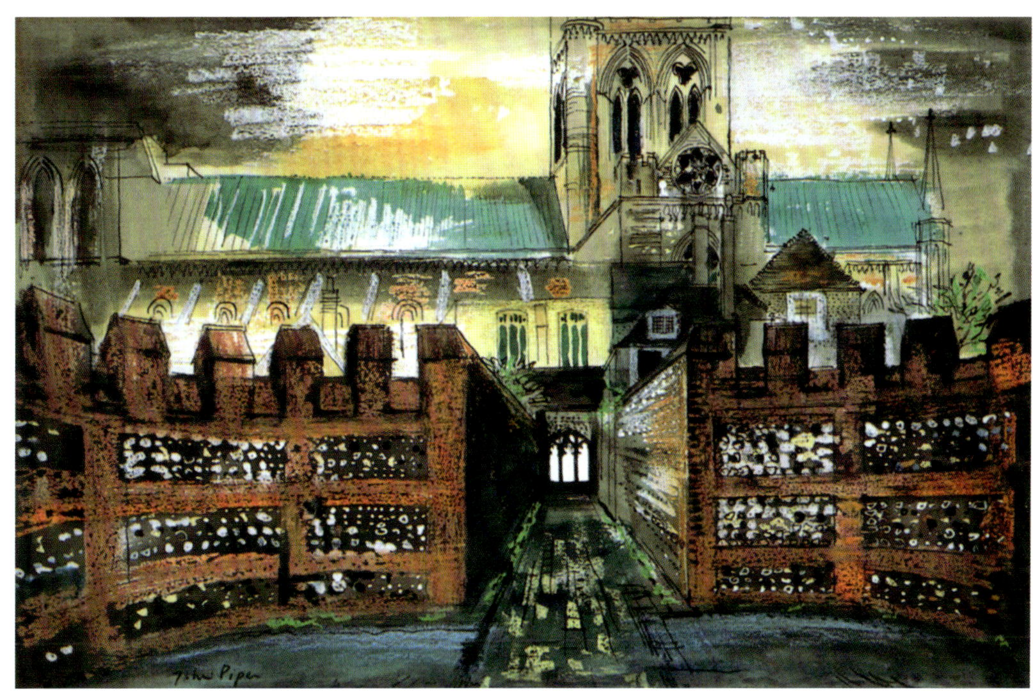

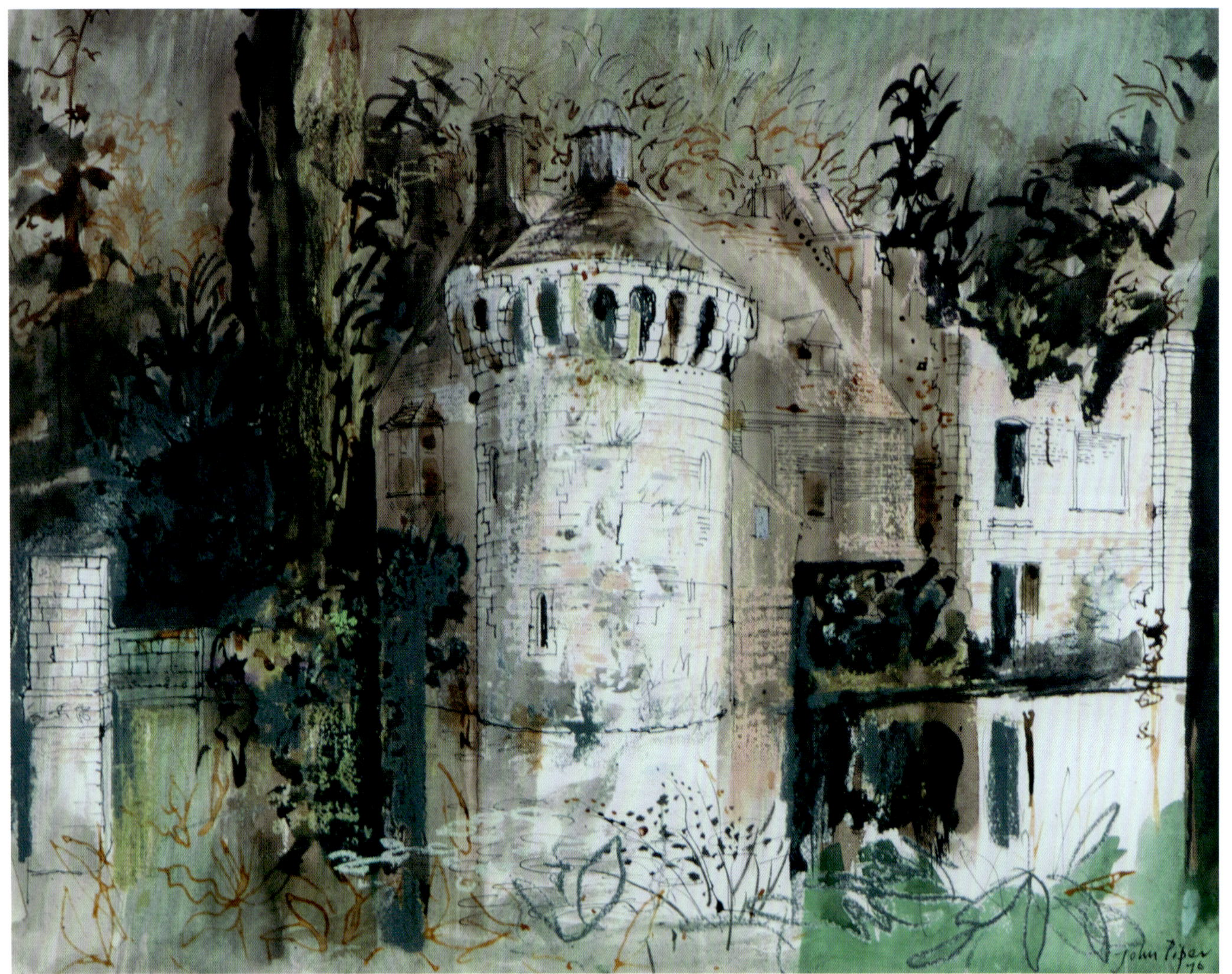

70. ***Old Castle, Scotney***

1976

Oil pastel and watercolour on paper
43 x 56 cm

Tne National Trust, Scotney Castle

71. ***Scotney Castle, Kent***
1976

Lithograph - Levinson 265
45 x 61 cm

Private collection

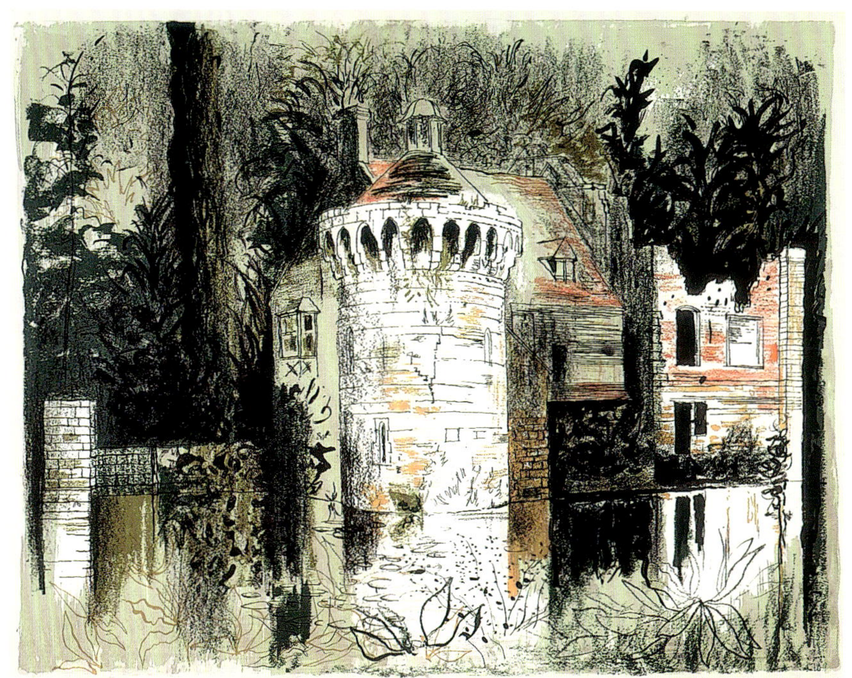

72. ***Scotney Castle, Kent***
1982

Portfolio of 6 etchings -
Levinson 343-348
(Levinson 344 illustrated)
21.3 x 40.6 cm

Private collection

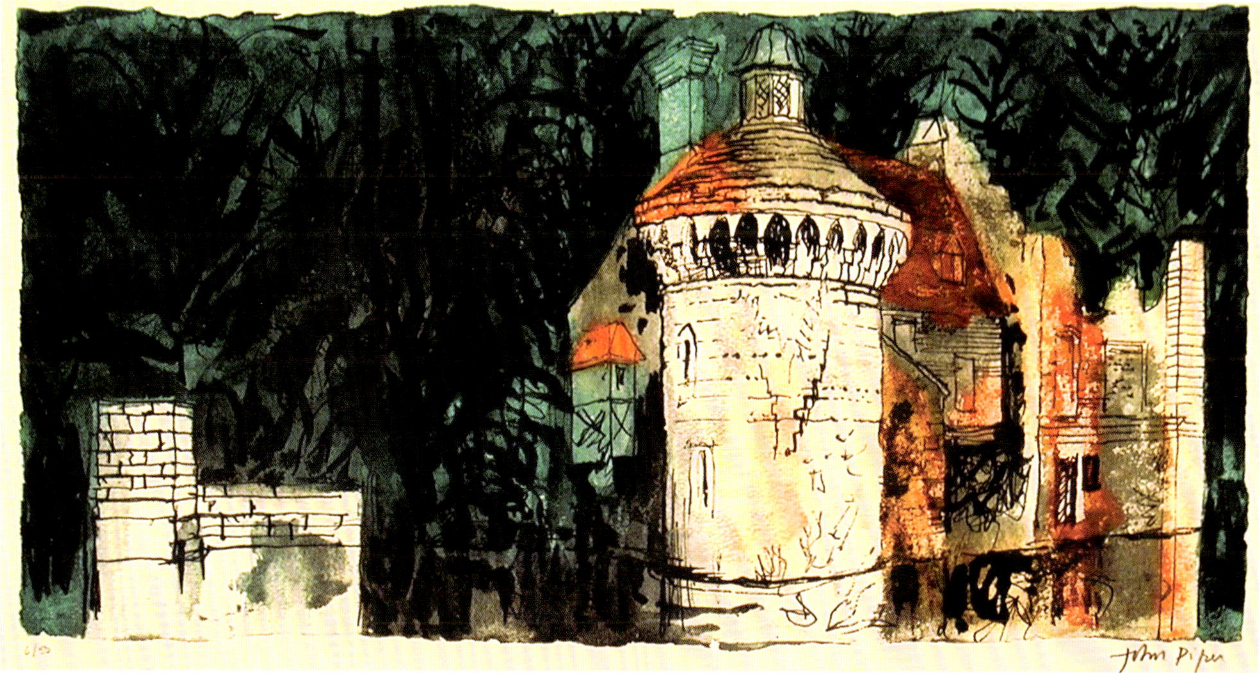

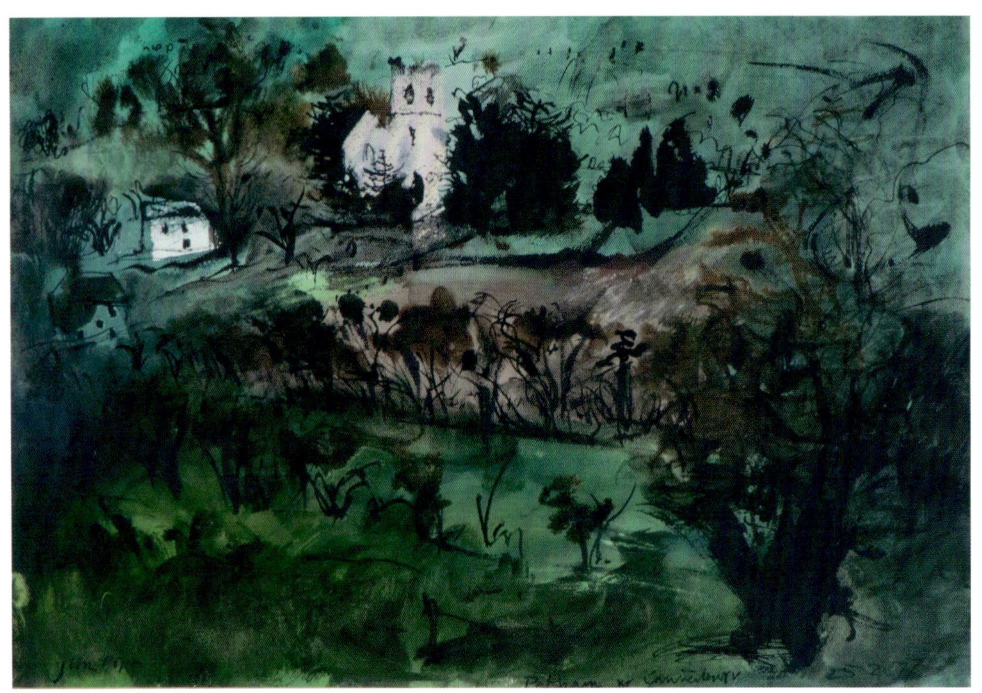

73. ***Petham, near Canterbury***
1977

Watercolour, bodycolour and black ink
40 x 58.2 cm

Canterbury City Council Museums and Galleries Service

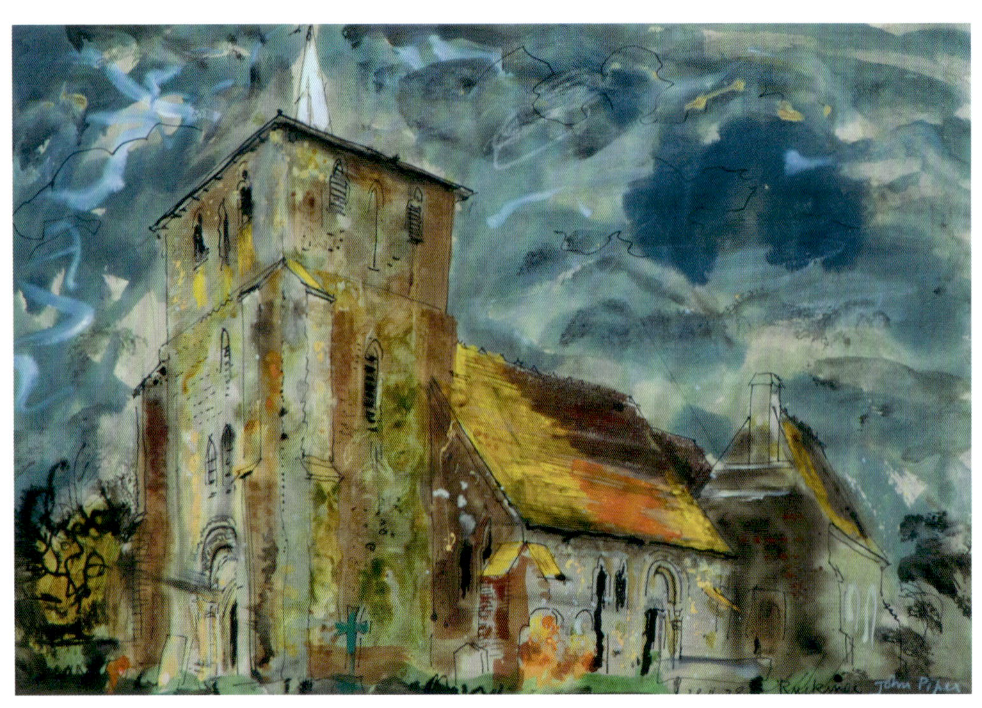

74. ***Ruckinge Church***
1978

Watercolour
38 x 56 cm

Rye Art Gallery

75. ***Dungeness***
1978

Gouache on paper
35.6 x 51 cm

Private collection

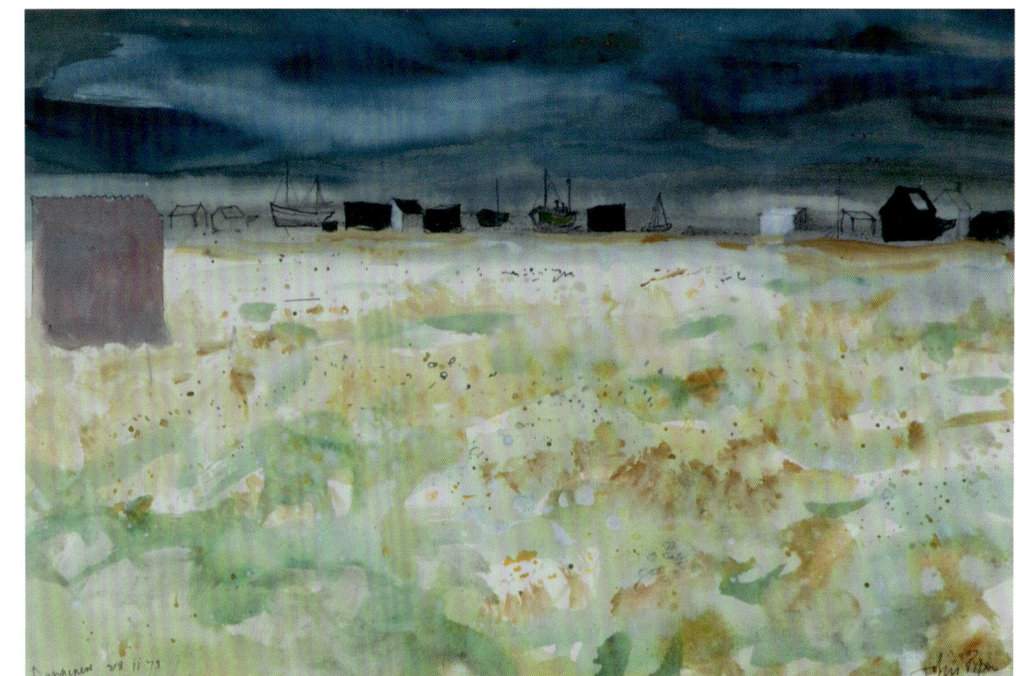

76. ***Romney Marsh Dyke***
1978

Black ink, watercolour, coloured crayons and gouache
39.4 x 50.8 cm

Private collection

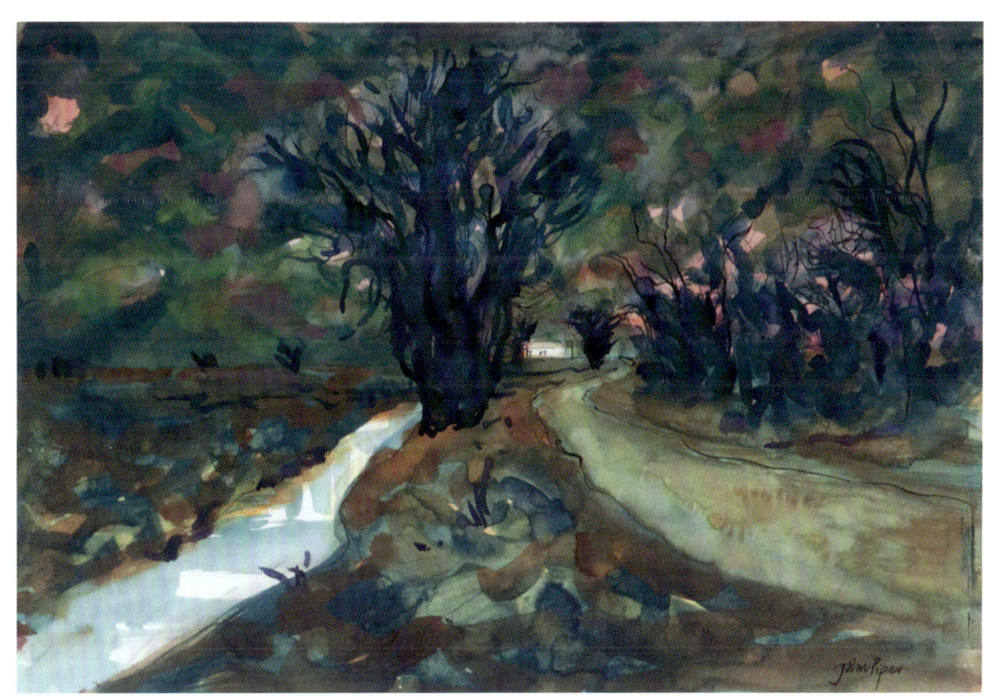

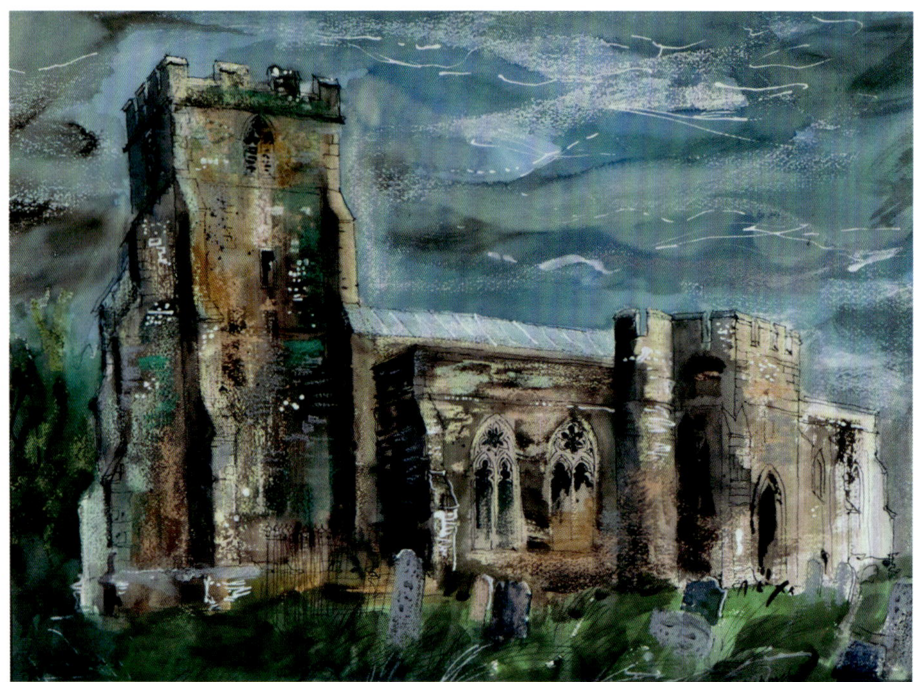

77. ***Ivychurch, Romney Marsh, Kent***
1982

Mixed media
45.7 x 63.5 cm

Private collection

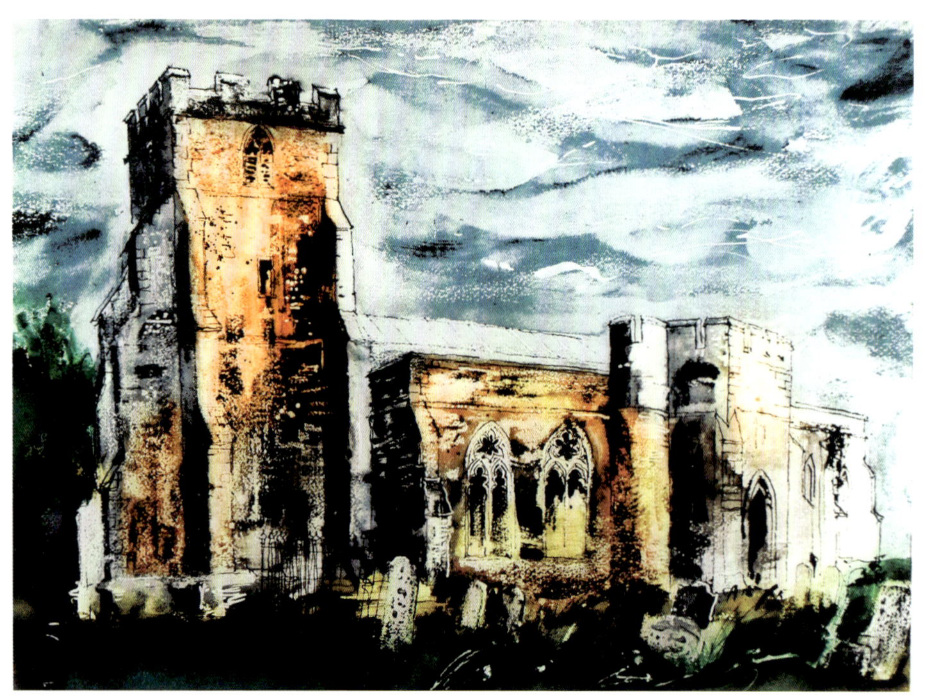

78. ***Ivychurch, Romney Marsh, Kent***
1983

Aquatint and etching -
Levinson 364
45 x 61.5 cm

Private collection

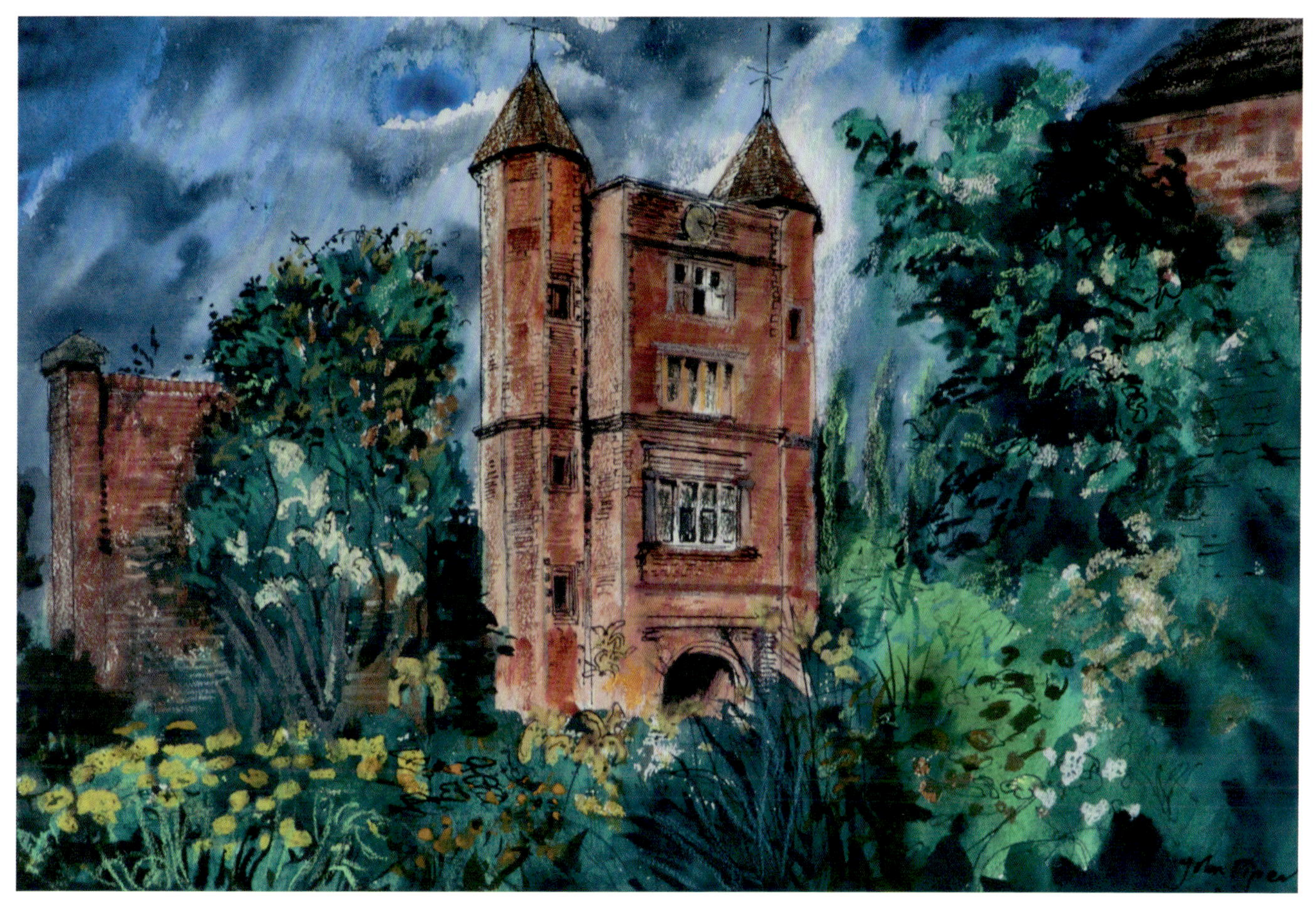

79. ***The Elizabethan Tower, Sissinghurst***
1984

Ink, watercolour and pastel on paper
37.5 x 56.5 cm

Private collection

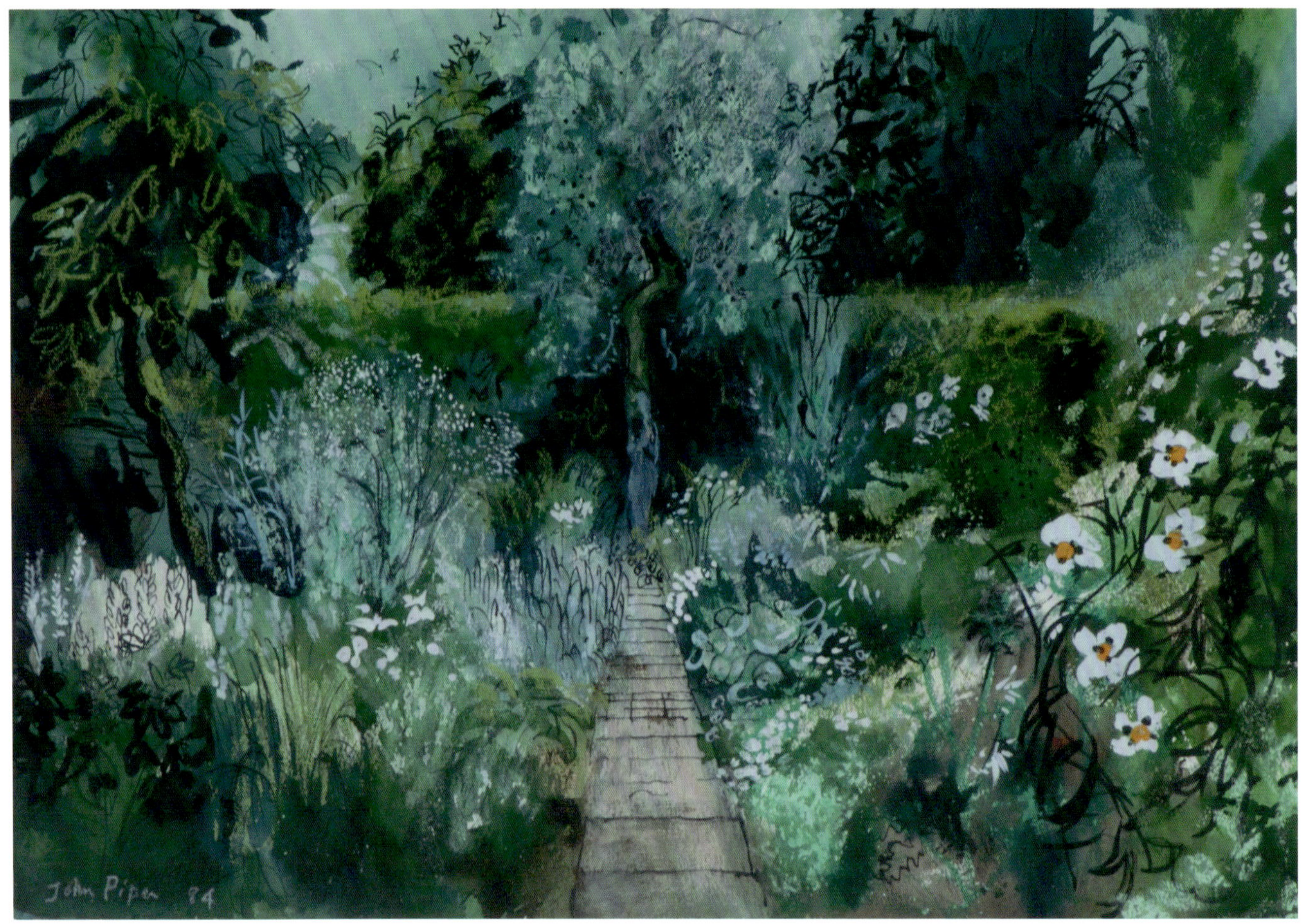

80. ***The White Garden, Sissinghurst***
1984

Ink, watercolour and pastel on paper
37.5 x 56.5 cm

Private collection

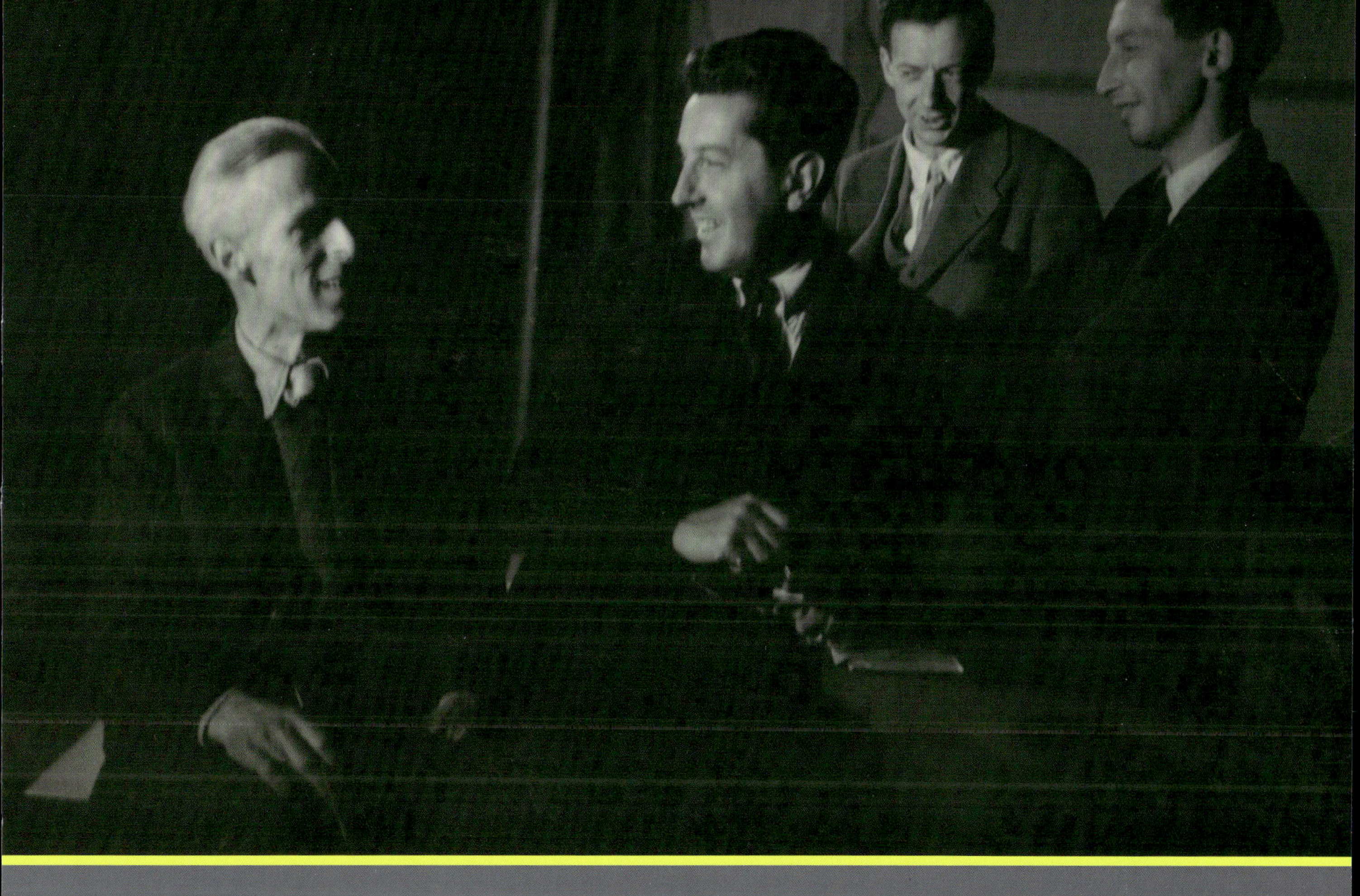

Commissions
in Kent & Sussex

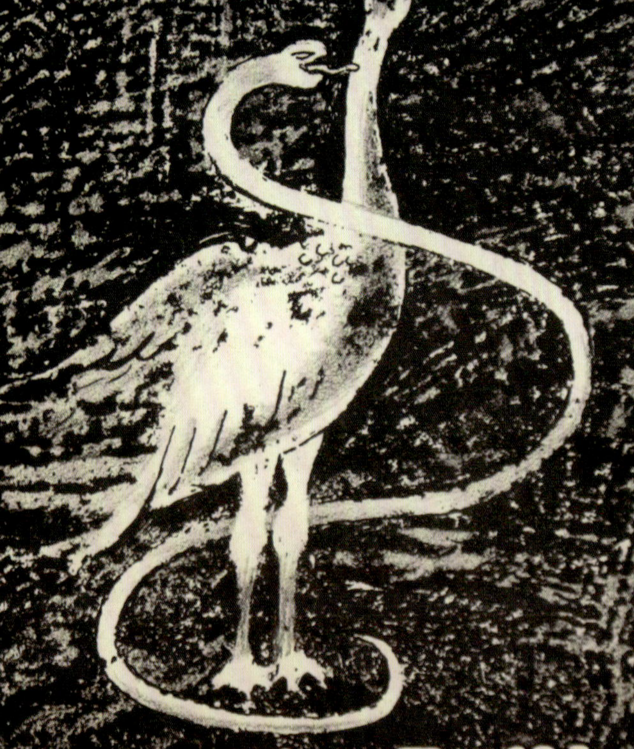
The Rape of
LUCRETIA
Benjamin Britten

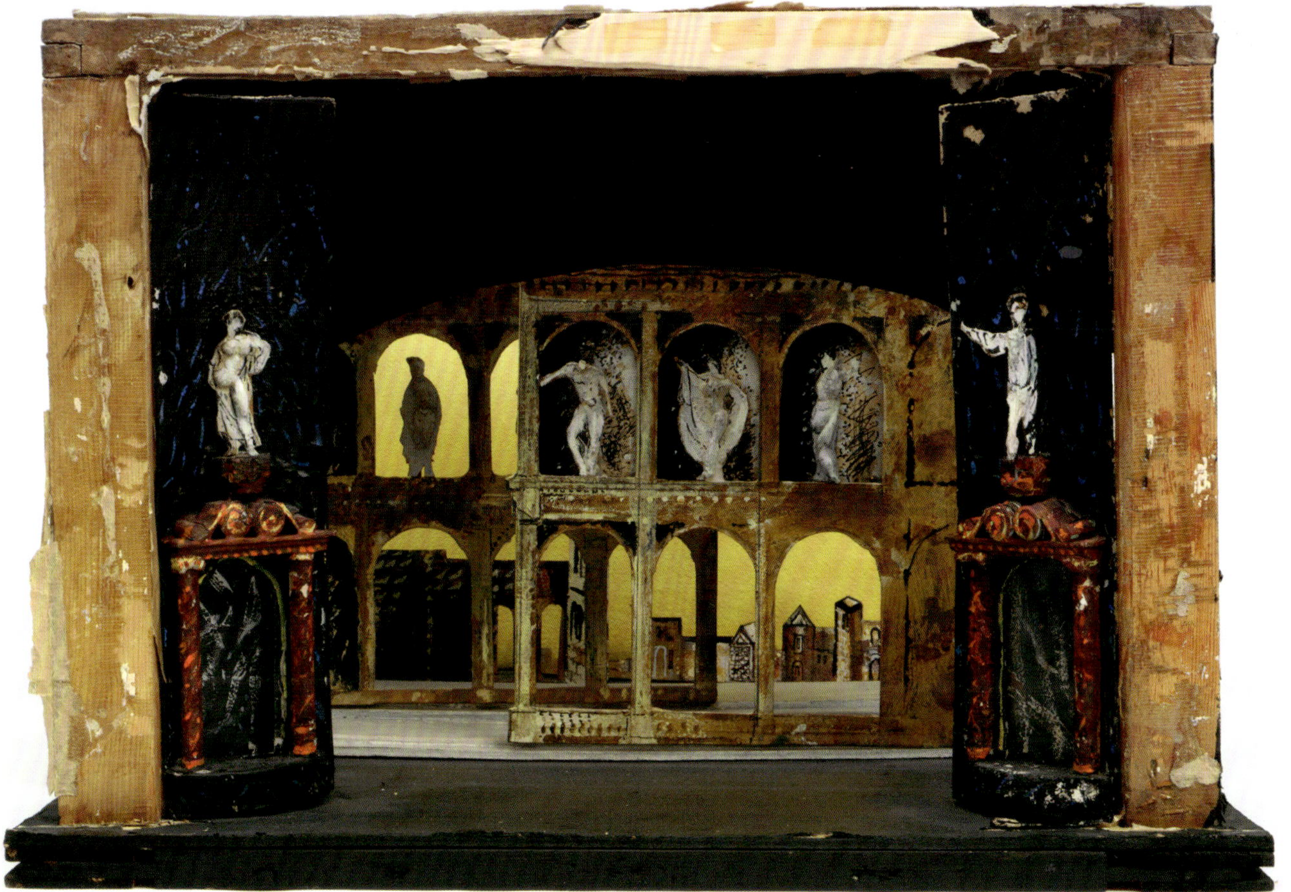

81. ***Cover for the Libretto 'The Rape of Lucretia'***

Lithograph
31 x 23.5 cm

Private collection

82. ***Set model for 'The Rape of Lucretia'***
1946

Painted cut card, annotations in ink, on wooden frame.
38.3 x 52.6 x 56 cm

V&A Theatre and Performance

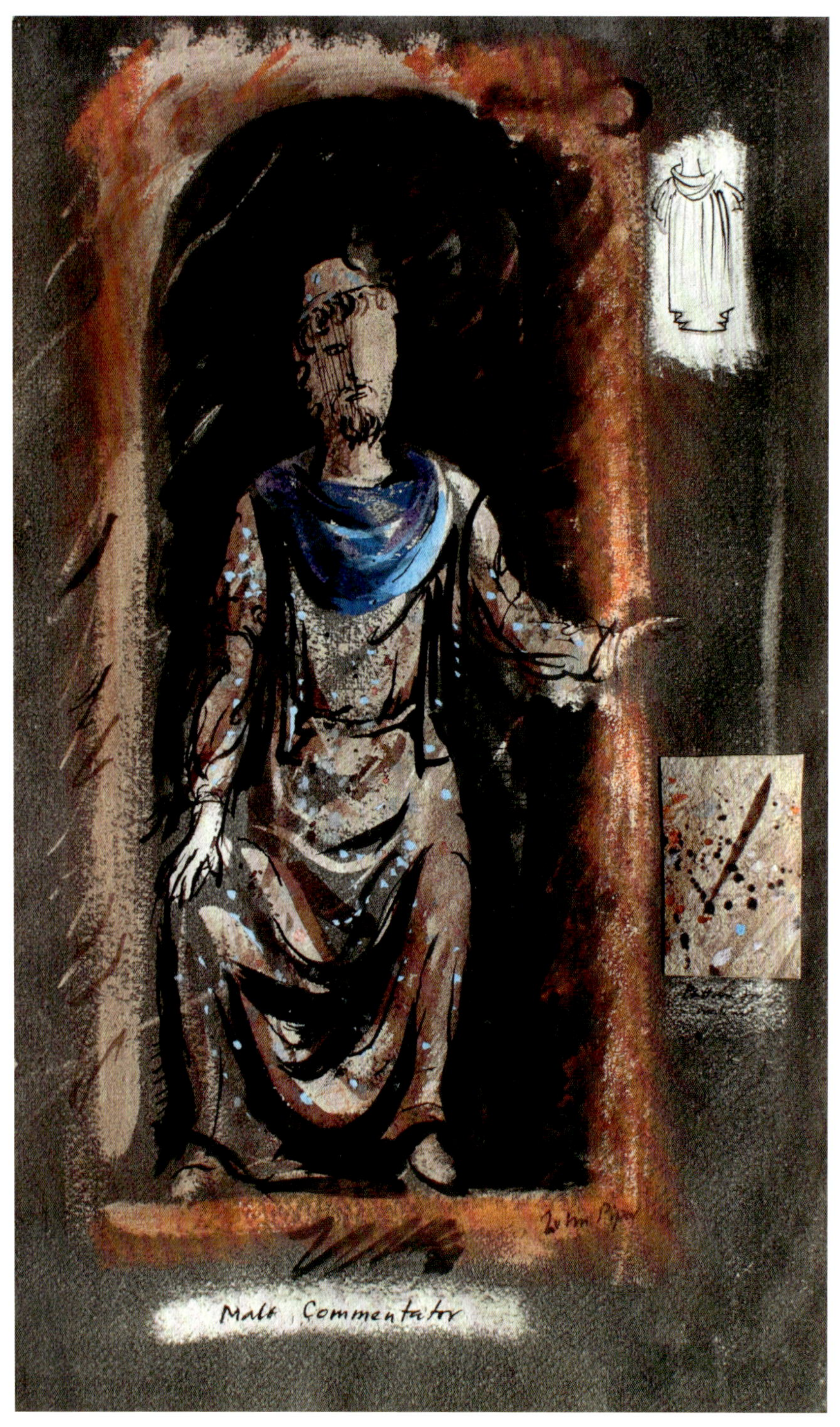

83. ***Costume design for 'The Rape of Lucretia' - Male Commentator***
1946

Watercolour, bodycolour, ink and collage
50.8 x 31.7 cm

Private collection

84. ***Costume design for 'The Rape of Lucretia' - Tarquin***
1946

Watercolour, bodycolour, pastel and charcoal
48.9 x 36.8 cm

Private collection

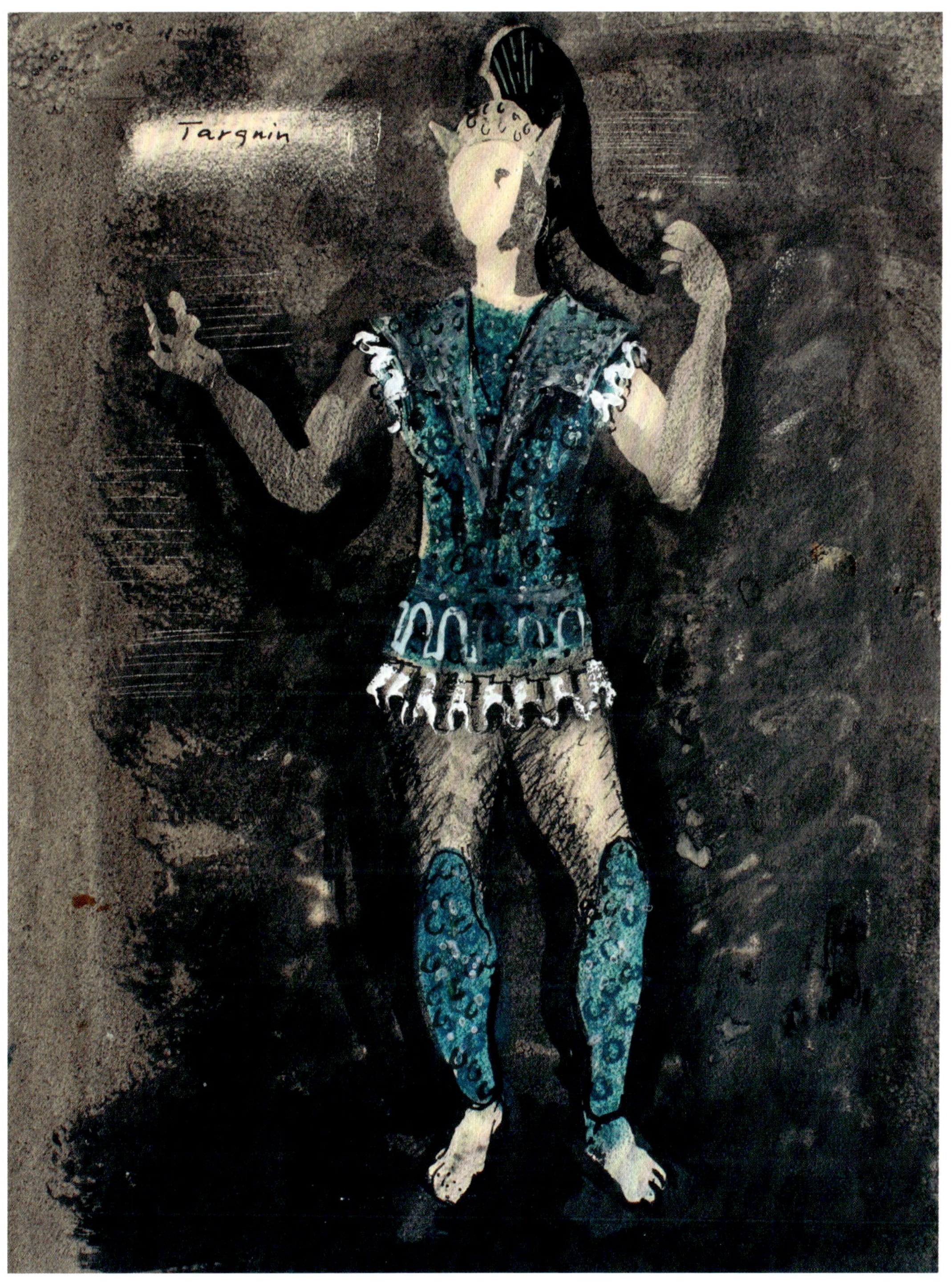
Tarquin

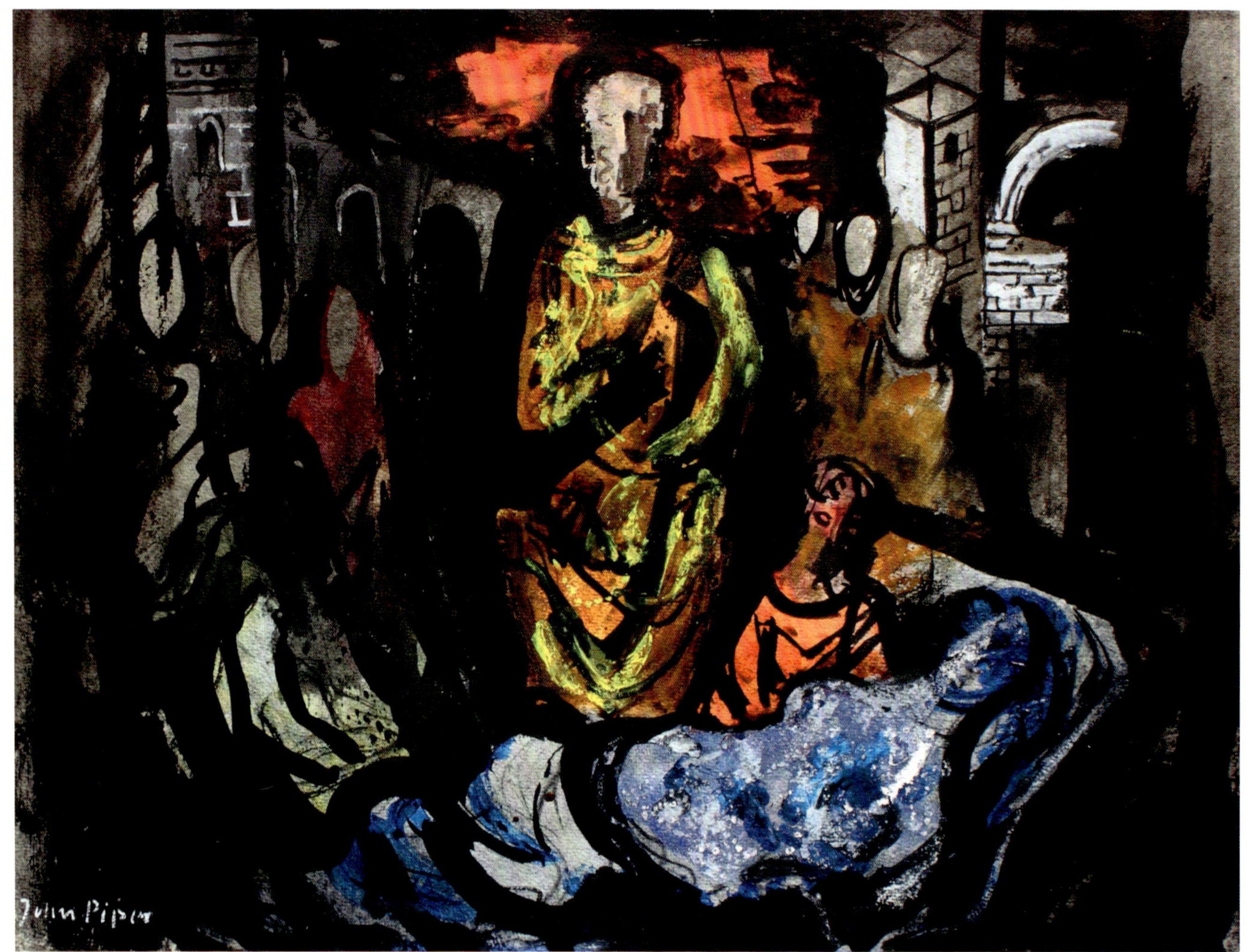

85. ***Design for frontcloth for 'The Rape of Lucretia'***
1946

Watercolour
35 x 47 cm

Private collection

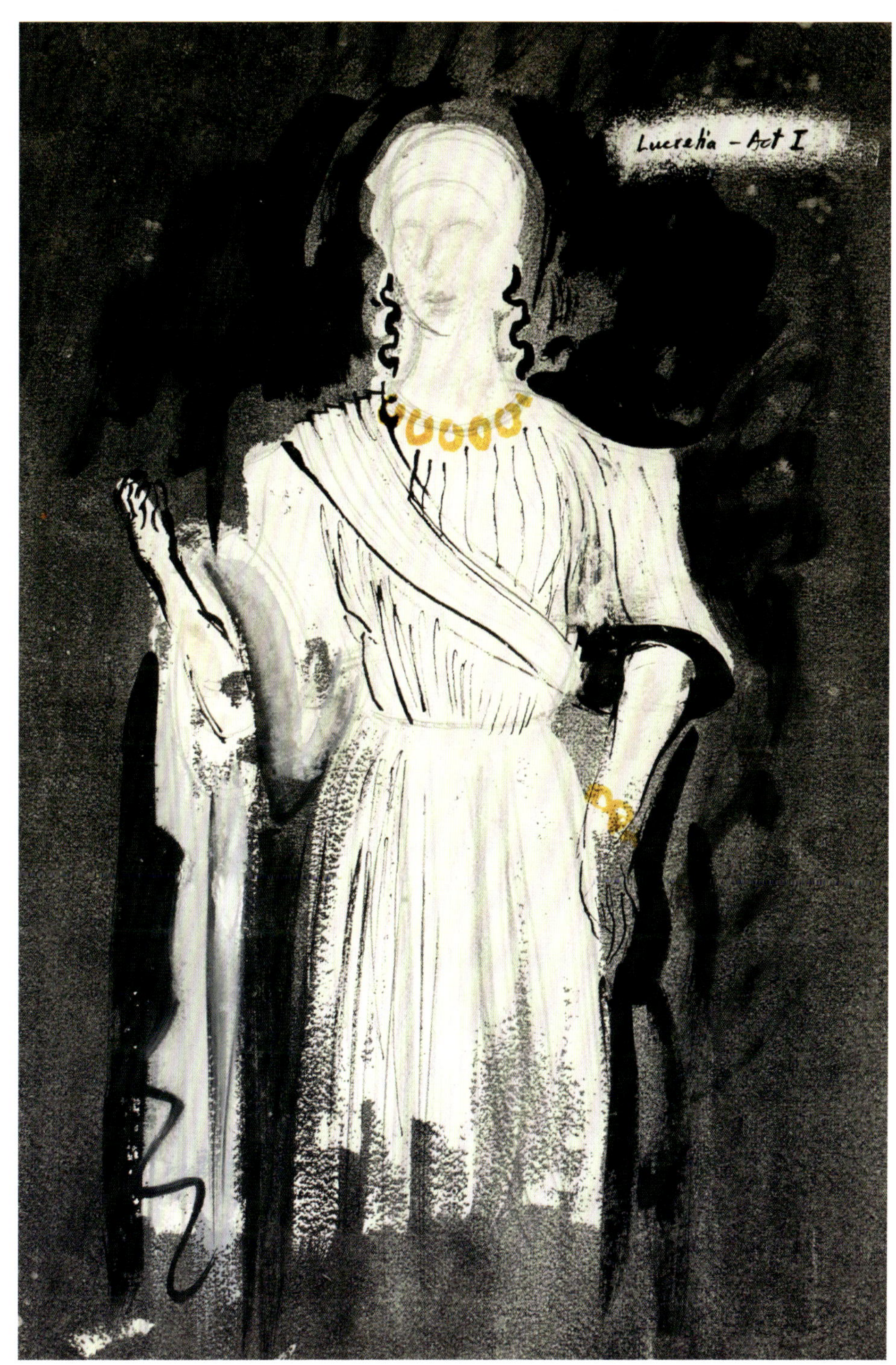

86. ***Costume design for 'The Rape of Lucretia' - Lucretia***
1951

Watercolour and ink on paper
44.5 x 30.7 cm

V&A Theatre and Performance

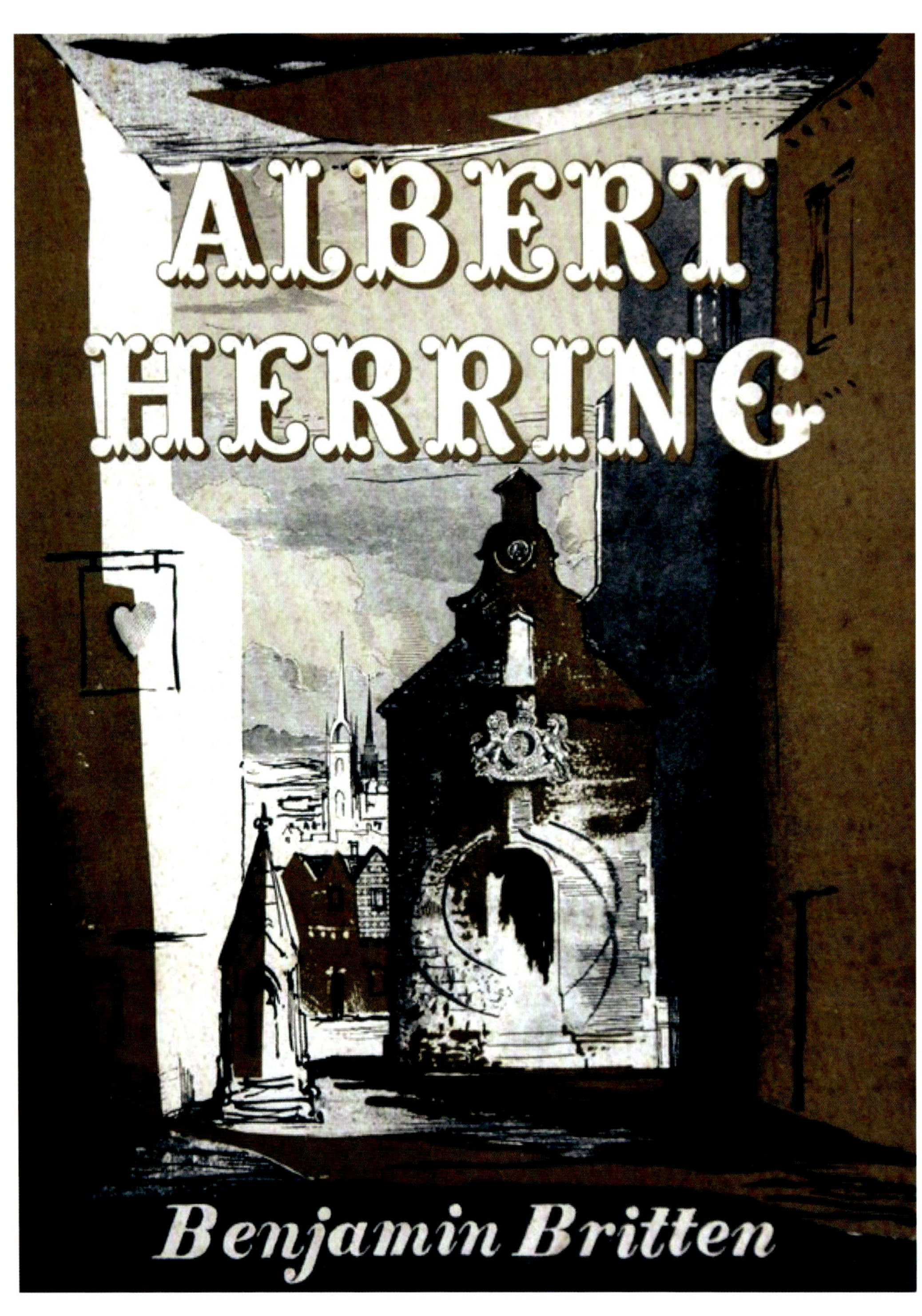

87. ***Cover for the Libretto 'Albert Herring'***

Lithograph
31 x 23.5 cm

Private collection

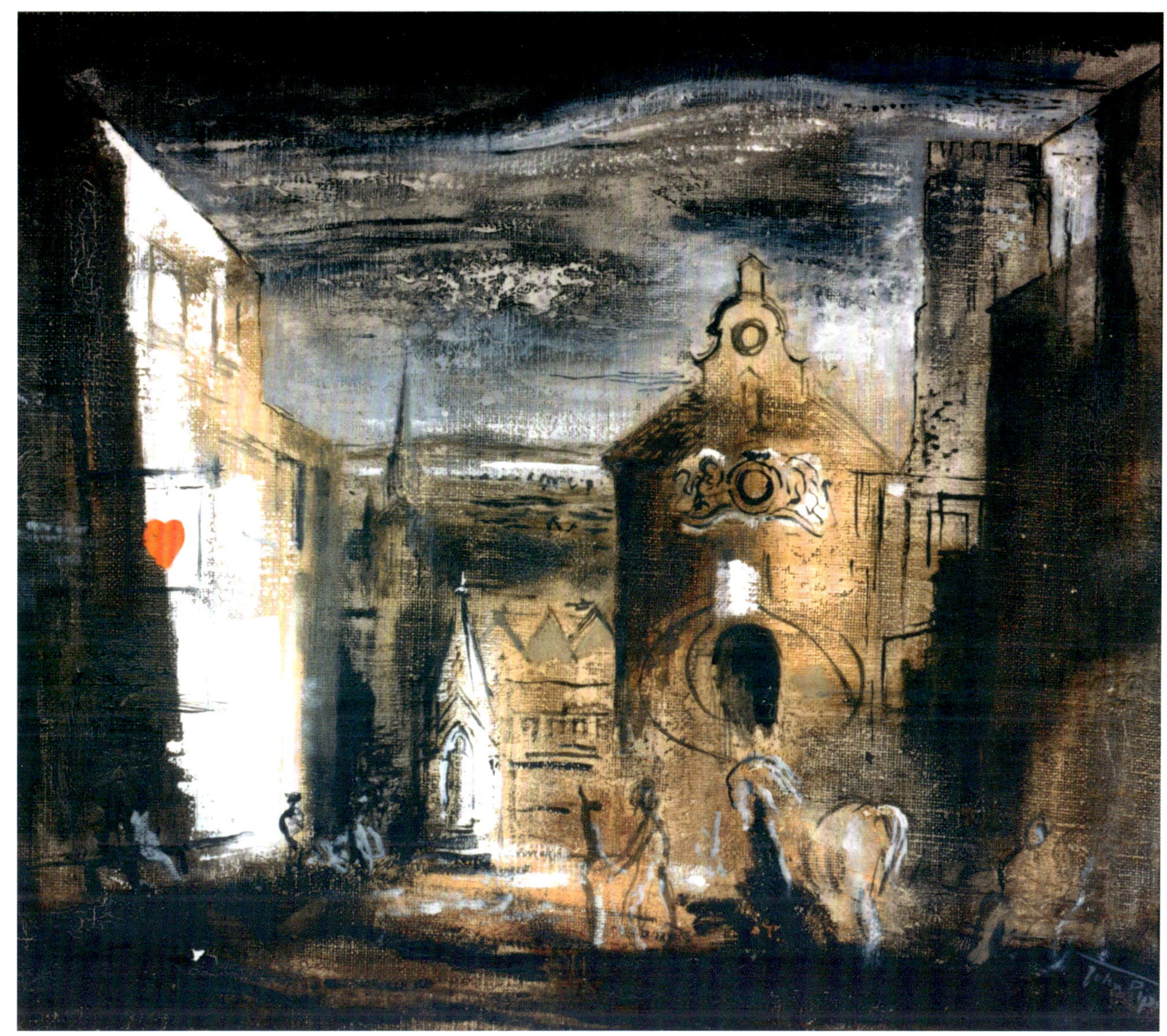

88. ***Loxford: painting from drop curtain - 'Albert Herring'***
1947

Oil on canvas
61.2 x 70.3 cm

Britten—Pears Foundation

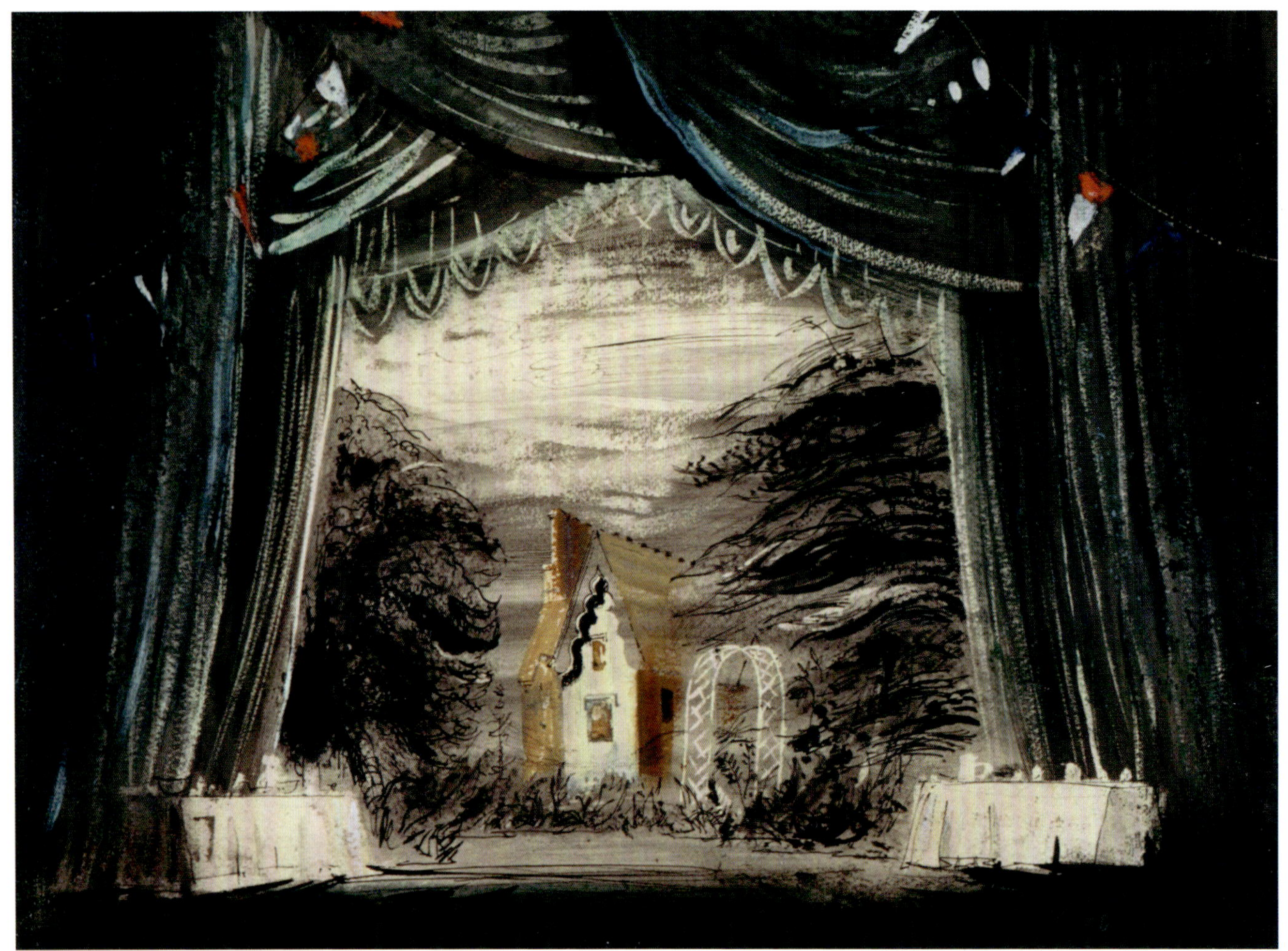

89. ***Set design for 'Albert Herring' - Marquee at the Vicarage***
1947

Black ink, watercolour and pastel on paper
38.2 x 53.3 cm

Britten—Pears Foundation

90. ***Set design for 'Albert Herring' - Lady Billows' House***
1947

Black ink, watercolour and pastel on paper
38.2 x 53.3 cm

Britten—Pears Foundation

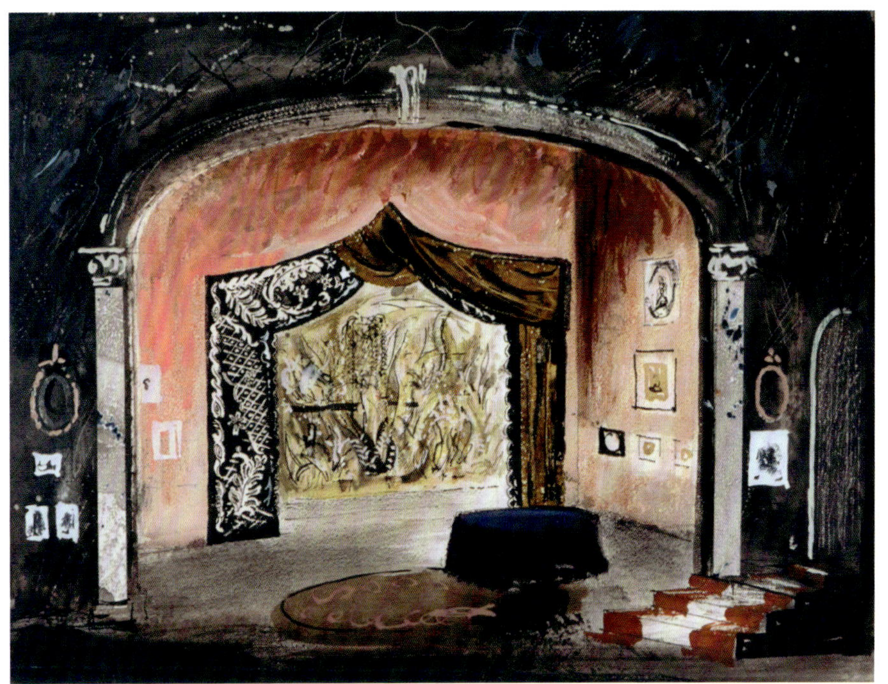

91. ***Set design for 'Albert Herring' - Miss Herring's shop***
1947

Black ink, watercolour and pastel on paper
38.2 x 53.3 cm

Britten—Pears Foundation

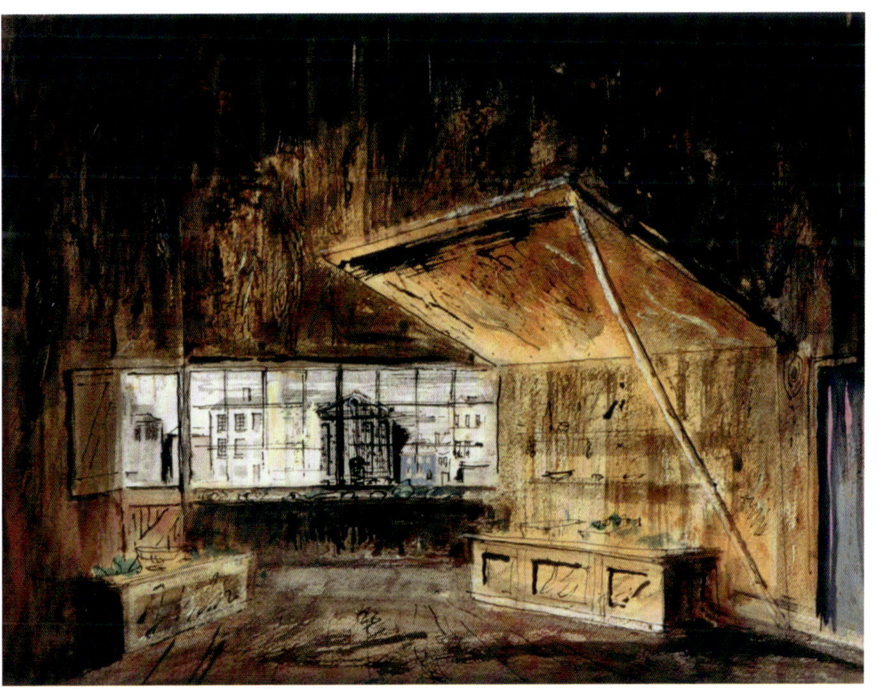

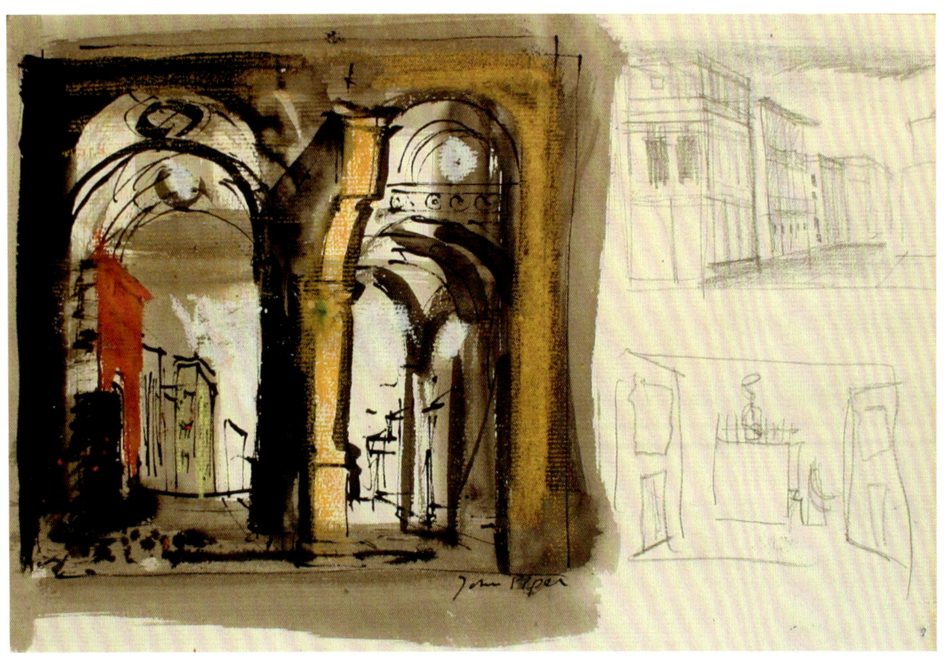

92. ***Design for 'Don Giovanni'***
1947

Ink and watercolour on paper
44.5 x 43 cm

Private collection

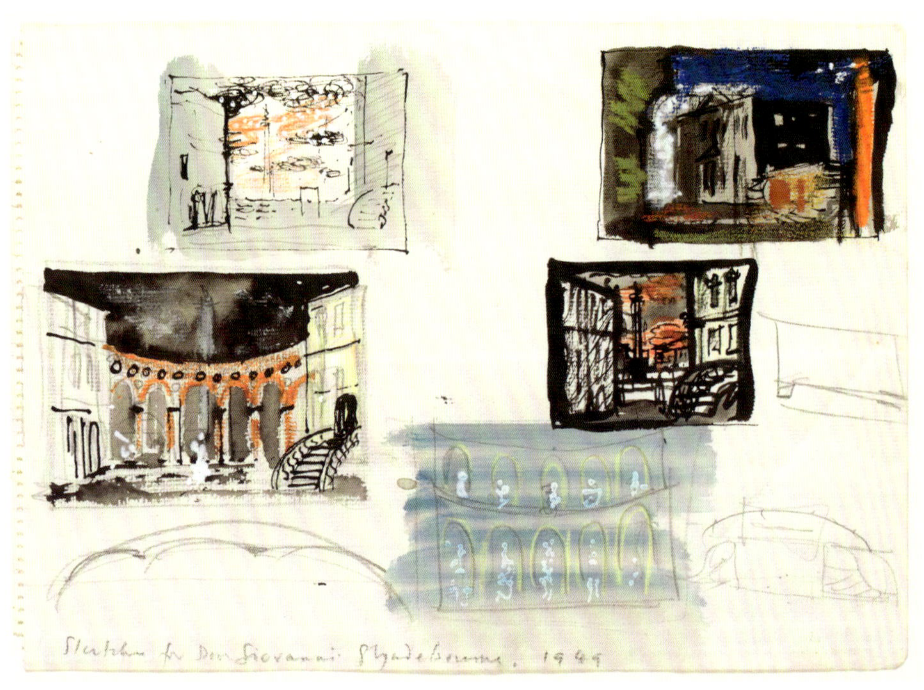

93. ***Design for 'Don Giovanni'***
1949

Ink and watercolour on paper
22.5 x 32.2 cm

V&A Theatre and Performance

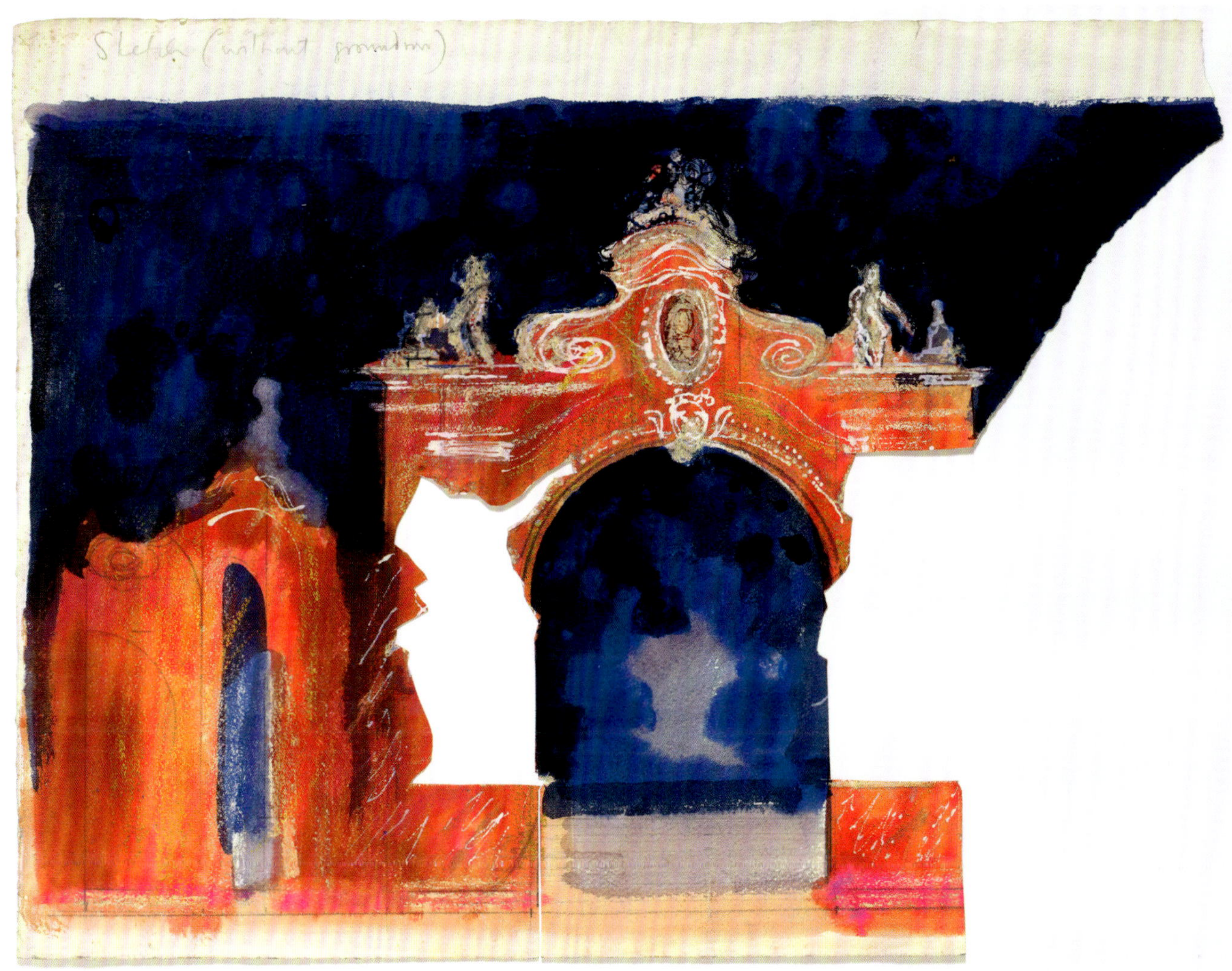

94. ***Design for 'Don Giovanni'***
1951

Ink and watercolour on paper
39 x 51.8 cm

V&A Theatre and Performance

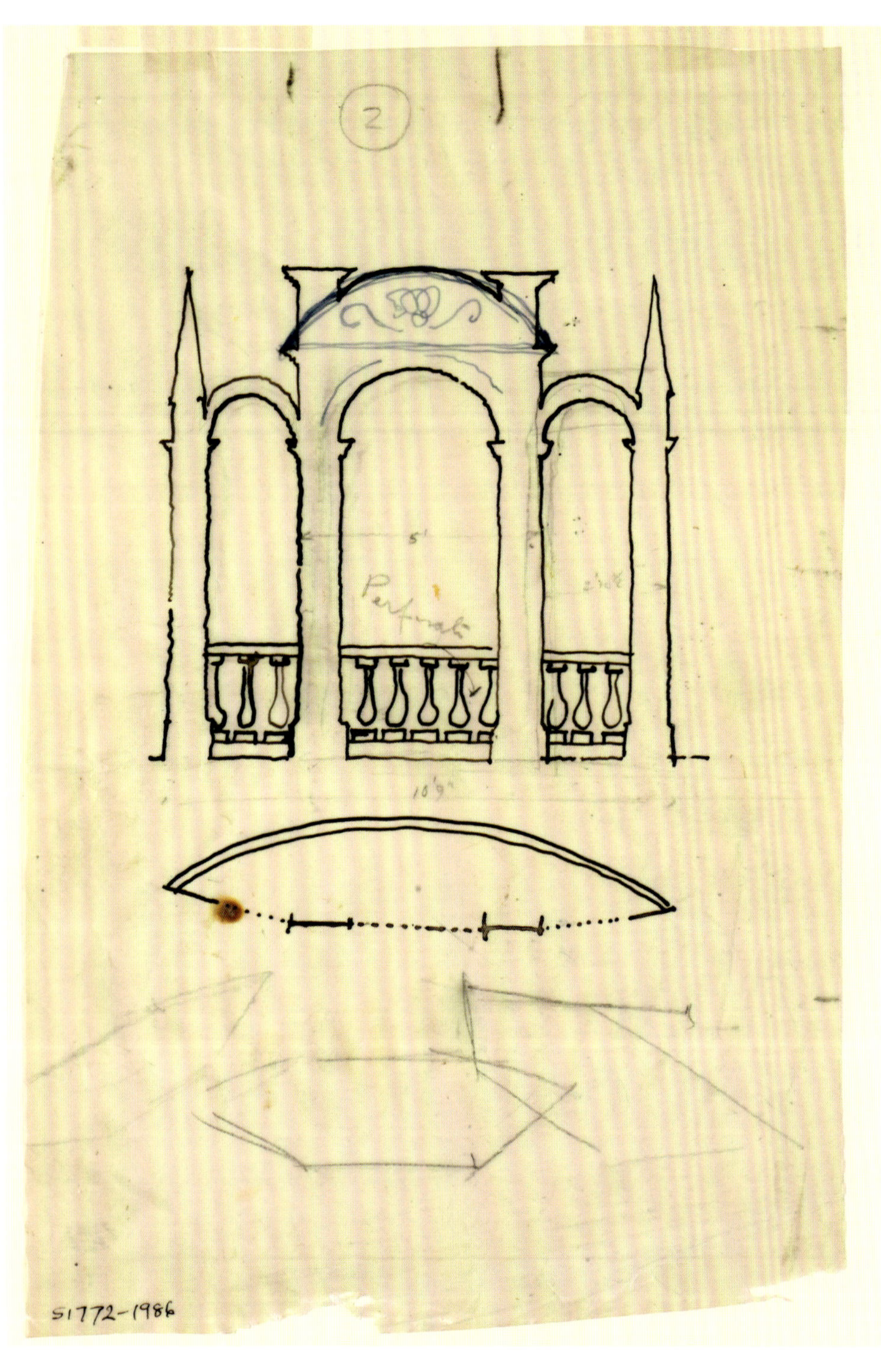

95. ***Design for 'Don Giovanni'***
1951

Ink and watercolour on paper
33.5 x 22 cm

V&A Theatre and Performance

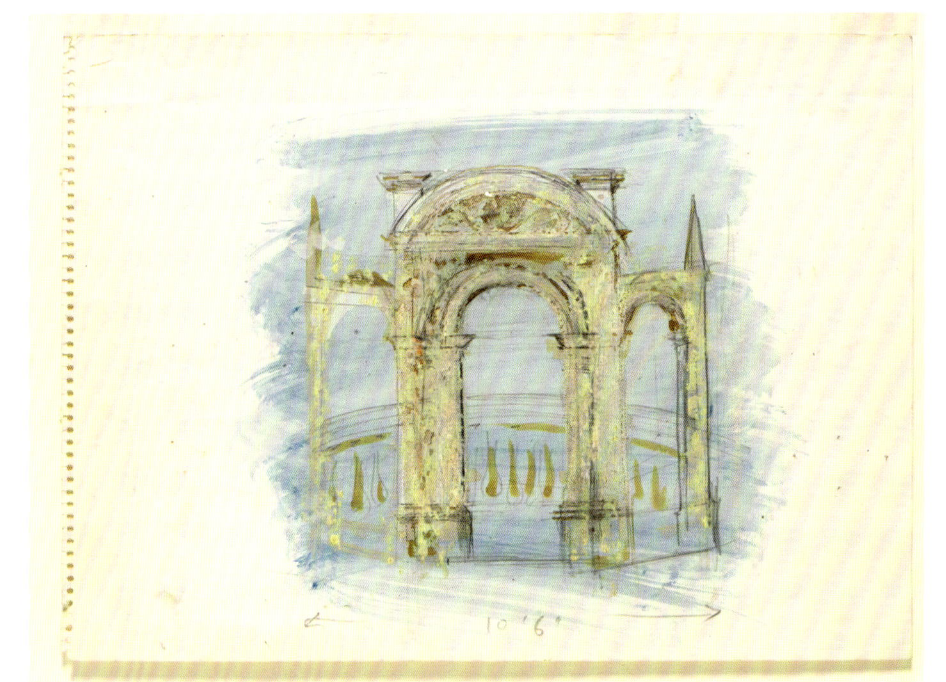

96. ***Design for 'Don Giovanni'***
1951

Ink and watercolour on paper
25.3 x 35.4 cm

V&A Theatre and Performance

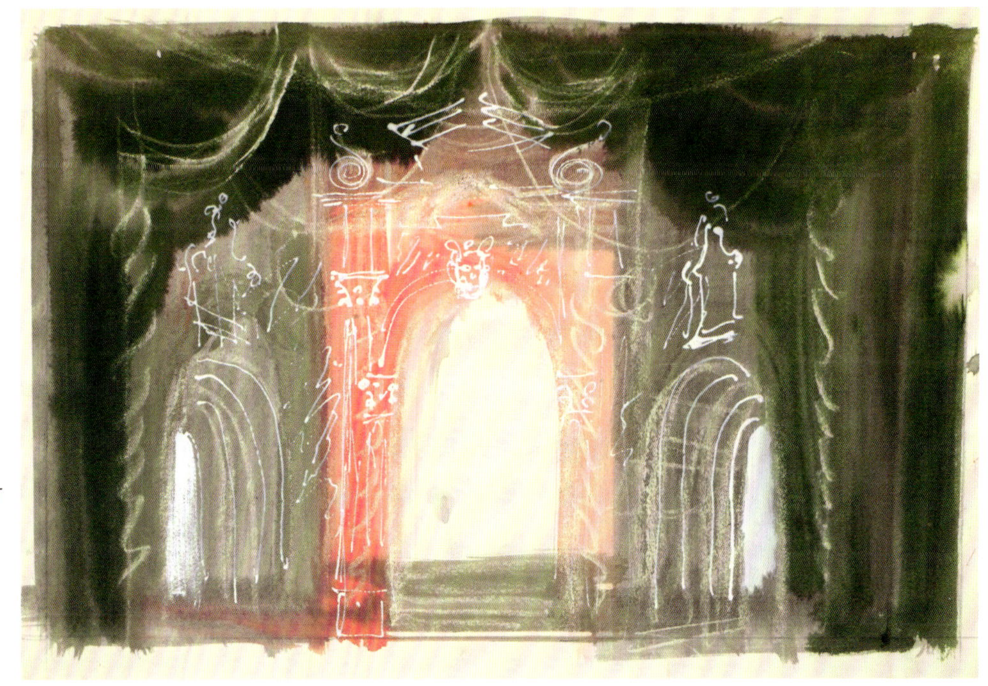

97. ***Design for 'Don Giovanni'***
1951

Ink and watercolour on paper
38 x 56 cm

V&A Theatre and Performance

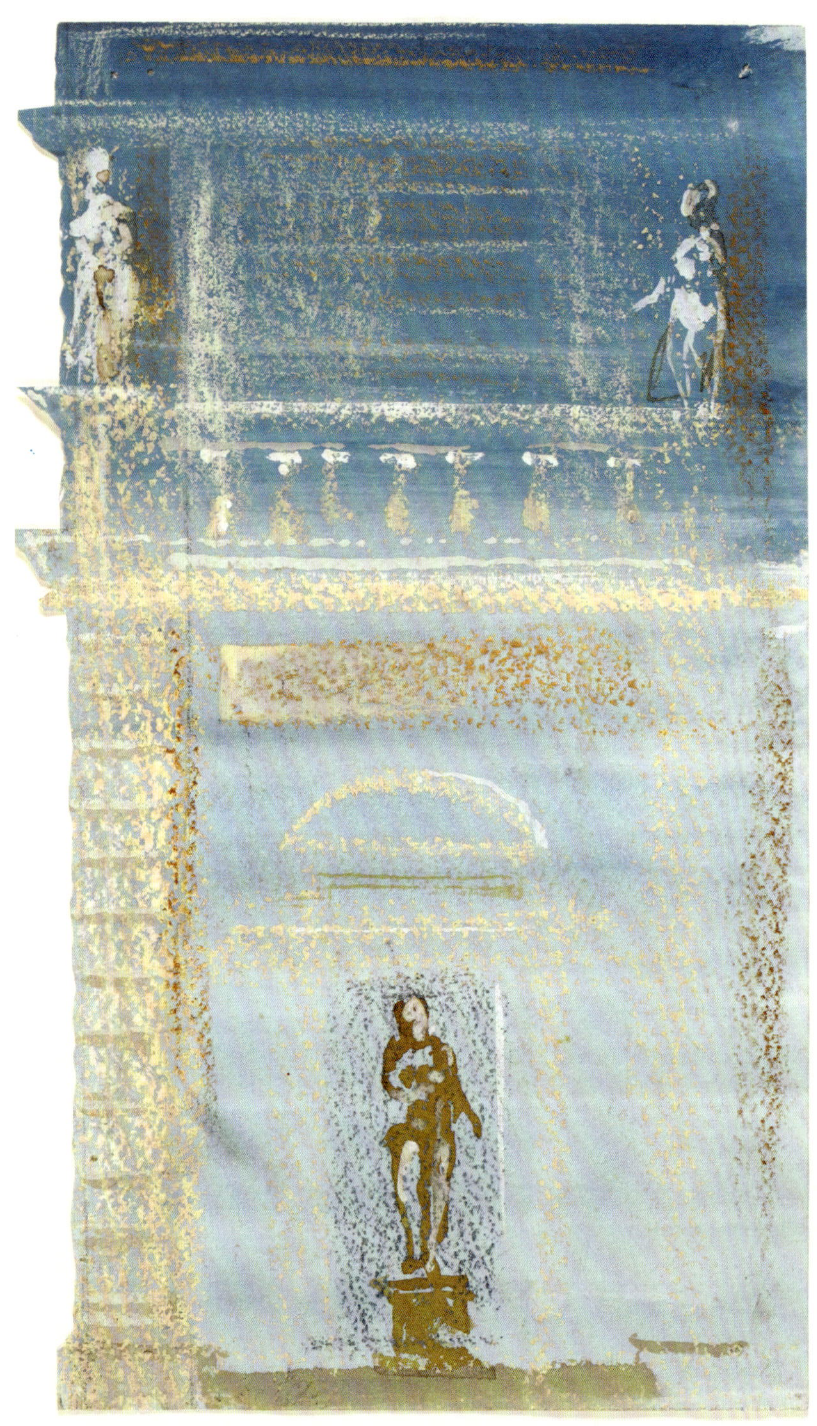

98. ***Design for 'Don Giovanni'***
1951

Ink and watercolour on paper
23.5 x 17.7 cm

V&A Theatre and Performance

99. ***Design for 'Don Giovanni'***
1951

Ink and watercolour on paper
26.7 x 15.5 cm

V&A Theatre and Performance

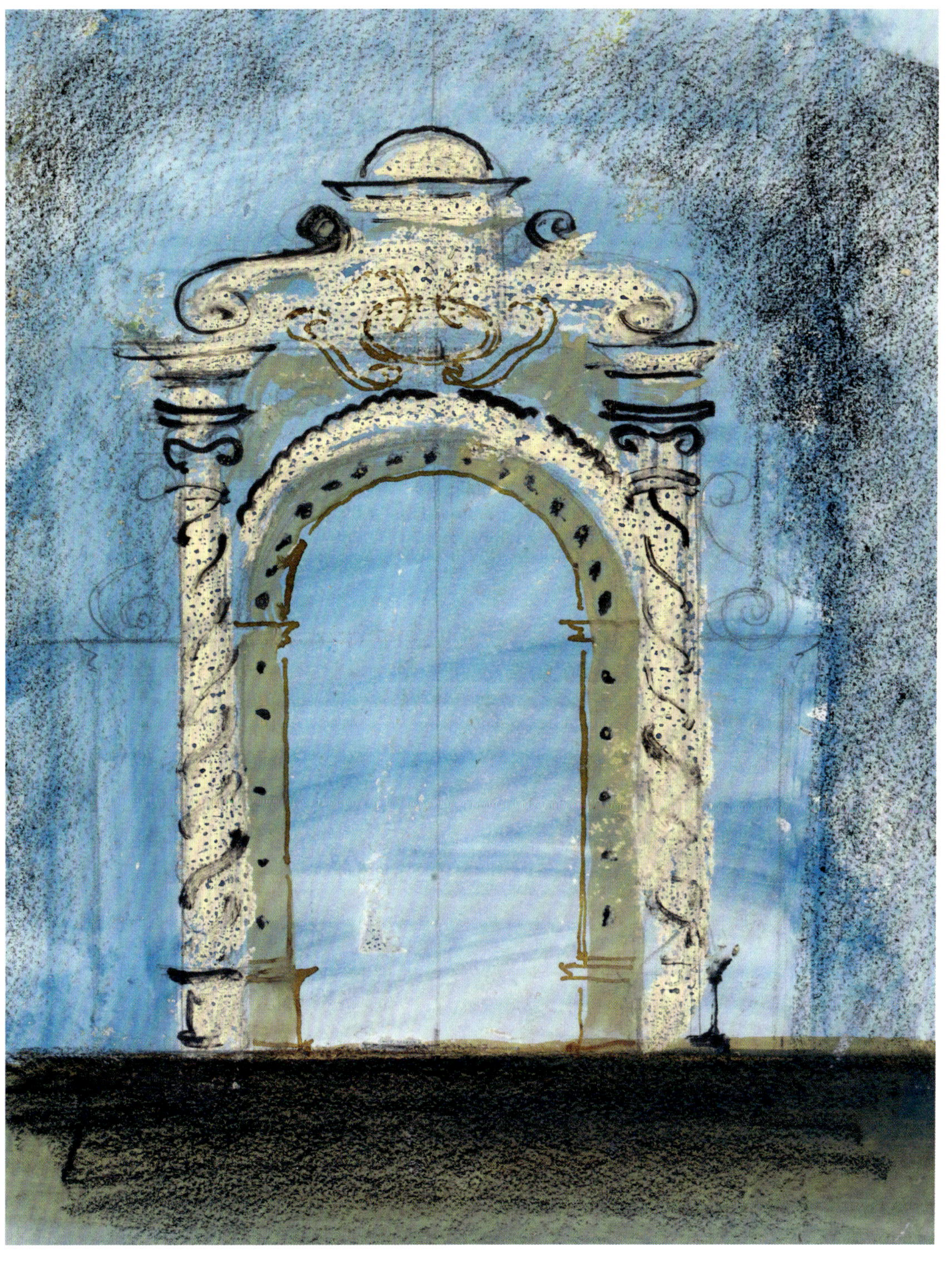

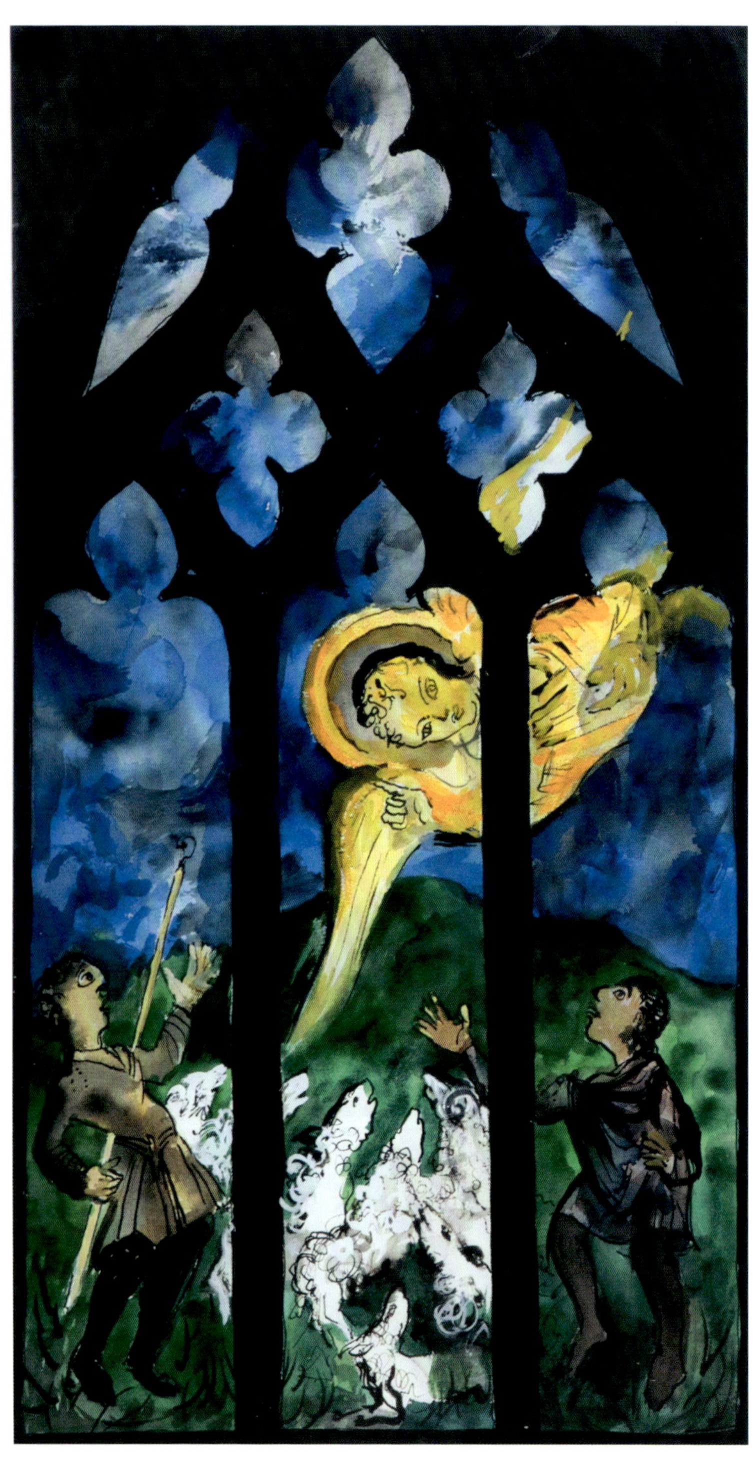

100. ***Sketch for 'The Annunciation to the Shepherds'***
1984

Watercolour, gouache
and ink on paper
38 x 68.5 cm

Private collection

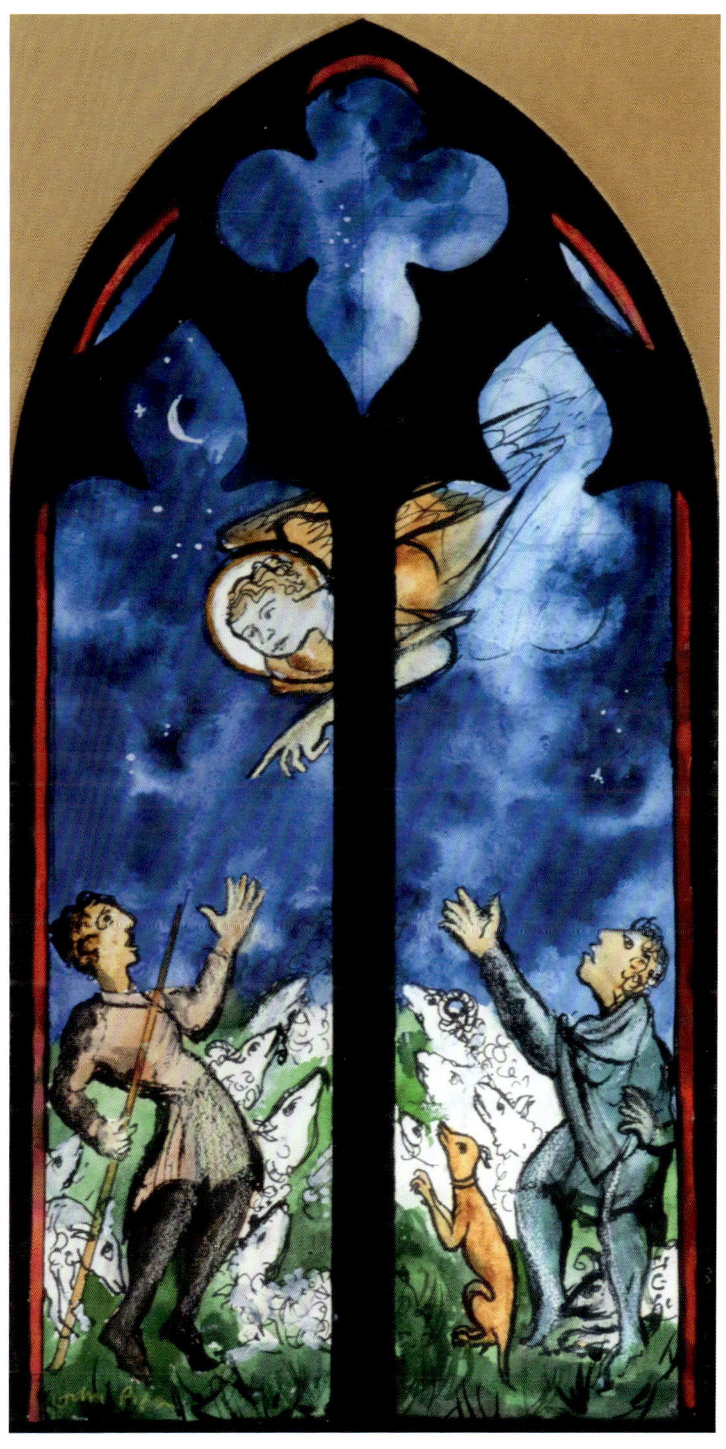

101. ***Sketch for 'The Annunciation to the Shepherds'***
1985

Gouache on paper
61 x 31.5 cm

Private collection

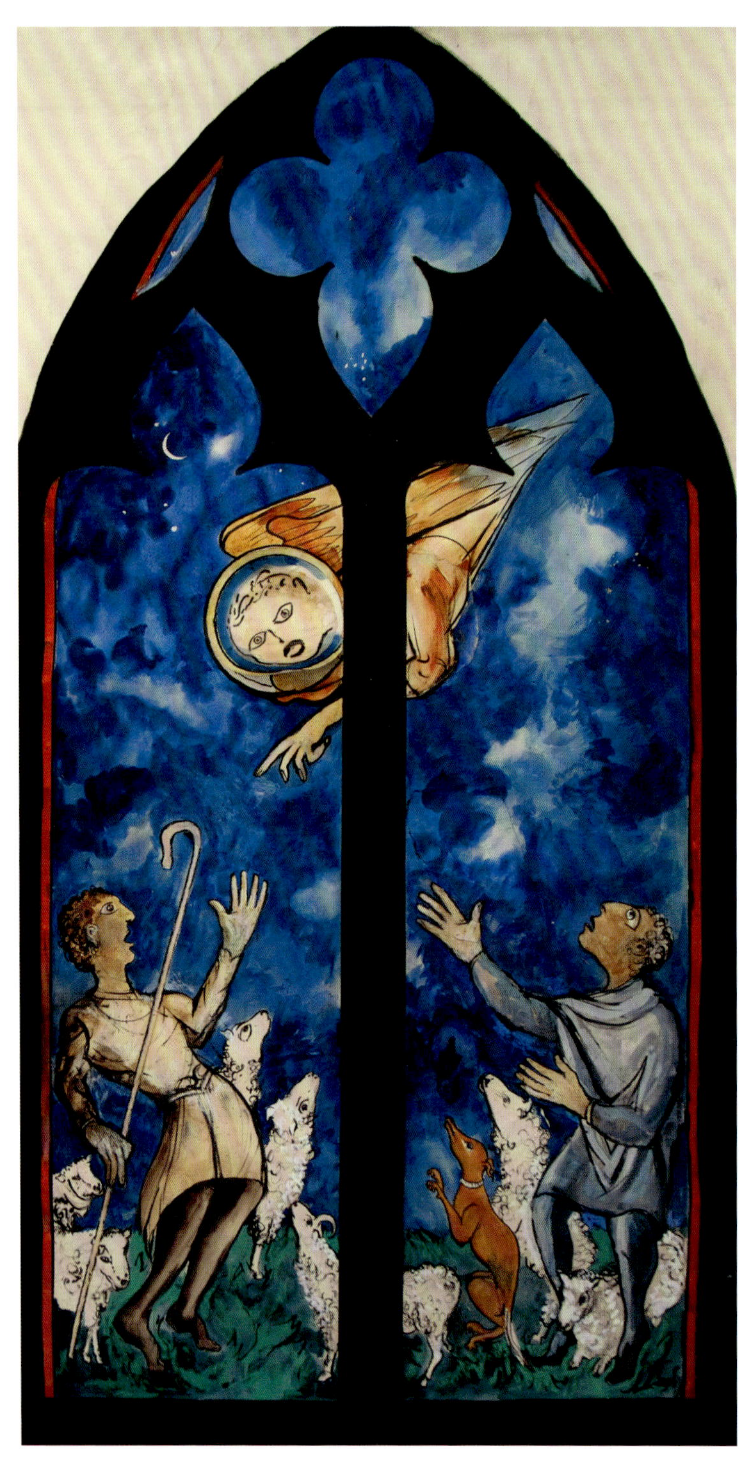

102. ***Cartoon for 'The Annunciation to the Shepherds' at the church of St Mary's, Lamberhurst***
1985

Gouache on paper
233 x 117cm

The Piper Estate

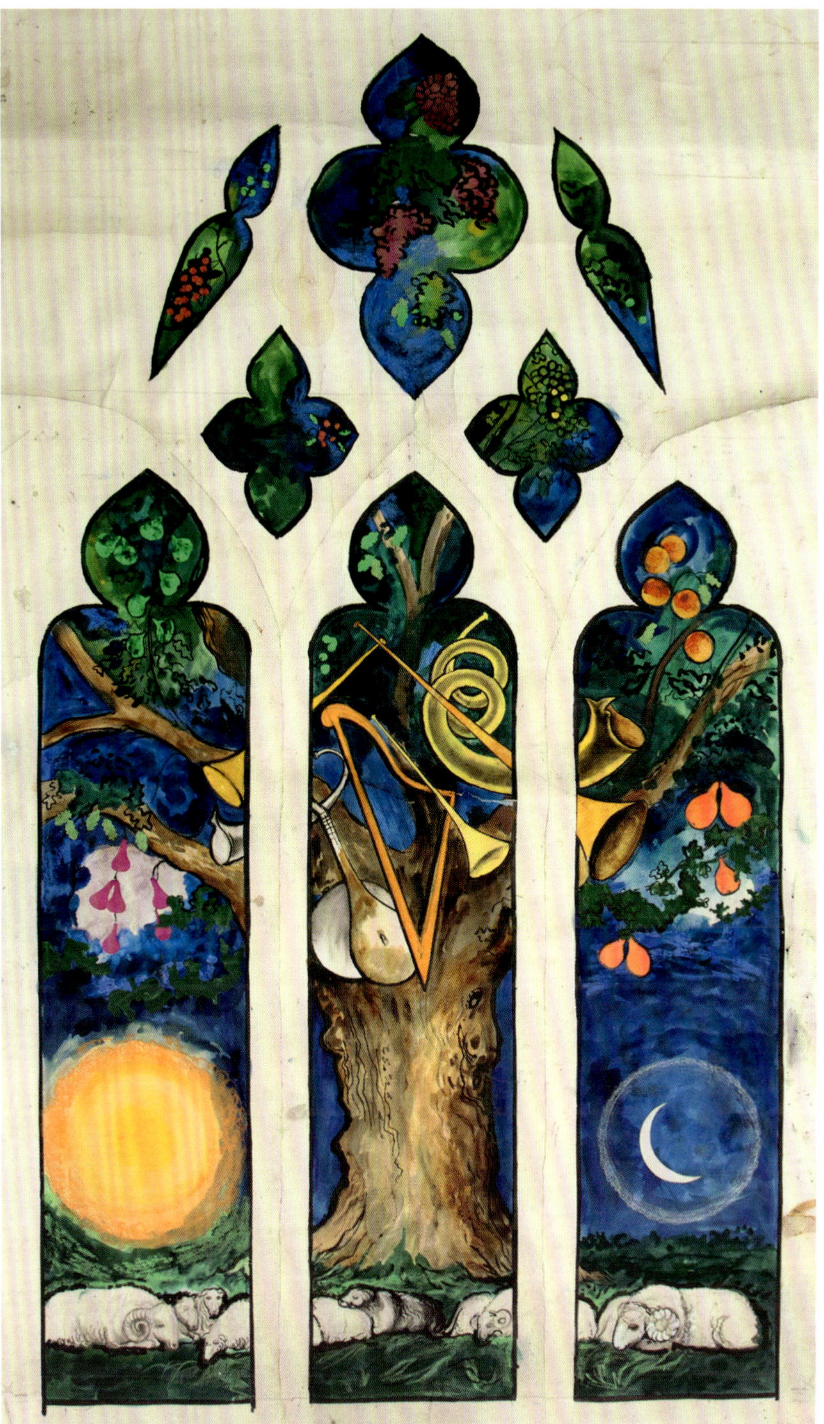

103. ***Cartoon for 'Homage to William Blake's The Book of Job' at the church of St Peter's, Firle***
1985

Gouache on paper
269 x 150 cm

The Piper Estate

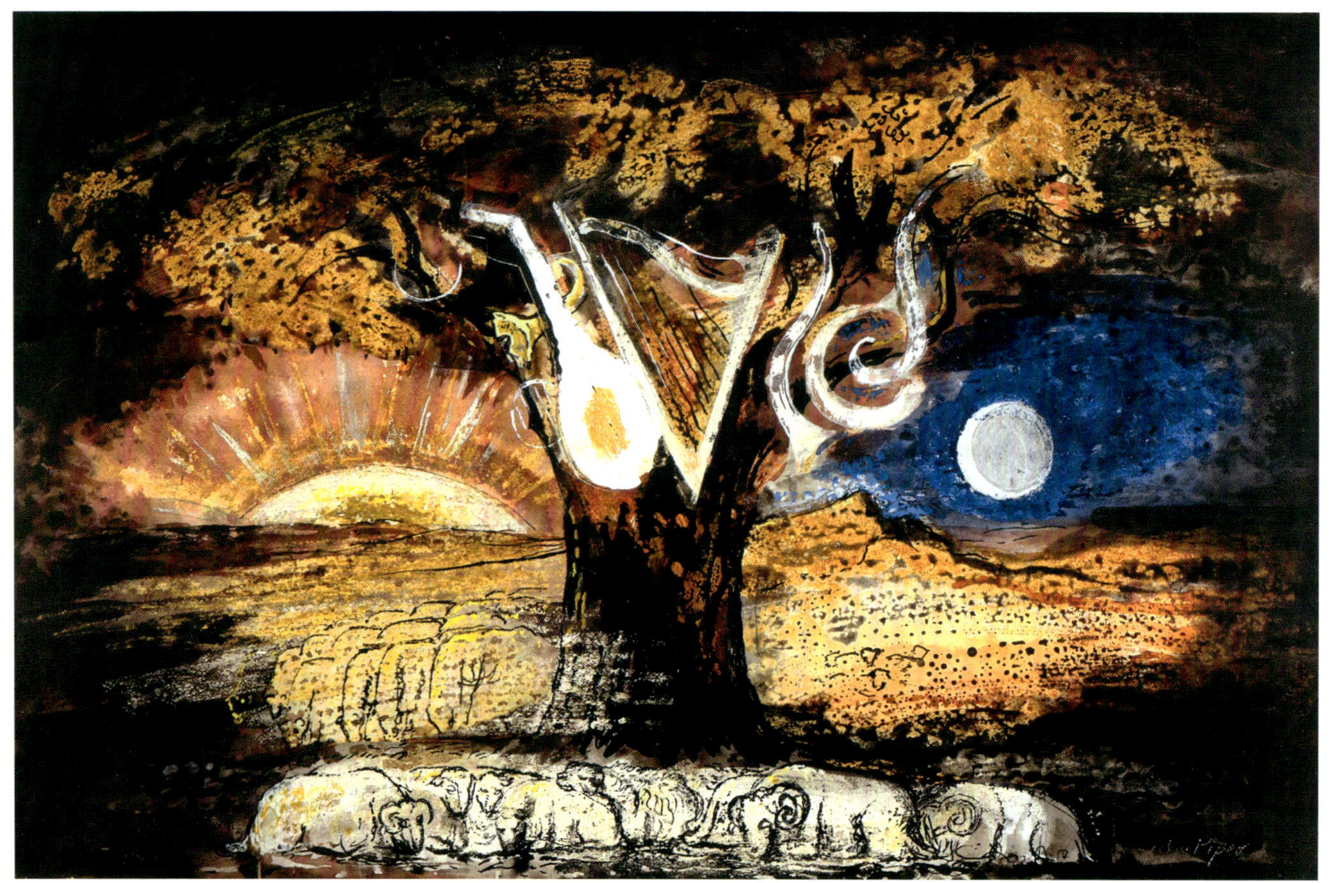

104. ***Design for the curtain 'Earth' - scene 1 of the ballet Job***
1948

Ink and gouache
38 x 53 cm

V&A Theatre and Performance

105. ***Preliminary design for Chichester Cathedral tapestry***
1965

Gouache and collage on paper
39.4 x 58 cm

Pallant House Gallery, Chichester (Hussey Bequest, Chichester District Council, 1985)

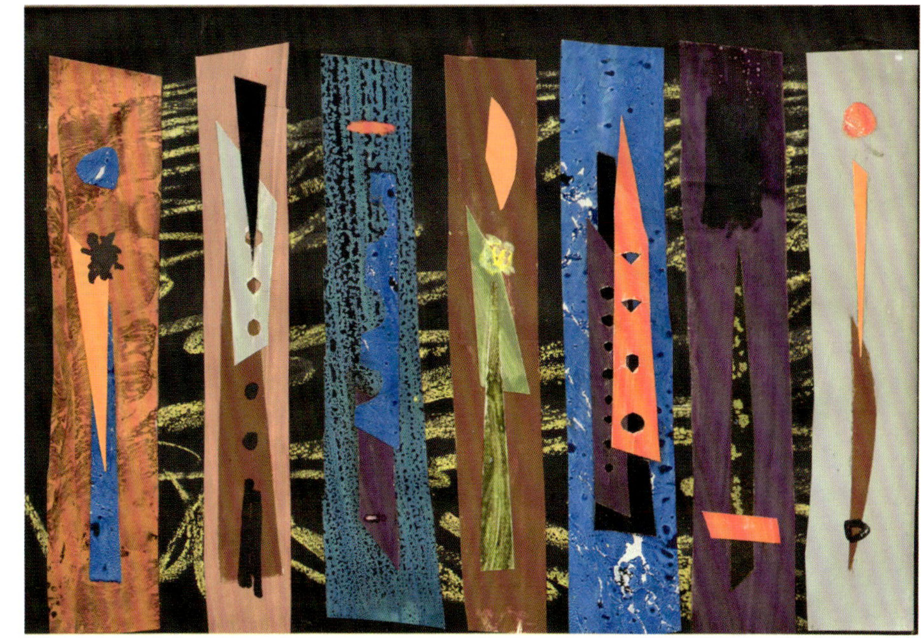

106. ***Sketch for Chichester Cathedral tapestry***
1965

Oil pastel, watercolour and gouache on paper
37 x 54.7 cm

Pallant House Gallery, Chichester (Accepted by HM Government in lieu of Inheritance Tax from the Estate of John & Myfanwy Piper. Allocated to Pallant House Gallery, 2002)

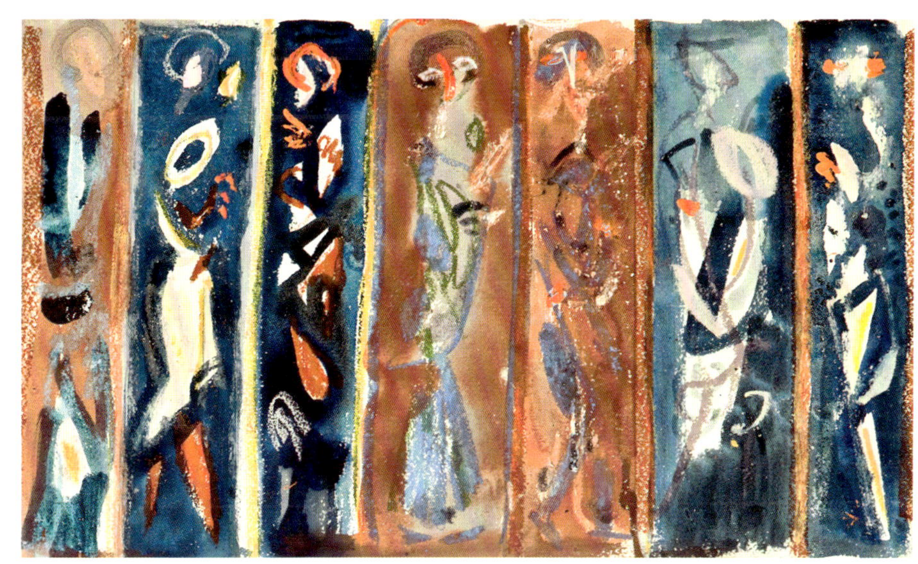

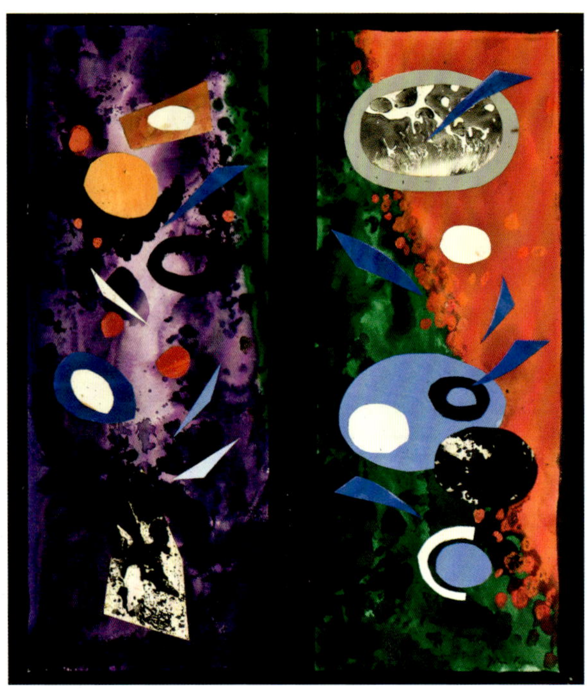

107. ***Studies for Chichester Cathedral tapestry: Earth & Air***
c. 1965

Collage and gouache on paper
75.5 x 58 cm

Pallant House Gallery, Chichester (Accepted by HM Government in lieu of Inheritance Tax from the Estate of John & Myfanwy Piper. Allocated to Pallant House Gallery, 2002)

108. ***Studies for Chichester Cathedral tapestry: St Matthew & St Mark***
c. 1965

Collage and gouache on paper
74.6 x 55.5 cm

Pallant House Gallery, Chichester (Accepted by HM Government in lieu of Inheritance Tax from the Estate of John & Myfanwy Piper. Allocated to Pallant House Gallery, 2002)

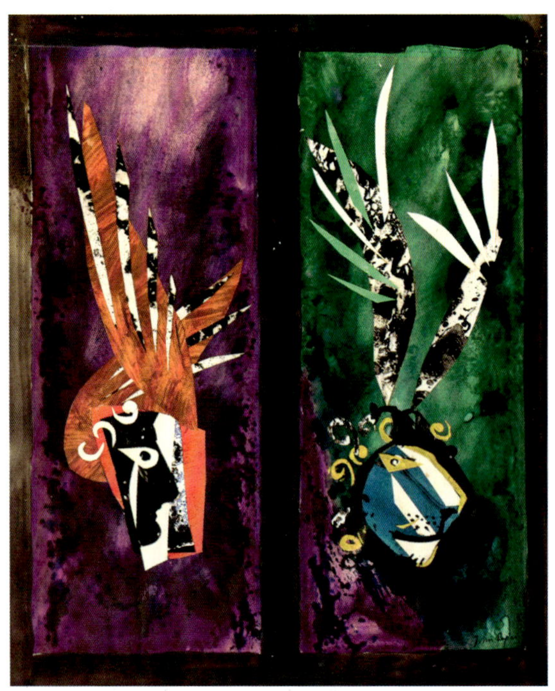

109. ***Studies for Chichester Cathedral tapestry: Fire & Water***
c. 1965

Collage and gouache on paper
75.7 x 55.8 cm

Pallant House Gallery, Chichester (Accepted by HM Government in lieu of Inheritance Tax from the Estate of John & Myfanwy Piper. Allocated to Pallant House Gallery, 2002)

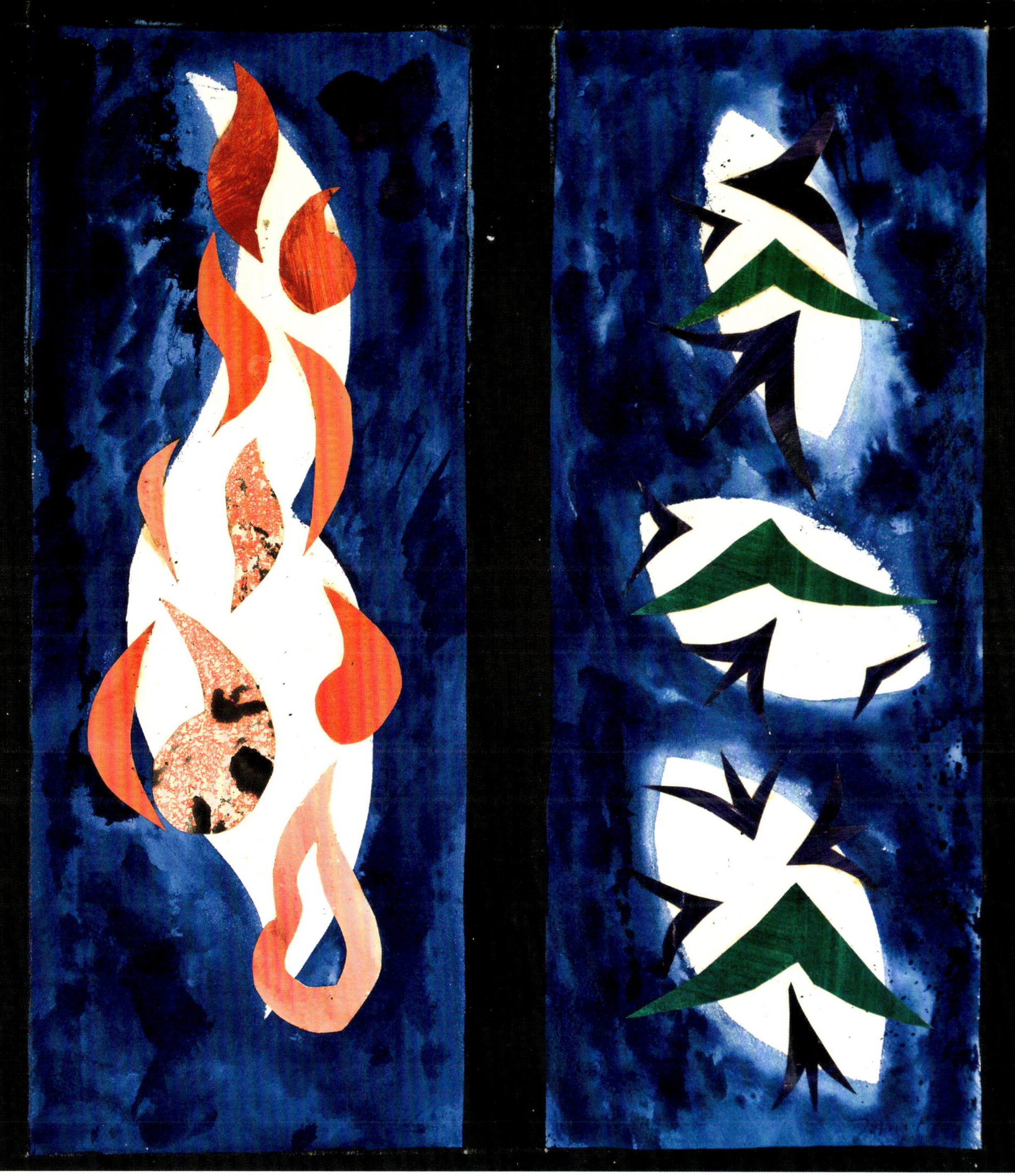

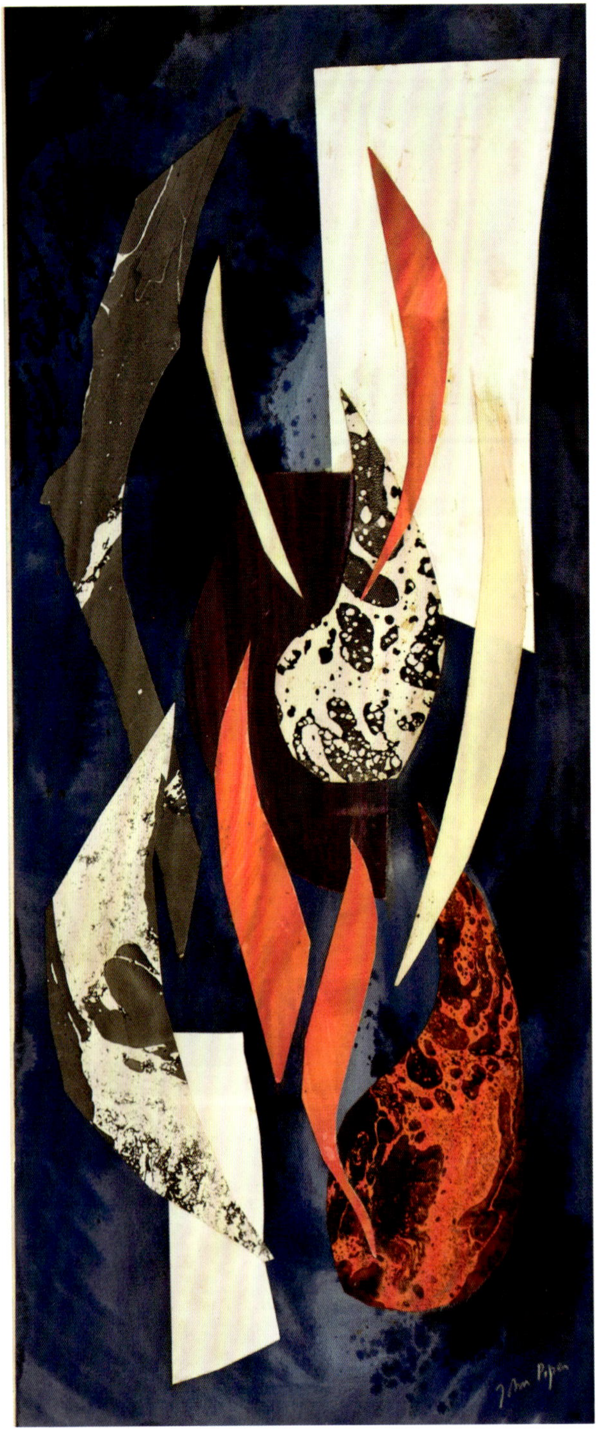

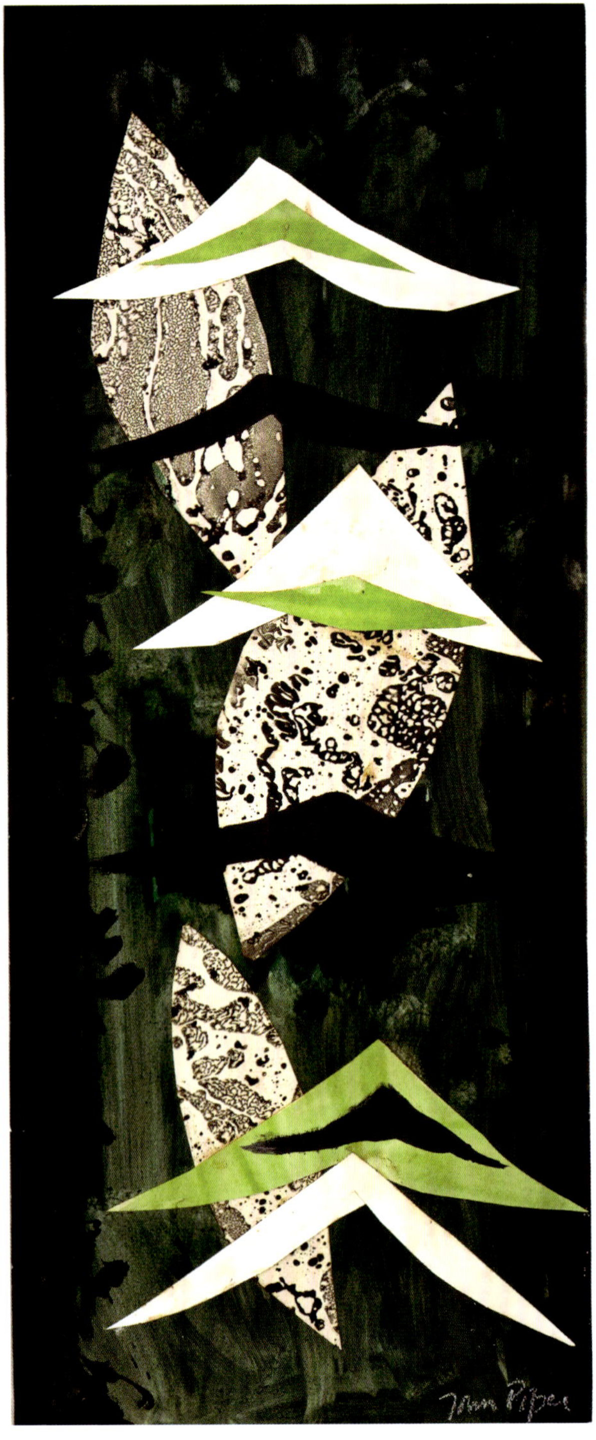

110. ***The Element of Fire***
c. 1965

Collage on paper
77.2 x 33.4 cm

Pallant House Gallery, Chichester (Accepted by HM Government in lieu of Inheritance Tax from the Estate of John & Myfanwy Piper. Allocated to Pallant House Gallery, 2002)

111. ***The Element of Water***
c. 1965

Collage on paper
77.5 x 45.3 cm

Pallant House Gallery, Chichester (Accepted by HM Government in lieu of Inheritance Tax from the Estate of John & Myfanwy Piper. Allocated to Pallant House Gallery, 2002)

112. ***Air motif from Chichester Cathedral tapestry***
1966

Oil and gloss on panel
122.3 x 58.1 cm

Pallant House Gallery, Chichester (Hussey Bequest, Chichester District Council, 1985)

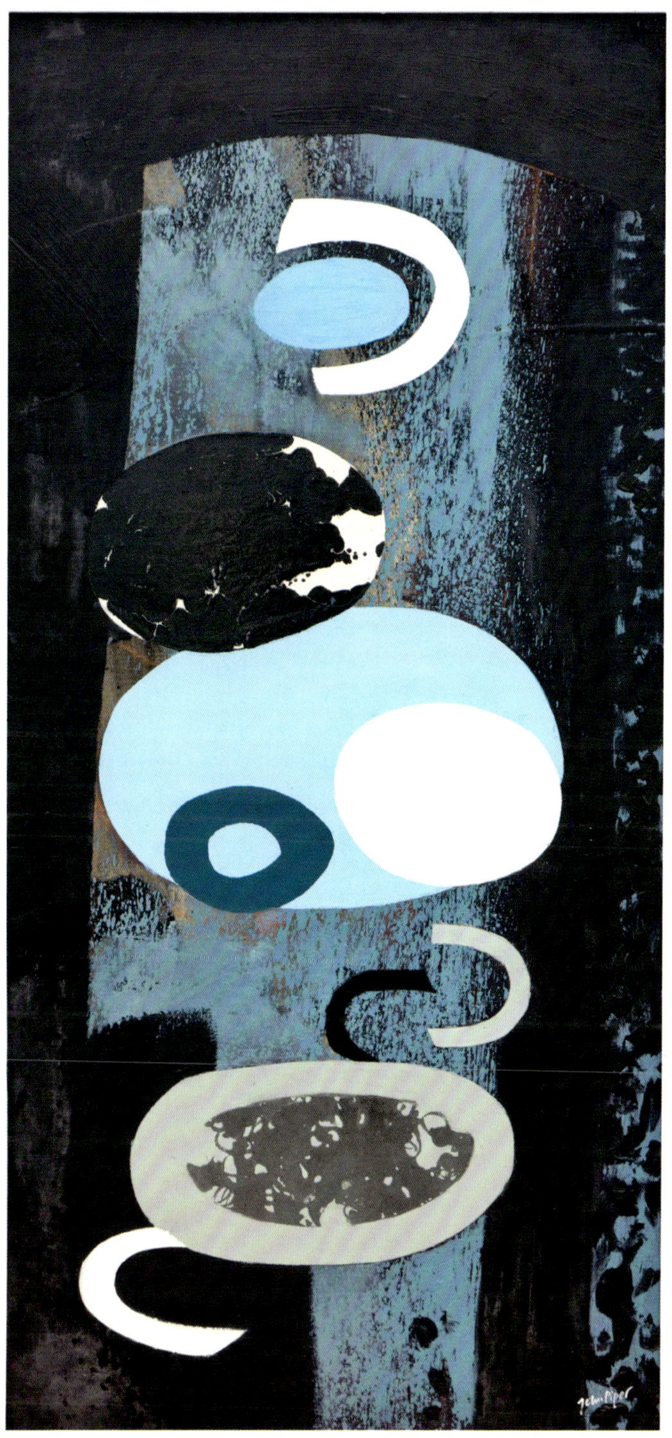

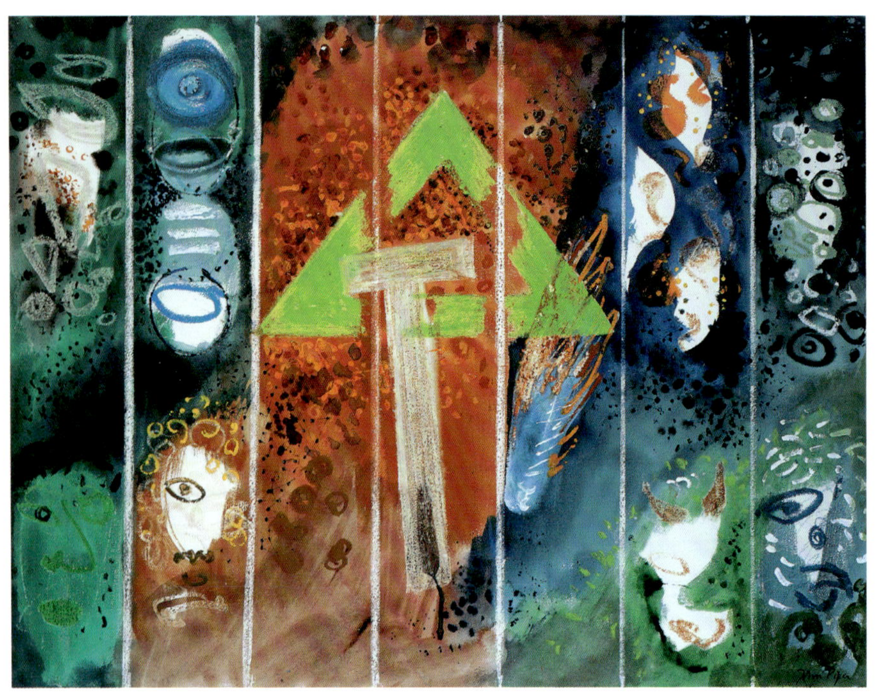

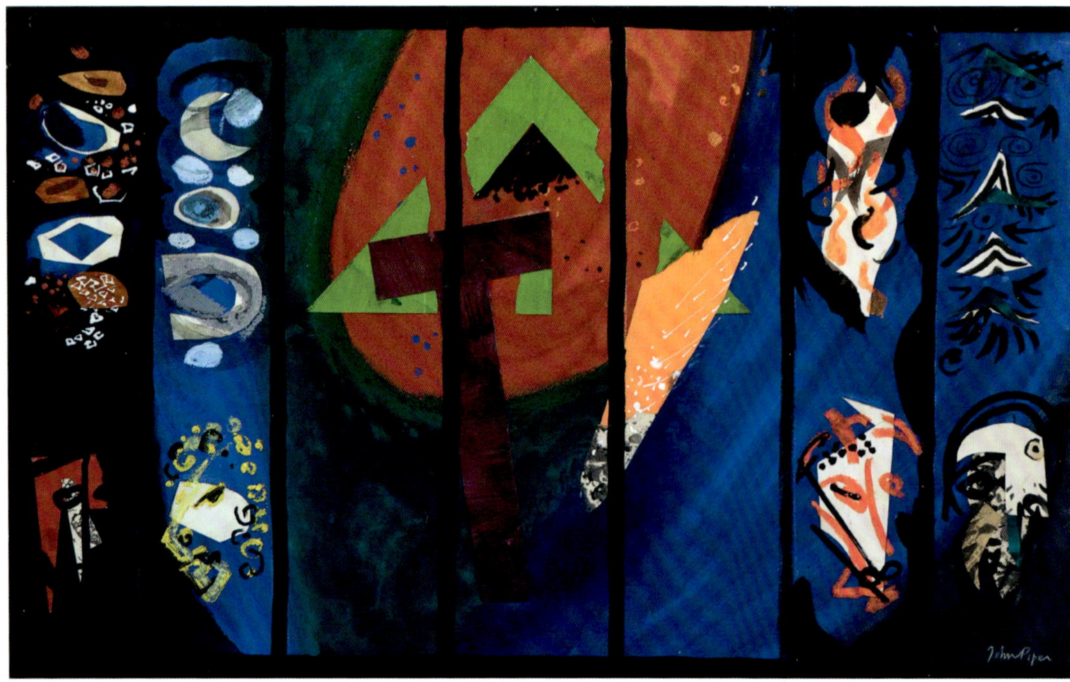

113. ***Study for Chichester Cathedral tapestry***
1965

Gouache, crayon and ink on paper
58.2 x 77.8 cm

Pallant House Gallery, Chichester (Accepted by HM Government in lieu of Inheritance Tax from the Estate of John & Myfanwy Piper. Allocated to Pallant House Gallery, 2002)

114. ***Design for Chichester Cathedral tapestry***
1965

Gouache and collage on paper
48 x 76.5 cm

Pallant House Gallery, Chichester (Accepted by HM Government in lieu of Inheritance Tax from the Estate of John & Myfanwy Piper. Allocated to Pallant House Gallery, 2002)

115. ***Sample Panel for St Luke from the Chichester Cathedral tapestry***
1965

Wool
221 x 93 cm

Pallant House Gallery, Chichester (Accepted by HM Government in lieu of Inheritance Tax from the Estate of John & Myfanwy Piper. Allocated to Pallant House Gallery, 2002)

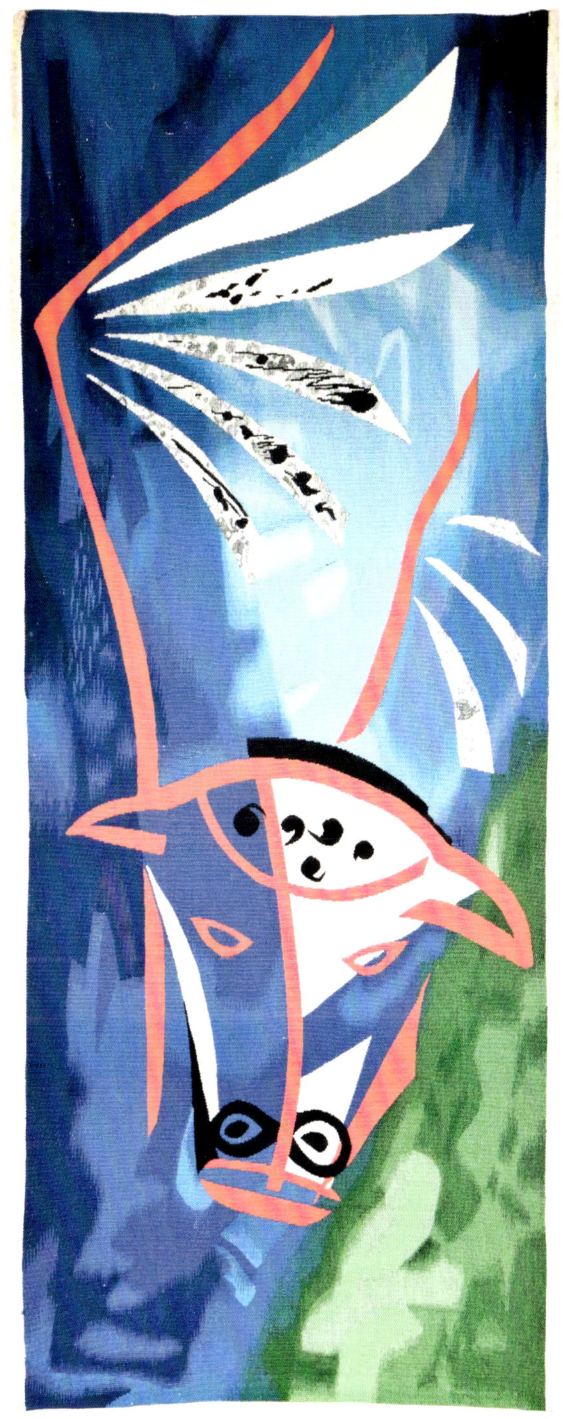

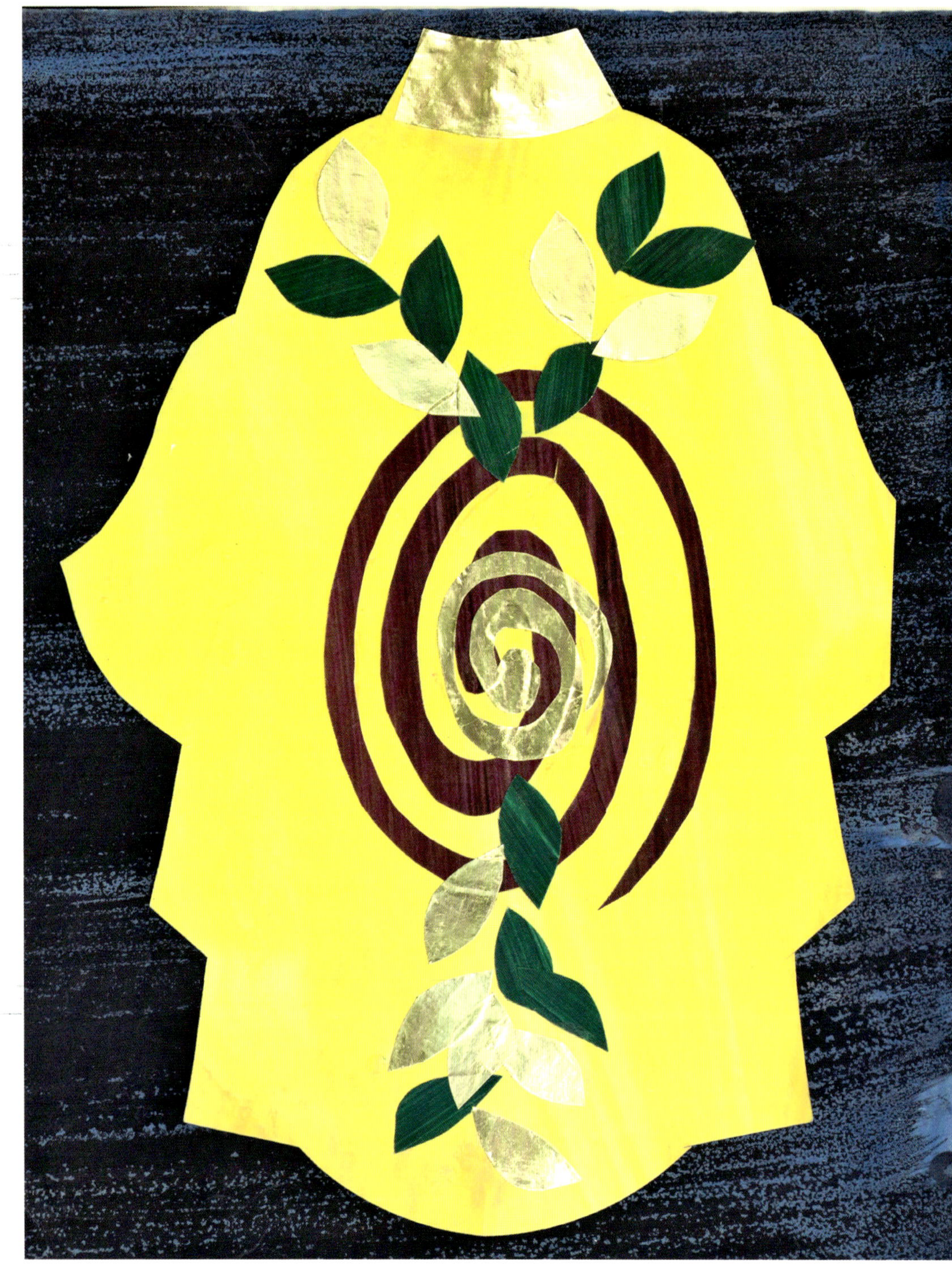

116. ***Preliminary design for Chasubles for Chichester Cathedral***
1967

Gouache and wax resist with collage on paper
40 x 27.5 cm

Pallant House Gallery, Chichester (Hussey Bequest, Chichester District Council, 1985)

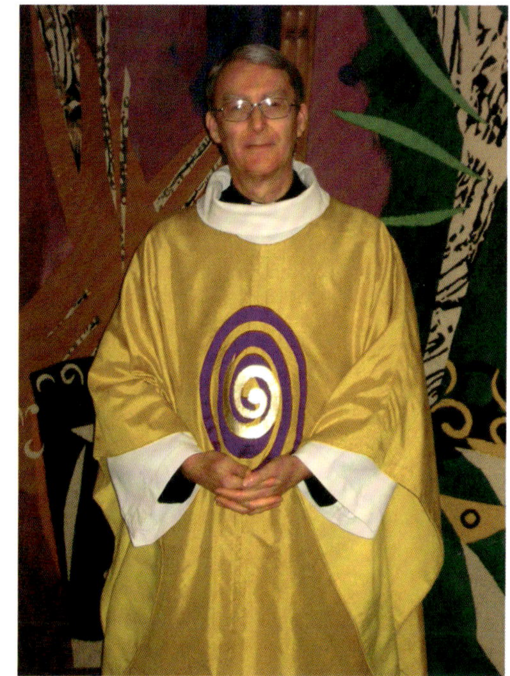

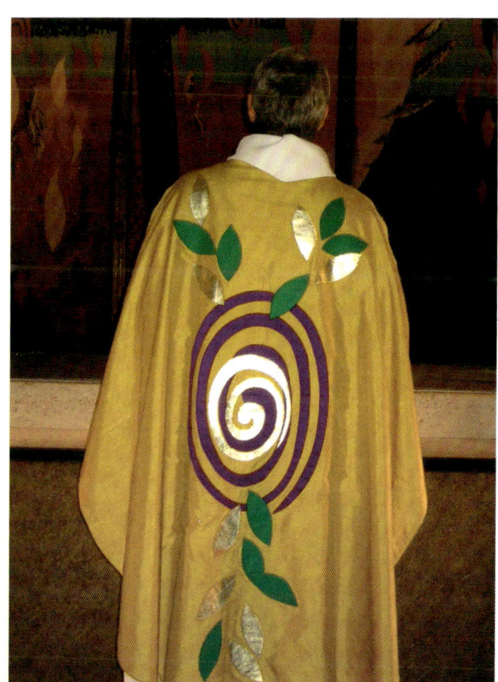

117. ***High Mass Vestments***
1967

Chichester Cathedral

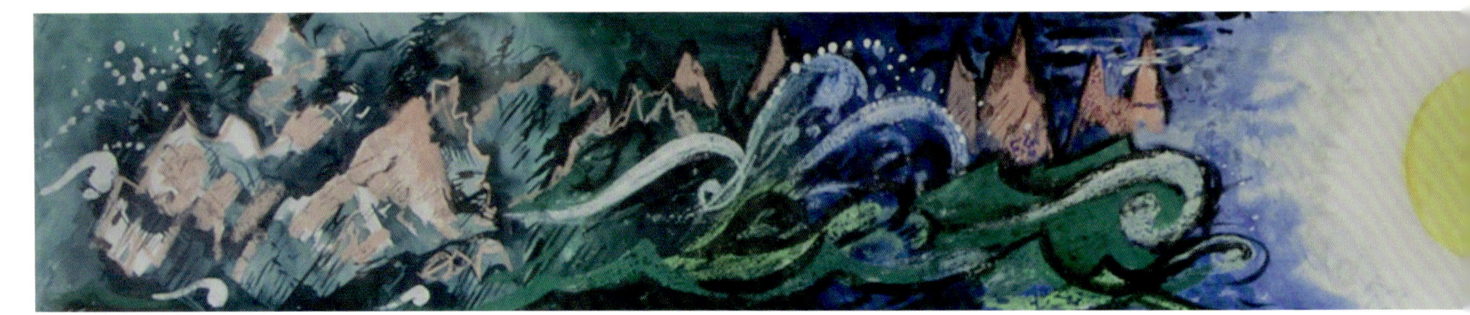

118. ***Study for the Meeting House, University of Sussex tapestry***
1976

University of Sussex

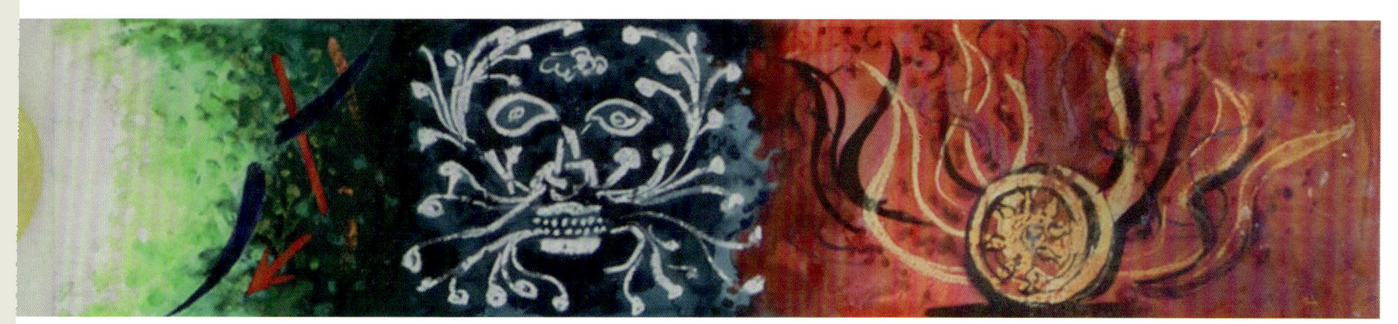

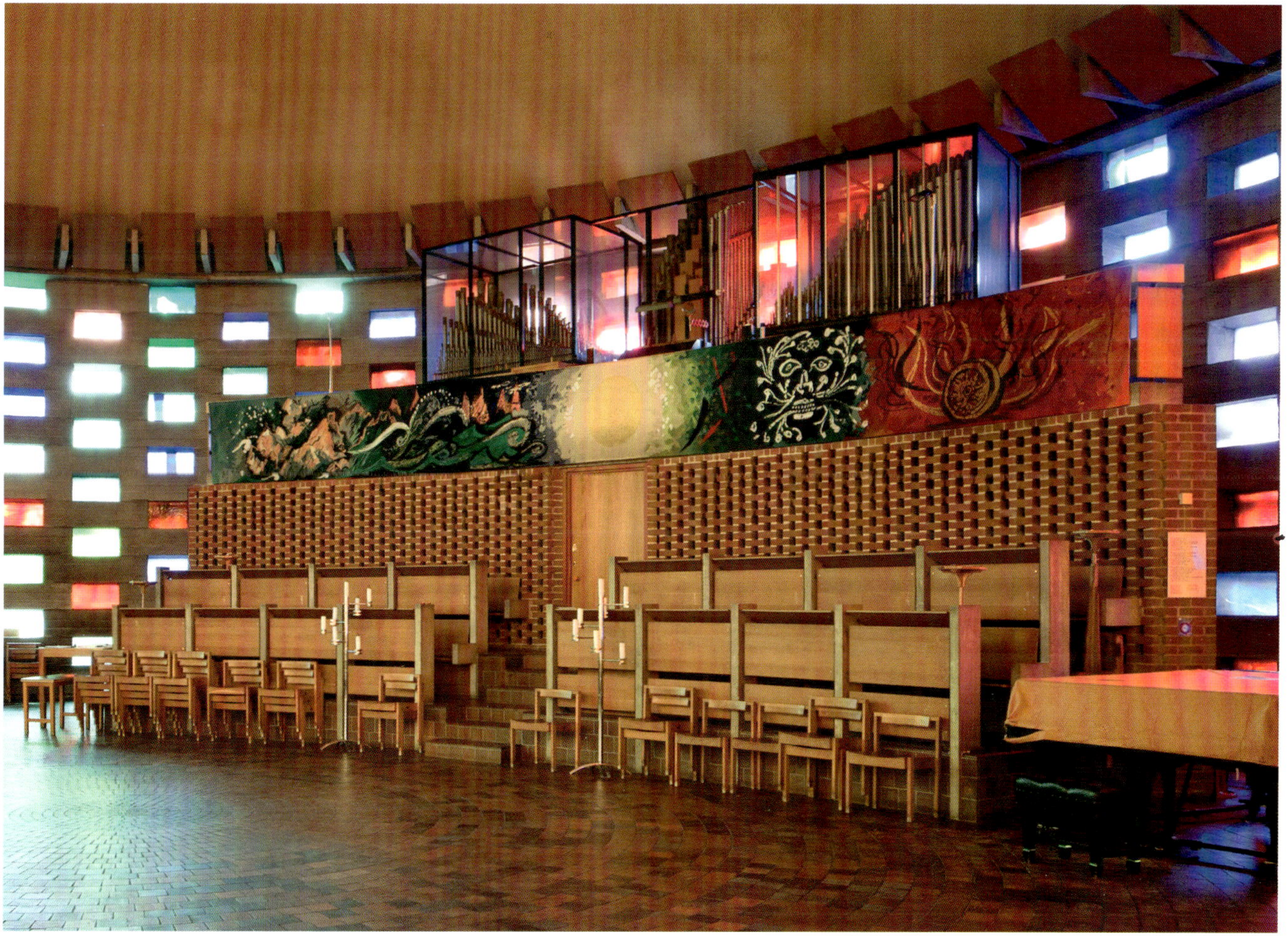

Image credits

Plates 1, 2, 22, 51-52, 56 © Tate, London, 2011
Plates 3-5, 8, 12, 14, 16, 18, 29, 81, 83-85, 87 George Richards
Plates 6, 19 Billy Fox
Plate 7 Huddersfield Art Gallery
Plates 9, 20, 25 Matthew Hollow
Plate 10 © Amgueddfa Cymru - National Museum Wales
Plates 11, 24, 35, 38-41, 43-44, 47-48, 53-55, 57-58,
61, 63, 66, 70, 73-77, 79-80, 100-103, 118 Michael Blissett / © Mascalls Gallery
Plates 13, 82, 86, 93-99, 104 © V&A Images / Victoria and Albert Museum, London
Plates 15, 21, 69, 105-116 Duncan McNeill Imaging / Pallant House Gallery
Plate 17 courtesy of River & Rowing Museum, Henley-on-Thames
Plates 26, 46 The Bridgeman Art Library
Plate 23 Kettle's Yard, University of Cambridge
Plates 27, 45, 49, 59 Sotheby's
Plates 28, 32-33, 42, 62, 65, 71-72, 78 Lund Humphries
Plate 30 Richard Green Gallery, London
Plate 31 Derby Museum & Art Gallery, 2011
Plate 36 Offer Waterman & Co
Plate 37 Leeds Museum and Galleries (City Art Gallery) U.K. / The Bridgeman Art Library
Plate 50 © Christie's Images Limited, 2011
Plates 60, 88-91 © Britten—Pears Foundation
Plate 67 Mark Heathcote / © Mascalls Gallery
Plate 68 The Trustees of Stansted Park Foundation
Plate 92 Abbot & Holder, London
Plate 117 Chichester's Dean and Chapter

Image on page 125 *The Meeting House, University of Sussex* by Mark Heathcote
Image on page 29 *John Piper, Sir Frederick Ashton, Benjamin Britten and Eric Crozier* by Edward Mandinian 1947 © V&A Images / Image courtesy of National Portrait Gallery, London
Image on page 93 *John Piper* by Lola Walker 1950s © Lola Marsden / National Portrait Gallery, London
Image on front cover *Clymping* 1953 Britten—Pears Foundation

Acknowledgments

Jo Wiltcher, Ian Beavis, Jamie Taylor and Katrina Burton - Tunbridge Wells Museum & Art Gallery; Emma Slocombe, Chlöe Tapping and Joe Lloyd - Scotney Castle.

Clarissa Lewis, Sebastian Piper, Henry & Luke Piper, Frances Spalding, David Fraser Jenkins, Hugh Fowler Wright, Stephen Laird, Alexandra Harris, David Heathcote, Nicholas Cranfield, Richard Ingrams, Julian Freeman, Orde Levinson, Peter de Rougemont, Patricia Jordan Evans - Bohun Gallery, Matthew Butler, Frank Collieson, Libby Horner, Sir Hugo Brunner, Robina Pelham Burn - Stephen Spender Trust, John Doyle.

Caroline Harding - Britten—Pears Foundation, Melissa Munro - Derek Williams Curator of Modern and Contemporary Art, Amgueddfa Cymru - National Museum Wales, Giles Baker-Smith - GBS Fine Art, Robert Hall & Andrew Charlesworth, Huddersfield Art Gallery, Andrew Kirk, Susan Catcher & Rebecca Wallace - V&A, Fiona Courage - University of Sussex, Craig Bowen - Canterbury City Museums & Galleries, Paul Mainds, Eloise Morton & Rachel Wragg - River & Rowing Museum, Henley-on-Thames, Philip Athill - Abbott & Holder Ltd, Matthew Edwards - Derby Museums & Art Gallery, Susan Morris - Richard Green Gallery, London, Emily Down - Tate Archives, Chlöe Thurbon - Chichester Cathedral, Simon Martin & Julie Brown - Pallant House Gallery, Isabelle Sambrook - Rye Art Gallery, Janet Sinclair - Stansted Park, Adam Nicholson, Viscount Gage, Deborah Gage, Peter Woolgar, Lord Sackville, Simon Lake - Leicester City Galleries, Rebecca Herman & Nigel Walsh - Leeds Museums and Galleries, Nicola Coleby and David Beevers - Brighton & Hove Royal Pavilion & Museums, Jill McNaught-Davis at National Trust, Pippa Jocomb & Megan Pockley - Christie's, Rachel Ross & Maureen Hooft Graafland - Sotheby's.

Alex Batten - Lund Humphries, Laura Summerton - Bridgeman Art Library, Amy Concannon - Dulwich Picture Gallery, Lucie Strnadova - Tate Enterprises Ltd, Melissa Atkinson - Rights and Images, National Portrait Gallery, Roxanne Peters - V&A Enterprises, Mark Heathcote, Michael Blissett.

Finally, thanks to my wife Vicky for accompanying me around Kent and Sussex searching for the site of John Piper's landscapes, as well as visiting galleries, collections and churches across the country much of the time whilst pregnant with Leo. This exhibition is a result of her support, encouragement and patience.